CREATURES *of* POSSIBILITY

CREATURES *of* POSSIBILITY

The Theological Basis
of Human Freedom

INGOLF U. DALFERTH
TRANSLATED BY JO BENNETT

B
Baker Academic
a division of Baker Publishing Group
Grand Rapids, Michigan

Published by Baker Academic
a division of Baker Publishing Group
P.O. Box 6287, Grand Rapids, MI 49516-6287
www.bakeracademic.com

Printed in the United States of America

Library of Congress Cataloging-in-Publication Data
Names: Dalferth, Ingolf U., author.
Title: Creatures of possibility : the theological basis of human freedom / Ingolf U. Dalferth ; translated by Jo Bennett.
Other titles: Umsonst. English
Description: Grand Rapids, MI : Baker Academic, a division of Baker Publishing Group, [2016] | Translation of: Umsonst. Tübingen : Mohr Siebeck, 2011. | Includes bibliographical references and index.
Identifiers: LCCN 2016027324 | ISBN 9780801098109 (cloth)
Subjects: LCSH: Theological anthropology.
Classification: LCC BL256 .D37513 2016 | DDC 233—dc23
LC record available at https://lccn.loc.gov/2016027324

16   17   18   19   20   21   22   7   6   5   4   3   2   1

To Hans Weder

Contents

✳

Preface to the 2016 English Edition

1. Creatures of Possibility

This book is the first of a series of studies I have written in recent years on questions of human life and existence.[1] It reconsiders the widely accepted thesis that human beings are what they are because they have to compensate for the many deficiencies of their biological nature through cultural artifacts such as technology, morality, and religion. There is no doubt a considerable amount of truth in this observation. But this is not the only way to read the evidence.

My proposal is to look at humans not as deficient beings but as creatures of possibility—*creatures* because I seek to understand them from a theological perspective, and creatures *of possibility* because we are creatures in the making whose actual becoming depends on possibilities beyond our control that occur in our lives as opportunities and chances that we can neglect and miss or take up and use. We are empowered and enriched, or disappointed and deprived, by the possibilities that break into our life and become opportunities for us to change for the better (positive opportunities) or for the worse (negative opportunities). It is only by relating to the possibilities played into our way that those possibilities become chances we can choose. But we

---

1. See Ingolf U. Dalferth, *Selbstlose Leidenschaften: Christlicher Glaube und menschliche Passionen* (Tübingen: Mohr Siebeck, 2013); *Transzendenz und säkulare Welt* (Tübingen: Mohr Siebeck, 2015).

would have no chances to choose from if there were no possibilities occurring in our lives in the first place. We are free because we can and must choose (freedom of choice) and act (freedom of action) in order to live a human life. And we are autonomous because we can and ought to determine the mode of our choosing and the way of our acting in moral terms (freedom as autonomy) if we want to live our human life together with others in a human way. But in all those senses our freedom depends on conditions that are beyond our control: we can choose and act and determine ourselves only against the backdrop of a basic passivity that characterizes our life and cannot be replaced or undone by anything we can do.

2. Freedom as Practice

Human freedom is not a capacity but a practice. Capacities are dispositional possibilities or potentialities: we can be x or do φ, and under the right circumstances we are x or do φ. Freedom is not a capacity in this sense. It is possible that we are free, but we do not have a capacity to be free. We are not free unless we practice our freedom, and we do not possess a capacity to be free whether we practice it or not. Rather, to be free is to practice one's freedom, and not to practice it is not to be free—whether we are hindered by circumstances or others, or because we fail to do it for other reasons.

When we practice freedom, we may or may not notice it. Not every choice is a conscious choice, and not every act is a conscious deed. The practice of freedom does not depend on knowing about or consenting to it. But when we are prevented from performing activities like going for a walk, or choosing, deciding, acting, thinking, or determining a way of living for ourselves, we cannot help but realize that our freedom also disappears. The cases are different, but the result is the same. Our freedom of choice withers away if there are no options from which we can choose, and our freedom of action dissolves if we are hindered from performing the relevant activities.

However, we cannot always blame others when we fail to practice freedom. Failures of autonomy can never be due to others, only to ourselves. We may be forced to commit an atrocity that we detest, but we cannot be forced to believe that something we know to be evil is good, or to determine ourselves in a way that contradicts the way we want to determine ourselves. If to be truly free is to be in control of the outcomes, then only God[2] is completely free, as Luther rightly insisted in opposition to Erasmus, and we are truly free only where we determine ourselves to choose and act in accordance with the maxim of the good will, as Kant secularized this insight. Only here are we in complete control of the outcomes and not dependent on the availability of options or on the availability of the occasion to act. If moral self-determination fails, it is due to us and not the fault of anybody else. Autonomy is an activity that cannot fail to achieve its end—if we practice it.

3. Passivity

The focus on activity in the discourse and practice of freedom has given passivity a bad name in mainstream Western culture.[3] Freedom is tied to activity, and those who cherish freedom often feel that they have to turn their back on passivity. As a whole industry keeps reminding us, in order to enhance our lives we must overcome passivity, step up our activities, and take matters into our own hands. In our culture, to be active is good, and to be passive is a deficiency to be overcome.

This book seeks to set the record straight. Christian theology has always resisted a one-sided focus on activity. The creative center of human life is not activity but passivity. Most of what we are we do not owe to ourselves. Our *Dasein* (existence) is not of our own making; our *Sosein* (existing in a particular way) is only in small part the result of what we do; and our *Wahrsein* (existing in the right way) does not result from what we do, but rather from something that befalls us (if

2. English grammar creates well-known problems about the appropriate third-person reflexive pronoun for God. Since Christians speak of God as Jesus did, and Jesus addressed God as father and not as mother, I shall use "he" and "himself" in this book wherever "God" or "Godself" sounds too clumsy. The reader ought not to conclude from this that I assume that God is male or that this gendered language is being used descriptively when applied to God.

3. See Juliane Schiffers, *Passivität denken: Aristoteles—Leibniz—Heidegger* (Freiburg im Breisgau: Karl Alber, 2014).

it does). We are made true, if we are, but we cannot make ourselves true, because we cannot step outside of ourselves and redo what has gone wrong. From beginning to end, and with respect to our *Dasein*, *Sosein*, and *Wahrsein*, our lives are molded by passivity. There is so much that happens to us and so little that we make happen. Before I can act as a self, I must become a self, and while I cannot be a self without acting, I cannot become a self by acting. In order to be able to live and act as an "I" in the nominative, I must first become a "me" in the dative (as in "to me"), as recent phenomenology reminds us. A primal passivity precedes all our activity. Before we can give, we must be a given, and before we can act, we must be an actuality.

However, we must be careful not to play off passivity against activity. Both are constitutive features of human life. But they occur in an order that must be respected and in ways that need to be distinguished.

The most important distinction is the one between horizontal (or contrastive) and vertical (or deep) passivity. Actual life as enacted in time and space is neither pure activity nor pure passivity; it is always a mixture of both, or, in Schleiermacher's words, a continual "interpenetration and succession of activity and passivity."[4] It has a passive side and an active side, a capacity to be affected by others (receptivity) and a capacity to affect others (activity), and the two are polar opposites that allow for different degrees of mixture. This is different in the case of deep passivity. This more basic passivity is not merely other than human activity; it is that without which there would be neither active nor passive processes in human life. It is a complete passivity *of* the life of human persons, not just a partial passivity *within* their lives.

4. Different Kinds of Becoming

The distinction between deep and contrastive passivity is frequently overlooked in theological accounts that claim there are no "dealings of God with us without us."[5] They construe the divine-human

4. Friedrich Daniel Ernst Schleiermacher, *The Christian Faith*, ed. H. R. Mackintosh and J. S. Stewart (London: T&T Clark, 1999), 41.
5. Karl-Heinz Menke, "Rechtfertigung: Gottes Handeln an uns ohne uns? Jüdisch perspektivierte Anfragen an einen binnenchristlichen Konsens," *Catholica* 63 (2009): 58–72. It does not help to construe God's self-determination as God's self-determination

relationship as an interaction between a divine and a human agent; they construe that interaction as a conjunction of divine and human activities; and they understand the mode of that interaction at the human pole (though usually not also at the divine pole) in terms of contrastive passivity and activity where the one cannot occur without the other. Not only is there no divine activity to which there is no corresponding human activity, but there is also no human passivity that is not tinged with human activity. In both respects the human person is seen as an agent who in principle is capable of acting in one way or another. There is no place in this picture for deep passivity.

However, even in ordinary life there are phenomena that do not fit such a view. You may become the heir to your uncle's fortune, but there is nothing you do to become this. And while it is true that you cannot be an heir and accept or deny your inheritance without being alive and able to act in some way or other, you do not become an heir by what you do but by what is done to you. To become an heir is to become one *mere passive* (in a merely passive way), as classical thinkers put it. This passive becoming makes you an heir, and only then are you able to act as an heir and accept or reject your inheritance. Passive becoming is indeed not without some relation to human activity. But the activity at stake is made possible by it and is not a receptive activity or active strand within the passive becoming. This is true of many other changes in human life as well, and it does not contradict the fact that you cannot live without being both active and passive, being affected by others and affecting others.

Moreover, we must distinguish between different kinds of becoming. Since the days of Aristotle, we have known that there is a difference between qualitative change and substantial becoming. It is one thing if a particular substance or entity (e.g., water) changes

---

to allow himself to be determined (or affected) by the free actions of his creatures as Menke does, making God say in effect: I allow you to affect me. This may be a way of showing what it means for God to be a creator. But it only underscores the prior activity of the creator and the deep passivity of the creature that precedes everything creatures do and can do as creatures. There is no created freedom of creatures that is not embedded in and dependent on a prior and one-sided creative freedom of the creator that corresponds to a deep passivity of the creature. Created freedom is only possible against the backdrop of deep passivity, for otherwise it wouldn't be *created* freedom (ibid., 64).

from one state (being hot) to another state (being cold), and quite another if some new entity springs up or comes into being. In the former case it makes sense to argue that the change is only possible because the entity at stake has the potentiality or capacity to be in either state: to become x or do φ is to have the capacity to become x or do φ. This is different in the second case. For a new entity to come into existence, there is no ὑποκείμενον or subject (substance) to be postulated that has the capacity to change from a potential to an actual state. All that is needed is a possibility that is actualized. To become actual is not a qualitative change but a modal change, and the modal change does not change the entity at stake; it changes the actual world in which it comes to exist. The world is changed in a different way when a new entity comes into being as opposed to when an entity changes from one state into another. In the latter case the entity participates in the change in some active way because the range of its potential actuality defines the possible changes it can undergo. In the former case, however, the entity that comes into being is not actively involved in its own becoming. It is the result of the becoming but not its agent. It is effected by what happens but is not co-effecting it. It is purely passively involved in the change from possibility to actuality, and it does not make sense to ascribe to it a potentiality or capacity for its becoming.

5. The Theological Importance of Deep Passivity

This is even more so with respect to human relations to God. To be created by God entails a purely passive becoming for the human (or any other) creature, as is to be saved by God. There is no living creature that is not active, and the same is true of living creatures who are saved. But the activity of the creature is not what creates or saves it; it is what follows from it. Only those who are created can and will act as creatures (or fail to do so), and only those who are saved can and will live as creatures who have been saved (or fail to live so). Thus, just as being a creature is experienced as deep passivity by the creature, so being saved is experienced as deep passivity by the one who is saved.

This is why it is wrong to claim that human beings must have an inherent capacity to relate to God or to elicit God's presence. Those who argue in this way construe the deep passivity of created existence in terms of a contrastive passivity within the realm of creation. But even if it were true that for every activity we perform we must possess a capacity to perform it (which would make the distinction uninteresting and superfluous), we can possess capacities only if we exist, and we cannot construe our existence as an activity that results from practicing a capacity that makes our existence possible. I may not be able to hear you without the capacity of hearing, but I do not need a capacity of existing in order to be able to come into existence. The modal distinction between possibility ("it is possible to φ") and capacity or potentiality ("it is possible for me to φ") does not translate to the deep passivity of coming into existence. If I exist, it is possible that I exist, but I do not have a capacity or potential to exist before I actually do.

The same is true of theological accounts of the *imago Dei* (image of God). They go wrong when they construe possibilities as capacities and grace as a built-in potentiality of the human creature. To call human beings the image of God is to say that it is possible that they become the locus where God's presence to his creation is realized and acknowledged (faith) or ignored and rejected (nonfaith) so that they can live the life of a creature of God or fail to do so. But even when God's presence is ignored or rejected, humans would still be the locus where this happens; and if they are God's creatures, they remain so regardless of what they do and how they relate to that presence. But it does not mean that they have a capacity to elicit God's presence, to be "inwardly open to God through an interior entry,"[6] or to have the capacity to be aware of their proximity to God or to possess a "primordial memory of the immemorial" that makes them restlessly, albeit unconsciously, strive for God and desire to "find stability and solidity" in God.[7] It is a modal mistake to turn possibility into capacity and to infer from the possibility of becoming aware of the presence of God a human capacity to do so. And it is a theological mistake to turn the *sola gratia* that makes us "all recipients, a priori, of the

6. Joseph Rivera, *The Contemplative Self after Michel Henry* (Notre Dame, IN: University of Notre Dame Press, 2015), 240.

7. Ibid., 221.

grace of God"[8] into a God-given capacity that humans possess qua human beings. Through God's grace we can become the locus where God's presence is known and acknowledged if it so pleases God, but we do not have a God-given capacity for such an acknowledgment that distinguishes us from all other creatures. We completely depend on the self-communication of God that makes us recipients of his self-communication. However, we do not need to possess a capacity to strive for it or to receive it in order that God may make his presence known to us. Where God's presence is acknowledged, it is not acknowledged because God is present and we have a capacity to acknowledge it. Rather, God is present in such a way that God creates the human condition of the possibility of acknowledging God's presence in the very act of our acknowledging or ignoring God's presence without the need of a pre-given or an a priori human capacity to do so. Not only the acknowledgment of God's creative presence but also the condition of the possibility of this acknowledgment is a gift of God and not a capacity of the creature. With the gift of his presence, God also gives the condition of the possibility of understanding and acknowledging it.[9] The emphasis is on a one-sided *solus Deus* and not on a cooperative *Deus et creatura*, on deep passivity and not on the interpenetration of divine giving and human receiving in a joint activity of Creator and creature.

6. *Solus Deus* and Deep Passivity

Reformation theology insisted on the *solus Deus* to safeguard accounts of creation and salvation from being misconstrued as a collaborative commerce between creatures and Creator. God is God and we are creatures. God is God in freely determining himself to be our Creator. We cannot determine ourselves to be God's creatures but only acknowledge (or ignore) the prior truth that God is our Creator. Whereas God's activity does not depend on us, we can never act without God, and nothing we can do can replace our utter dependence on the prior activity of

8. Ibid., 247.
9. Cf. Søren Kierkegaard, *Philosophical Fragments: Johannes Climacus*, ed. and trans. H. V. Hong and E. H. Hong (Princeton: Princeton University Press, 1985), 14–19.

God. To be a creature is in no sense the result of anything we can do, and the same is true of being saved from our blindness and ignorance about our existential situation before God. In creation and salvation God is the sole center of activity, and we partake in it in utter passivity.

This bears on everything. Classical Protestant theology in the Baroque period sought to show this by spelling out the *solus Deus* in terms of *sola gratia*, *solus Christus*, *solo verbo*, and *sola scriptura* in the whole structure of dogmatics. Thus the prolegomena focused on *sola scriptura*, the doctrine of God (*De Deo*) on *solus Deus*, theological anthropology (*De Homine*) on *sola gratia*, Christology and pneumatology (*De Principiis Salutis*) on *solus Christus*, and ecclesiology and sacramental theology (*De Mediis Salutis*) on *solo verbo*. In each case the emphasis is on a creative divine activity that corresponds to a deep passivity on the human side that must not be construed in terms of the contrastive activity and passivity in human life. Where the Reformers spoke of a cooperation between God and human creature in sanctification, they did so against the backdrop of a prior, ultimate, and absolute creative activity of God in creation and salvation (justification) and a corresponding deep passivity of the human creature. We owe our *Dasein* not to ourselves but to God, and while we are responsible for our *Sosein*, we will only live in a true way if we acknowledge our basic passivity by incorporating it in the mode of our *Sosein*. We cannot do this by our own powers but only through the help and guidance of God's Spirit, and therefore we cannot achieve the *Wahrsein* of our *Sosein* by what we do but rather only by what befalls us.

This is why the distinction between deep and contrastive passivity is all-pervasive in theological accounts of human life. It informs the biblical imagery of talking about the human situation before God, in particular in Christian accounts of the fundamental change from the old life of sinners to the new life of faith and trust in God. The change occurs in human lives that continue in many ways as before. But it is not merely a change from one state to another within an identical life (a qualitative change to another phase of one's life); rather, it is a change from an old life to a new life that leads across an abyss that in no way can be crossed by the creature, only by the Creator (a substantial change to a new life). To underline the difference, Paul construes that change in Romans 6 as a change from death to life that mirrors the death and resurrection of Jesus Christ: We were "buried with him through baptism into death in order that, just as Christ was raised from the dead through the glory of the Father, we too may live a new life" (Rom. 6:4 NIV). Just as in Christ's case the continuity through death was not due to Christ himself but to "the glory of the Father," so too in our case the continuity from the old to the new life is not to be sought in anything in our lives but exclusively in the saving activity of God. God alone is active here, whereas we are utterly passive. Just as we are born into this life without our collaboration, so too we are born into the new life without our cooperation. We are the ones who benefit from that which is done to us. But we are no cooperators in it, and we have no capacity or potentiality for it. We can only describe it retrospectively as the surprising occurrence of the creative deep passivity to which we owe our life and who and what we are. This deep passivity is beyond anything we can replicate or transform in our own activity. In actual life we cannot enact it; we only represent it symbolically. This is what the Christian sacraments do: They signify the true reality of the new life that humans owe to God, but they do so through symbolic actions that present more than they perform and say more than they show. They disclose meaning and possibilities that point beyond the contingent realities of actual life, and in doing so they manifest the divine creativity of the deep passivity to which we owe our lives.

Acknowledgments

I am grateful to Jo Bennett for the excellent translation of the book. The art of translation is greatly to be admired, and so is a translator who masters the art of translation in the way she does.

Marlene Block has been of invaluable help in assisting with the proofreading. I am deeply indebted to her.

I am also thankful to Baker Academic for considering the manuscript for publication and to Dave Nelson and Brian Bolger for being such considerate and helpful editors. The art of editing is increasingly becoming obsolete in a world of do-it-yourself publishing on internet platforms. I am glad to have had a chance to work with editors who know what they are doing.

Preface to the 2011 German Edition

*

What is a human? Who are we? What can we be? And what do we want to be? Each of these questions has more than one answer, and each answer throws up further questions. What can, should, and may we know, do, or hope? What can or must we become? What do we want to become? What have we made ourselves into, and what have others made us into? What might we have been if we had not become what we are? What did we actually want to be? And what could we become if we ceased to be merely what we have become?

This book does not provide an answer (or at any rate not just one answer) to any of these questions. But they all revolve around this single starting point: we exist. But who are we, or what? We will never really know the answer if we pay attention only to what we can or cannot do, to what we can or cannot make. We are always more than we can do, be, or become on our own initiative. We are not merely deficient beings with a past; we are beings of possibility with a future.

This future is not to be decided purely on the basis of what we do or fail to do, but first and foremost on the basis of what we cannot do. It is not the undoubtedly remarkable competence of our knowledge and actions that is the defining characteristic of our humanity, but our less obvious, but no less remarkable, creative passivity, which we cannot make up for or compensate for with any activity of our own, but which we must draw on in all the activities and passivities of our life. We only are insofar as we are becoming. But we always become more than we or others can make us, and more than we can become of ourselves. We live from a surplus of the possible that is not limited to what we actually are or could have been. What defines our humanity is not our reality and its possibilities ("Become what you are!") but rather the unforeseeable that comes our way as we live our lives, opening up possibilities that without the unforeseeable would never have been either conceivable or accessible ("Become what you can never be of your own accord!"). We live from possibilities over which we have no control. We are—in a radical sense—beings of possibility.

How are we humans to organize our thinking if we are thus perceived as beings of possibility, living from the creativity of our deep passivity more than from any contrastive activity or passivity? This is the key question addressed in the philosophical and theological reflections that follow. Following an introduction to the subject (chapter 1), I will develop the theme in six case studies relating to the current debate over the nature of our humanity (chapter 2), the phenomenon of gift (chapters 3 and 4), the problematic of sacrifice (chapter 5), our understanding of the incarnation (chapter 6), and human passivity (chapter 7). I will do this in conversation with Luther (chapters 1 and 2), Kant (chapter 1), Schiller (chapter 5), Lessing (chapter 7), Nietzsche (chapter 7), Marion (chapter 4), Derrida (chapter 5), and Blumenberg (chapter 6), to name just a few. Each study will consider a specific aspect of the theme. They do not build successively on each other but can each be read as a stand-alone study. Taken together, however, they shed light on the range of problems against the background of which this subject needs to be considered.

The book deals with material from the following publications: "*Mere passive*: Die Passivität der Gabe bei Luther," in *Word—Gift—Being: Justification—Economy—Ontology*, ed. B. K. Holm and P. Widmann (Tübingen: Mohr Siebeck, 2009), 43–71; "Alles umsonst: Zur Kunst des Schenkens und den Grenzen der Gabe," in *Von der Ursprünglichkeit der Gabe: Jean-Luc Marions, Phänomenologie in der Diskussion*, ed. M. Gabel and H. Joas (Freiburg/Munich: Herder, 2007), 159–91; "Selbstaufopferung," *Theologische Literaturzeitung* 133 (2008): 1155–68; "Vom Denken der Menschwerdung: Zur relecture der Inkarnation bei Hans Blumenberg," in *Incarnation*, ed. M. M. Olivetti (Padova: CEDAM, 1999), 221–31; and "Die

Selbstverkleinerung des Menschen," *Zeitschrift für Theologie und Kirche* 105 (2008): 94–123.

I would like to thank the publishers for their permission to incorporate this material into the process of thinking the subject matter through and updating and revising it. Publications are always interim results that are intended to be taken further in both the author's and the readers' own thinking. For there can be no end to the thought process, and nothing is ever conclusively thought through.

I am grateful to my publishers, especially Mohr Siebeck, for their interest in the subject of this book. And I would like to thank my assistant Dr. Stefan Berg, who performed a great service in handling the proofreading and indexing.

This book is dedicated to my friend and colleague Hans Weder as a farewell upon his retirement from his professorship. In his teaching and his publications he gave constant emphatic reminders that *umsonst* is the *basso continuo* of the New Testament. May this recollection also serve as a reminder of this.[1]

---

1. The present text is the English translation of Ingolf U. Dalferth, *Unsomst: Eine Erinnerung an die kreative Passivität des Menschen* (Tübingen: J. C. B. Mohr-Paul Siebeck, 2015). The German word *umsonst* has no immediate English equivalent. It has the double meaning of "for nothing" (for free, in vain) and it is used frequently in economic discourse in the sense of "free of charge." Throughout the German text I employ *umsonst* to describe the sheer gratuitousness of the gift of salvation.

Abbreviations

AA   Immanuel Kant, *Gesammelte Schriften*, Ausgabe der Königlich Preußischen Akademie der Wissenschaften. Citations using "A" or "B" refer to the first or second edition of Kant's writings, respectively. Citations from the Prussian Academy edition will be given by volume and page number.

KSA   Friedrich Nietzsche, *Sämtliche Werke: Kritische Studienausgabe in 15 Bänden*. Edited by Giorgio Colli and Mazzino Montinari. Munich and New York: de Gruyter and deutscher Taschenverlag, 1980.

RGG   *Die Religion in Geschichte und Gegenwart*. 4th ed. Edited by Hans Dieter Betz et al. Tübingen: Mohr Siebeck, 1998–2007.

ThLZ   *Theologische Literaturzeitung*

WA   *D. Martin Luthers Werke*. Weimarer kritische Ausgabe. 120 vols. 1883–2009.

ZThK   *Zeitschrift für Theologie und Kirche*

1

From Deficient Being to Beings of Possibility

An Introduction

1. Compensating for Our Deficiencies

We have become used to viewing humans as deficient beings who would have no chance in their struggle for existence if they did not know how to compensate for the weaknesses of their biological nature through the use of technology, morality, the media, religion, and culture. Had we not learned to think in the subjunctive and pray in the optative, we would scarcely still be alive in the indicative. If we did not constantly explore the impossible and achieve the as yet hardly possible, we would long since have ceased to be a reality. And had we not subjected ourselves to a morality in which self-interest is restricted by the common good, we presumably would long since have ceased to exist, because we in effect would have annihilated ourselves.

In a long history, none of that was likely to have happened without a large dose of self-abuse and self-violation, as Nietzsche surmised

with good reason.[1] Nonetheless, in view of the way in which their
biological nature fails to conform to their natural environment, it
would seem that human beings have only been able to survive by
creating, as a "second nature,"[2] their own environment using technology, their social world using morality, their cultural world using
media tools, and a transcendent world using religion. Only in this
way could they wrest from the hostile world in which they found
themselves a human-friendly world in which they could live together
with others in tenuous security. And it was even longer before they
began to shape their world in a way that provided conditions that
were not just human-friendly but also worthy of human beings, so
that they did not simply act negatively, to avoid danger, but positively,
to realize what was deemed "human."

To achieve all this—to evolve from an animal into an "interesting
animal"[3]—there is no question but that they had to behave in a deliberately anti-ecological manner. Whereas other animals adapt to
their environments and make themselves at home in their ecological
niches, human beings have learned to adapt their environments to
suit themselves and to shape them according to their needs. It is only
because humans have become animals who create and think that we
are still here.

2. Self-Abolition

But not for much longer, perhaps. The transition from animal to human
apparently has elevated human beings to the point where they are
showing signs of forgetting that as humans they are also animals and
belong to an overall life context that they have not engendered, but
that engenders them. Initially, this development seemed promising: the

1. Friedrich Nietzsche, *Zur Genealogie der Moral*, KSA 5:245–412. English
translation: *On the Genealogy of Morals*, trans. W. Kaufmann and R. J. Hollingdale
(New York: Vintage Books, 1989), 13–163.

2. Friedrich Nietzsche, *Morgenröte*, Buch 1, §38; Buch 5, §455, KSA 3:45 and 275.

3. Friedrich Nietzsche, *Zur Genealogie*, 5:266 (*Genealogy*, 33). See also Nietzsche,
Der Antichrist: Versuch einer Kritik des Christentums, §14, KSA 6:180. English
translation: *The Anti-Christ, Ecce Homo, Twilight of the Idols, and Other Writings*, ed. Aaron Ridley and Judith Norman, trans. Judith Norman (2005; repr.,
Cambridge: Cambridge University Press, 2006), 12.

very thing that looked like a biological weakness turned out to be an anthropological strength. The human biological failure to conform to our environment has resulted anthropologically in an openness to the world, which in turn has provided the stimulus for the continual crossing of frontiers. There is nothing that humans cannot shape and reshape. They stop at nothing when responding to their creative urge—not even at the human species itself.

But here they find themselves overstepping a categorical boundary and not just a boundary of degree. Overextended humans began shaping their environments in partial and risky ways in order to reduce the probability that their hostile environment would bring about their annihilation. What they had initiated, under a compulsion to find relief and out of a need for compensation, is no longer limited today to their environment (*Umwelt*) and social world (*Metwelt*), but extends to their very selves, to the point that humankind is in danger of self-annihilation through an unbridled removal of the limits on its compensatory urge. It is not just our natural environment that we shape to suit ourselves, with all the ecological consequences with which we must struggle today. We also view our human social world as a field of experimentation, where, under the pressures generated by modernity, human relationships are subjected to constant "modernization" through our social, political, legal, economic, and media constructions, whose cumulative collateral damage we often can barely keep in check. And we are in the process of making our very selves the subjects of a comprehensive biological design experiment whose parameters we have not really mastered and whose outcome is wholly uncertain, since those who began it will not be those who will have to live with its consequences. Not only will they be numerically different but they will also differ in principle; they will not just be different people from those who began the experiment, they will be entirely other, because what we call "human" today will no longer be what will be termed "human" by then.

It is not sufficient to view this as a mere technical problem of mastering the technologies necessary for redesigning the human being. The problem lies deeper, and it is a problem of principle. It is not simply a question of perfecting the human being; it is a question of the concept of the human by which one is orienting oneself. When the necessity for humans, as highly vulnerable deficient beings, to "transform their deficiencies into opportunities for survival"[4] is extended, it leads *ad absurdum* not just to the human-friendly design of the environment and social world in which human beings find themselves, but beyond to human beings themselves. This means that it is not merely human beings who are modified, but the concept of what is human in itself. What would a human-friendly design of a human being look like if humans themselves can no longer be distinguished from the human design? One cannot treat everything as a designable environment without driving the compensatory design process into a paradoxical self-abolition.

It therefore seems imperative that we distinguish between two present-day developments that frequently are conflated. It is one thing to regard media, materials, technology, and culture as extensions of the body that shift the conventional boundaries between the body and its environment, between humans and their surroundings, requiring them to be redefined. This can still be understood as an expression of the prosthetic enhancement or "prosthetic extension" of the human, which by "'organ relief' [*Organentlastung*] and 'organ supersession' [*Organüberbietung*] . . . turns the human being into the 'God of prosthetics.'"[5] But it is quite another thing for humans to convert themselves into an environment that can and should be designed. For, in doing so, we do not only give fresh definitions to the concepts "environment" and "human"; we withdraw the distinction between humans and their environment, the distinction that generated the pressure to compensate that necessitated the progression from biology to anthropology. This rebound of the design process onto the designers themselves is not just a further stage in the extension of the sphere of his drive to shape his environment; it also results in the decomposition of the dichotomy between human and environment, since it is not just that the environment is now conversely extended

4. A. Gehlen, *Man: His Nature and Place in the World*, trans. Clare McMillan and Karl Pillemer (New York: Columbia University Press, 1988), 39.

5. R. Kaehr, "Joachim Castella: Studien zur Thematik 'Kalkül und Kreativität,'" (n.p.: SelectedWorks, 2001), 12, http://works.bepress.com/thinkartlab/22/. Cf. S. Freud (*Civilization and Its Discontents* [New York: W.W. Norton & Company, 1989], 44) points out that through the use of auxiliary organs man has, "as it were, become a kind of prosthetic God. When he puts on all his auxiliary organs he is truly magnificent; but those organs have not grown on to him and they still give him much trouble at times."

into the human person, but that both the environment and the human person are made to vanish along with the distinction between them. Where once there were human beings and an environment, only the material and media of production remain. It is no longer possible to speak of a human-friendly human design any more than one can speak of a human-friendly environmental design. Where everything has been transposed into the subjunctive, the distinction between indicative and subjunctive disappears, just as it does where everything is kept in the indicative. Of course both are only boundary concepts. But life is impaired both when we attempt to measure every possible thing by what is actual, and when we believe that we should keep our focus on the possible free from every orientation toward the actual. Both approaches can only result in driving the life out of life. The operation may have been a success, but the patient is dead.

3. Original Passivity

In the face of these unhappy prospects, it is worthwhile venturing a different view of the human person, not considering the person as a deficient being but rather as a being of possibility. This is particularly appropriate when one considers the human person from a theological point of view, reflecting on the person not simply as one living being among others but also as a living being before God. In theological terms, the basic modality is possibility and the distinction between the possible and the impossible, rather than reality and the distinction between reality and the nonreal.[6] It is the enrichment of his life through the possibilities that come his way, rather than the inadequacy of his deficient reality, that is most interesting about the human from a theological point of view.

This alters both the anthropological perspective as well as what comes into view. As deficient beings, humans are in danger of working themselves up into a frenzy of activity and thus destroying themselves.

6. See Ingolf U. Dalferth, "*Possibile Absolutum*: The Theological Discovery of the Ontological Priority of the Possible," in *Rethinking the Medieval Legacy for Contemporary Theology*, ed. Anselm K. Min (Notre Dame, IN: University of Notre Dame Press, 2014), 91–130.

By putting everything indicative, even themselves, into the subjunctive so that they only pay attention to what could be or could have been, and no longer to what is and will be, humans turn themselves into the object of their creative frenzy and undermine the basis of their activity. As a being of possibility, on the other hand, the essence of the human person's creativity does not manifest itself in a compensating activity in the struggle for survival in a world hostile to humans, but rather in a passivity that is more fundamental than all human activity and passivity. This fundamental passivity is not merely other than human activity; it is that without which there would be neither active nor passive processes in human life. It is a passivity *of life*, not just a passivity *in the life* of the human person, since, in contrast to the latter, it is the prerequisite for, not a corollary of, activity in life.

More than all activity and passivity in life, this passivity of life is the center of creativity from which humans live. It is the boundary point that no human activity can overstep and turn into a self-performed activity. We can shape our contingency, and we can reshape the conditions of others' contingency beyond recognition, but we cannot make ourselves the contingency or engender ourselves. Our lives are based on a passivity that lies behind all our activities and that we can never transform into our own activity.

For that very reason this passivity preserves the deficient beings that we are from escalating our own activities to the point where we destroy ourselves through it. There is nothing about our existence that we cannot reshape. We are not compelled to be as we are. We could be different, or we even could not exist. But if we exist, then we are not what we are because of ourselves, but because of others—because of what our parents, doctors, midwives, and many others do. Yet, even if we owe our existence to others, their activity manifests itself to us, who owe our existence to it, not as activity but rather as a passivity that for us is inescapable: we *have come to exist*.

This original passivity is written into our lives existentially, and nothing can remove or cancel it. When we recognize, secondarily, that others have made us, this cognitive insight does not override our existential passivity; rather, it presupposes and confirms it. It is only on the basis of this insight that we can know and say that we are *because* we have become (the existential perspective of those who experience their lives) and that we became what we are *because* others and we ourselves have made us what we are (the cognitive perspective of those who reflect on their lives). But this cognitive statement is secondary and presupposes the existential perspective. We were not there when we came into existence, which means that our becoming, as part of the process of living our lives, is not accessible to us primarily and decisively in activity mode, even the activity of others, but rather only in the mode of our own passivity: we have come to exist, and we did not make ourselves. If this applies to us, however, then it applies to others as well, in which case passivity is an essential feature of human existence that must not be suppressed but given thoughtful consideration if one is seeking to understand human beings from the perspective of their experience of themselves and not simply as one object among others.

4. Unavailable Possibilities

This point gives rise to the following reflections. We can only be because we have become, and we only are for as long as we are becoming. This becoming cannot be understood wholly as doing unless a critical dimension of our life and experience of ourselves is grayed out. Our becoming and what we become is never completely merged with what was before us or with what we ourselves and others have made us. We live from a surplus of the possible, which cannot be derived from or traced back to the activities of others and our own activities, but which consistently exceeds these realities and the possibilities inherent in them. We do not just become what others can make us or we can make ourselves, nor do we become what we can become simply because we are what we have become. Rather, we are constantly becoming more and becoming something other than merely that, because something new and unexpected takes place—new life when we begin our existence, and something new within our life when possibilities come our way that could not have been derived from our life hitherto or from everything we currently do or refrain from doing. As beings of possibility, humans live from possibilities that they do not initially have at their disposal, that they cannot provide or create for themselves, and that others cannot give them because others do not have them at their disposal but must be given them. We do not have these possibilities in such a way that we need only actualize them; rather, their occurrence interrupts our actualization processes by making possible something new, something that is more than the other that was already possible before.

This does not mean that one is compelled to engage with these possibilities or give attention to them. One can ignore them. But one cannot contrive, devise, or fabricate them. They cannot be anticipated; they take us by surprise; they are unforeseeable and unexpected, without specific purpose, unprovoked, unmerited, gratuitous. They are what turns every moment of life into an adventure, both in the positive and the negative sense. Human life is full of new beginnings throughout and cannot be planned in advance. The desire to be able to plan and control it completely is a clear, sometimes understandable, but fortunately futile attempt to drive the life out of life. It founders on the very thing that makes life worth living: on the possibilities that cannot be pinned down as calculable probabilities, but are wholly improbable. Any attempt to calculate them is futile (*umsonst*). For they happen unconditionally (*umsonst*). Only the conditional can be actively formed, and then only if the conditions under which it can occur can be created or its occurrence can be prevented. By contrast, we are passively exposed to the unconditional. It eludes the effects of our activity. But this is the source of the creativity of our passivity and hence also the possibility of our activity.

How are we humans to organize our thinking if we are perceived in this sense as beings of possibility, living from the creativity of our passivity more than from any actual activity or passivity? That is the central question addressed in the reflections that follow.

2

Of Humanity and God

The Perspective of Reason
and the Wider Perspective of Faith

1. *Animal Rationale*

The classical philosophical definition of the human being is *animal rationale*, a living being endowed with reason. Humans are distinguished from other living beings by the fact that they are endowed with reason in its wider sense of λόγος, νοῦς, νόησις, διάνοια, *ratio, mens, intellectus*. They are not mere animals but rational animals.

Ever since Kant, German-language philosophy has customarily differentiated between *Vernunft* (reason) and *Verstand* (understanding). *Vernunft* (νοῦς, that is, νόησις, *intellectus, raison, reason*) is understood critically as the capacity for reflective self-thematization (determination of the character and boundaries of *Vernunft*), understood theoretically as the ability to recognize and assess associations in context (rational cognition), understood practically as the capacity for self-determination (autonomy), and understood hermeneutically as insight into the governing principles of different practical contexts, guided by distinctions such as one/many (ontology), truth/falsehood (knowledge), good/evil (ethics), beautiful/ugly (aesthetics), and the like. It is distinguished from *Verstand* (διάνοια, *ratio*, *entendement*, understanding), which is characterized theoretically as the capacity for thought and cognition, the faculty of comprehension (abstract formation of concepts), of judging (connecting concepts to form judgments), and of deduction (valid inference of judgments from other judgments); hermeneutically, it is characterized as the faculty of understanding, which can grasp the meaning of signs, symbols, words, and concepts and the sense of complexes of signs, sentences, judgments, actions, and groups of phenomena. In contradistinction to sensory intuition, which applies to the singular, *Verstand* (understanding) is concerned with the particular and the general; and in contradistinction to *Vernunft* (reason), which has unity and interrelation as its goals, understanding is concerned with multiplicity and diversity. In the literal sense of *Verstand* there are echoes of the Old High German *firstān*, *firstand* (to stand in front of or around something, to master or take hold of it; or, figuratively, to grasp, comprehend, apprehend, perceive, penetrate),[1] and in the same way, in the literal sense of *Vernunft* there are echoes of the old *ferniman* (to hear, perceive correctly, register; or, figuratively, to process what has been registered).[2] Just as *Verstand* is a conceptual condensation of the process of grappling with and reaching out in discernment for what "one is standing in front of," so too *Vernunft* is a conceptual condensation of the assimilation of those things from which one takes in, learns, and understands. If one extends this idea systematically, one can say that with *Verstandesverstehen* (intellectual understanding) it is the reference to something that is given prominence, whereas with *Vernunftverstehen* (rational insight) it is the reference to others. Where nothing has been given and nothing is present, there is no intellectual understanding; where there is no communication with others, there is no rational insight. Hence, *Verstand* stands for relatedness to something other, whereas *Vernunft* stands for openness to others.

The etymological connotation clarifies what has always been the nub of the philosophical definition of the human being. The anthropological

1. Jacob Grimm and Wilhelm Grimm, *Deutsches Wörterbuch*, s.v. "Verstand," http://woerterbuchnetz.de/DWB/?sigle=DWB&mode=Vernetzung&hitlist=&patternlist=&lemid=GV0457.

2. Ibid., s.v. "Vernunft," http://woerterbuchnetz.de/DWB/?sigle=DWB&mode=Vernetzung&hitlist=&patternlist=&lemid=GV0296.

definition of humans as rational beings does not tie them down; on the contrary, it sets them in motion by pointing them beyond themselves. It is an abbreviated form of the open indeterminacy of humans, not of a rigid, prescriptive ontological definition of humanness. Human reason does not just give humans a special status among animals; it is the decisive factor that raises the one above the other.

We lose sight of the above if we construe this definition of humanness purely logically instead of ontologically and epistemologically. If one understands the term *rational* as the description of an attribute R, which one can define using the set of characteristics "$R_1 \ldots R_n$," and if one also understands *animal* as an abbreviated formula for a set of attributes "$P_1 \ldots P_n$," which, taken together, characterize what we call "living being," then the whole term *animal rationale* can be understood as a conjunction of the attributes "$P_1 \ldots P_n$ & $R_1 \ldots R_n$" that a being must necessarily and sufficiently exhibit in order to be properly called "human." The term *human* thus is understood as a complex predicate H, which can accurately be used to describe something if the following statement is true. "There is an x that is H," and this is always the case when x exhibits the attributes "$P_1 \ldots P_n$ & $R_1 \ldots R_n$." This formal reading conceals the *philosophical problem* underlying this definition: from what angle, against what background, and with what interest is what we call "human" defined here? When we describe it as "$P_1 \ldots P_n$ & $R_1 \ldots R_n$," how does this differentiate it from anything else and relate it to anything else? Does "$P_1 \ldots P_n$" represent the context in which "$R_1 \ldots R_n$" is to be understood? If so, a human being's rationality would be an expression of his animality. Or conversely, should we understand "$P_1 \ldots P_n$" within the context of "$R_1 \ldots R_n$"? In that case the animality of the human being would be apprehended as the expression of his rationality. So where should we begin so that we do not misunderstand the human being but rather comprehend him within the context of everything else? Should we understand human reason from the perspective of human animality, or human animality from the perspective of human reason? Is the human being a rational animal or an animal instance of reason?

Questions of this nature led the philosophical tradition to an inversion of perspective that was fraught with consequences from its earliest stages. In order to understand humans correctly as living beings endowed with reason, one must conceive of them as rational *animals*. The normative hermeneutical context for understanding human beings is not their animal nature (animality), but their reason (rationality). The human person is not an animal endowed with reason but rather a rational being, singled out by his animal nature and limited in the use of his reason by being tied to his animal life form. His reason—not his animal nature—constitutes his normative *genus*, and his animal nature—not his reason—constitutes the *differentia specifica* (specific difference) most appropriate to him.

But this means that reason is the truly decisive factor in the life of the human being. With the aid of their reason, human beings can keep the animal functions of their souls and bodies under control; that is to say, they can live their lives in a manner that is "correct," "good," or "upright." By well-ordered communal life (ethics, ethical principles), economic life (economy, economics), and public life (government, politics), they can create out of the imponderability of nature and the accidents of life a habitat in which, despite a hostile environment, they are able to live in an "upright," "good," and "safe" manner within the bounds of their human possibilities.[3] Hence, the more human beings foster and nurture their capacity for reason—not surrendering to their animal emotions, passions, and desires, but taking care, in their personal lives as well as in social, economic, and public communal life, to do "what is right," which is to say, the socially apposite, the morally good, the economically right, and the politically just—the more they will be leading a truly human life.

2. The *Animal Rationale* as *Imago Dei*

From time immemorial, this representation of the human person has been taken theologically as an interpretation of the biblical reference to the human being as *imago Dei* (the image of God).[4] Humans are

3. Wherever all that we traditionally take for granted regarding these common life forms (in other words, the traditional ethos, economy, and system of government) is called in question, we are faced with tasks of reflection and decision that lead to the formation of disciplines of thought such as ethics, economics, or politics.

4. There is no need to go into the complicated history of this interpretation here. It merits separate treatment. See Christoph Markschies, "Gottebenbildlichkeit. II. Christentum," 4th ed., 3:1160–63; Wolfhart Pannenberg, "Gottebenbildlichkeit und

related to God in that they are endowed with reason, but they manifest their likeness to God as in a mirror obscurely, because they are
animals and not (only) reason, as God is. This interpretation of the
doctrine of human beings created in the image of God, which took as
its reference point the image of human beings as animals endowed with
reason, had disastrous consequences for the interpretation of human
creatureliness and sin. The creation-theological distinction between
God and humankind became associated in a confusing way with the
hamartiological distinction between true humanity as intended by God
and fallen humanity as it actually is; the human faculty of reason was
linked with human God-relatedness, whereas the human animal nature
was linked with the human state of separation from God. Thus the
problem of sin was read into the animal nature of humankind, with
the far-reaching consequence that every animal and physical impulse
was suspected of separating and turning human beings away from their
Creator. Conversely, relationship with God became focused entirely on
reason, with the equally far-reaching consequence that reason became
the definitive touchstone for determining whether it was possible to
treat God seriously as God and the human person seriously (or even
at all) as God's creation. The current debates surrounding the neuroscientific naturalization of central aspects of this view of reason (free
will, self-determination, and responsibility) speak for themselves.[5]

Bildung des Menschen," in *Grundfragen Systematischer Theologie: Gesammelte Auf-
sätze* (Göttingen: Vandenhoeck & Ruprecht, 1980), 2:207–25; Eberhard Jüngel, "Der
Gott entsprechende Mensch: Bemerkungen zur Gottebenbildlichkeit des Menschen
als Grundfigur theologischer Anthropologie," in *Entsprechungen: Gott—Wahrheit—
Mensch: Theologische Erörterungen* (Munich: Chr. Kaiser, 1980), 290–321; Ingolf U.
Dalferth and Eberhard Jüngel, "Person und Gottebenbildlichkeit," in *Christlicher
Glaube in moderner Gesellschaft*, ed. Franz Böckle, Franz-Xaver Kaufmann, Karl
Rahner, and Bernhard Welte (Freiburg: Herder, 1981), 24:56–99; Klaus Koch, *Imago
Dei: die Würde des Menschen im biblischen Text* (Göttingen: Vandenhoeck & Ru-
precht, 2000); Ingolf U. Dalferth, "Mit Bildern leben: Theologische und religionsphi-
losophische Perspektiven," in *Die Unvermeidlichkeit der Bilder*, ed. G. v. Graevenitz
et al. (Tübingen: Mohr Siebeck, 2001), 77–102; Claudia Welz, "Imago Dei—Bild des
Unsichtbaren," *ThLZ* 136 (2011): 479–90.
    5. See D. Evers, "Hirnforschung und Theologie," *ThLZ* 131 (2006): 1107–22; Evers,
"Neurobiologie und die Frage der Willensfreiheit," in *Naturwissenschaften und Theologie: Methodische Ansätze und Grundlagenwissen zum interdisziplinären Dialog*,
ed. J. Weinhardt (Stuttgart: Kohlhammer, 2010), 102–23; T. Dennebaum, *Kein Raum
mehr für Gott? Wissenschaftlicher Naturalismus und christlicher Schöpfungsglaube*

This development has become possible because reason, as the characteristic that differentiates humankind from animals (the human/ animal distinguishing feature), is simultaneously understood to be the supreme characteristic linking humans with the divine or with God (the human/divine common feature). Meanwhile, conversely, humankind's animal nature is seen as the definitive distinguishing characteristic that differentiates it from God and the divine (the human/ divine distinguishing feature) and links it with the rest of creation (the human/animal common feature). By virtue of their reason, humans are living beings who are able to orient themselves toward the true, the good, the beautiful, and the eternal, beyond all impermanence, half measures, falsehood, evil, and shortcomings. In their reason, in the *apex mentis* (summit) of their souls, they can touch that which is inaccessible to all other living beings: the divine immutability. Their capacity for reason thus makes manifest both what differentiates them from other animals and, simultaneously, what they hold in common with the divine and with God. It is a common feature that does not apply in the same way to both humans and God, but, because of the animal nature of the rational human being, it is modified by the difference between infinite and finite, immutable and mutable, divine and earthly, or—within the sphere of Jewish, Christian, and Islamic thought—Creator and created. Human beings are neither merely animals nor gods; they are related to worms but also to angels.

This singles human beings out, but it also puts them in a permanently precarious position. Neither mere animals nor wholly angels, they are compelled to find their identity on the border between two orientation points, neither of which they can lose sight of, lest they fall headlong and fail to achieve their potential. For whenever they want to be more than they are, behaving as if they were angels, they in fact become less than they are: inhuman animals. And whenever they want to be less—in other words, mere animals—they do not even achieve the level of animal life. "Man is neither angel nor brute, and

(Würzburg: Echter, 2006); A. L. C. Runehov, *Sacred or Neural? The Potential of Neuroscience to Explain Religious Experience* (Göttingen: Vandenhoeck & Ruprecht, 2007); U. Schmidt, "Glaube und Gehirn: Eine theologische Auseinandersetzung mit gegenwärtigen Ergebnissen und Trends der Hirnforschung," *Deutsches Pfarrerblatt* 12 (2009), http://pfarrerverband.medio.de/pfarrerblatt/archiv.php?a=show &id=2731.

the unfortunate thing is that he who would act the angel acts the brute," Pascal remarked appositely in his *Pensées*.[6] And from this state of affairs Kierkegaard drew the conclusion that human beings are faced with the unending task of solving an insoluble paradox that they cannot evade but can never solve: "The human person is a synthesis of the infinite and the finite, of the temporal and the eternal, of freedom and necessity—in, short a synthesis."[7] He can only be this by becoming it, and this is precisely what is impossible. In order to live as a true human, the human being must exist as a synthesis of the infinite and the finite even though there can be no relationship between infinite and finite. But if human beings are obliged to become what they cannot become, then they are an existential impossibility, a living paradox in person.

3. The Philosophical Critique of Modernity

Since the end of the eighteenth century, this emphasis, among others, has led to the entire philosophical-theological tradition of thought surrounding the concept of *animal rationale* being subject to criticism in a whole variety of ways. Questions raised include both what we should understand by human reason or rationality, and what the animal nature of the human being comprises and what its hallmarks are. In addition to dualistic approaches, which hold on to the irreducible double identity of human beings as physical and spiritual, body and soul, animal and rational,[8] there have arisen idealistic approaches, which seek to integrate the human being's animal nature into a more comprehensive concept of reason, as well as naturalistic approaches, which attempt to comprehend every aspect of humanness, including

6. Blaise Pascal, *Pensées*, ed. Michel Le Guern (Paris: Gallimard, 1977), frag. 572, p. 370.

7. Søren Kierkegaard, *Die Krankheit zum Tode*, ed. H. Diem and W. Rest (Munich: dtv, 1976), 31.

8. These designations are by no means identical in meaning. Rather, they are explained and formalized differently by different approaches. What they have in common, however, is the belief that it is only possible to conceive of human beings in the light of two perspectives that are not mutually reducible and cannot be rooted in a third common perspective from the differentiation of which they could be understood.

human reason and spiritual activity, on the basis of a dynamic evolutionary understanding of the human being's animal nature.

Thus Kant points out emphatically and with significant implications that it is wholly inadequate to look for the uniqueness of the human being only in his "humanity" (rationality) as distinct from his "animality," and not also in his "personality, as a rational *and at the same time accountable* being" to be differentiated from both of the former.[9] This accountability or personality is not simply another aspect in addition to his animal (living) nature and rational (human) nature; it only comes into consideration when one alters one's perspective so as to view the human being not merely as a "*Thiermensch* [human animal]" but also as a "*Vernunftmensch* [rational human being]."[10] Considered from the first perspective he is, with all his capability of understanding, a relatively insignificant animal; from the second, in contrast, he is a rational being worthy of respect.

> In the system of nature, a human being (*homo phaenomenon, animal rationale*) is a being of slight importance and shares with the rest of the animals, as offspring of the earth, an ordinary value (*pretium vulgare*). Although man has, in his reason, something more than they and can set his own ends, even this gives him only an extrinsic value in terms of his usefulness (*pretium usus*). This extrinsic value is the value of one man above another—that is, his price as a ware that can be exchanged for these other animals, as things. But, so conceived, man still has a lower value than the universal medium of exchange, namely money. . . . But a human being regarded as a person, that is, as the subject of a morally practical reason, is exalted above any price; for as a person (*homo noumenon*) he is not to be valued merely as a means to the ends of others or even to his own ends, but as an end in himself, that is, he possesses a dignity (an absolute inner worth) by which he exacts respect for himself from all other rational beings in the world. He can measure himself against every other being of this kind and value himself on a footing of equality with them.[11]

9. Immanuel Kant, *Die Religion innerhalb der Grenzen der bloßen Vernunft*, AA 6:26 (emphasis added). Cf. Johannes Schwartländer, *Der Mensch ist Person: Kants Lehre vom Menschen* (Stuttgart: Kohlhammer, 1968).
10. Immanuel Kant, *Metaphysik der Sitten*, zweiter Teil, "Ethische Elementarlehre," Erster Teil, Zweites Hauptstück, §11, AA 6:435.
11. Ibid., 6:434–35. English translation: Immanuel Kant, *The Metaphysics of Morals*, ed. M. Gregor (Cambridge: Cambridge University Press, 1996), 186.

As a *Verstandestier* (an animal capable of understanding), a human being is only different from other animals to a relative degree. But as a rational being—that is to say, "in view of the claim *to be an end in himself*"—he has attained a position of "*equality with all rational beings*, whatever their rank."[12] Of all animals, he alone is a person and is thus in a position "to perfect himself in accordance with the ends that he sets himself; with the result that, as an animal endowed with the capacity for reason (*animal rationabile*), he is able to turn himself into a rational animal (*animal rationale*)."[13] This means that a human being is not already an *animal rationale* but must first become one. He can only become one by making himself into one. He can only make himself into one by training his "human animal self" in reason. To achieve this, he will set for his activity only those goals that are consistent with his dignity as an end in itself. He does not have to live this way. Nor can he be compelled to live this way. He can only choose to do it of his own free will. If he does not choose to do it, he remains a "human animal" of minor importance within nature as a whole. If, on the other hand, he does so choose, then "his insignificance as a human animal may not infringe upon his consciousness of his dignity as a rational human being,"[14] and, despite all his shortcomings, he proves himself a perfectible being with an open horizon.[15]

This redefinition of reason, with its focus on the fundamental distinction between understanding and reason, pushes open a door. Like Kant, albeit not always using his arguments, many nineteenth- and twentieth-century writers argued for a reassessment of what was meant by human reason and, indeed, by reason overall. This question is variously answered by Fichte and Hegel, Schleiermacher and Schelling, Whitehead and Hartshorne, Heidegger, Wittgenstein and Adorno, Habermas, Foucault, Derrida, Lyotard, Ricoeur, Rorty, and Welsch.[16]

12. Immanuel Kant, *Muthmaßlicher Anfang des Menschengeschlechts* (1786), A 11–12, AA 8:114.

13. Immanuel Kant, *Anthropologie in pragmatischer Hinsicht* (1798), A 315, AA 7:321.

14. Kant, *The Metaphysics of Morals*, 186.

15. What Kant says about the human person as "he" applies in the same way to the human person as "she."

16. See the overview in W. Welsch, *Vernunft: Die zeitgenössische Vernunftkritik und das Konzept der transversalen Vernunft* (Frankfurt am Main: Suhrkamp, 1996).

4. The Current Naturalistic Critique

Still others, particularly Nietzsche, follow Darwin in insisting that human beings must be understood in all their aspects, including their rationality, from the perspective of their animal nature. The human being is "the *as-yet undetermined animal*."[17] In contrast to Kant, and without taking account of his critical differentiation between understanding and reason, Nietzsche does not see the basis for this anthropological openness and indeterminacy in the dignity of the human being as an accountable rational being, but rather, conversely, in his animal nature. The human being is counted "unadorned and without metaphor, among the animals,"[18] and is to be conceived of wholly and exclusively as an animal. As Nietzsche puts it:

> We have changed our minds. We have become more modest in every way. We have stopped deriving humanity from "spirit," from "divinity," we have stuck human beings back among the animals. We see them as the strongest animals because they are the most cunning: one consequence of this is their spirituality. On the other hand, we are also opposed to a certain vanity that re-emerges here too, acting as if human beings were the great hidden goal of animal evolution. Humans are in no way the crown of creation, all beings occupy the same level of perfection. . . . And even this is saying too much: comparatively speaking, humans are the biggest failures, the sickliest animals who have strayed the most dangerously far from their instincts—but of course and in spite of everything, the most *interesting* animals as well! . . . People used to see consciousness, "spirit," as proof that humanity is descended from something higher, that humanity is divine; people were advised to become *perfect* by acting like turtles and pulling their senses inside themselves, cutting off contact with worldly things and shedding their mortal shrouds: after this, the essential element would remain, the "pure spirit." We are more sensible about all this too: we see the development of consciousness, "spirit," as a symptom of precisely the relative *imperfection* of the organism, as an experimenting, a groping, a mistaking, as an exertion that is sapping an unnecessarily

17. Friedrich Nietzsche, *Jenseits von Gut und Böse*, drittes Hauptstück, §62, KSA 5:81. English translation: *Beyond Good and Evil: Prelude to a Philosophy of the Future*, trans. Walter Kaufmann (New York: Vintage Books, 1989), 74.

18. Ibid., Fünftes Hauptstück, §202, 5:124 (*Beyond Good and Evil*, 115).

large amount of strength away from the nervous system,—we deny that anything can be made perfect as long as it is still being made conscious. "Pure spirit" is a pure stupidity: when we discount the nervous system and the senses, the "mortal shroud," *we miscount*—nothing more![19]

Even our human spirit and our reason are nothing but functions of our animal nature and to be strictly subordinated to our instincts.[20] This is the conclusion drawn by current cultural and scientific research. The "faith in the dignity and uniqueness of man, in his irreplaceability in the great chain of being, is a thing of the past—he has become an *animal*, literally and without reservation or qualification—he, who was, according to his old faith, almost God ('child of God,' 'God-man')."[21] Like all animals, however, this "human animal"[22] is basically governed by one thing: his "will to live" (thus Schopenhauer),[23] or, as Nietzsche expresses it, his *"Will to power."*[24] This will is the basic Dionysian driving force in the human life, even where, guided by questionable ascetic ideals, it turns against itself, becoming a "hatred of the human, and even more of the animal, and more still of the material," this "horror of the senses, of reason itself."[25] Even in the perverted form of a *"will to nothingness*, an aversion to life, a rebellion against the most fundamental presuppositions of life," it is nevertheless true that "it is and remains a *will*! . . . man rather will *nothingness* than *not* will."[26] Human animals have to be understood from the perspective of this basic impulse of life, not from that of the questionable forms of culture and morality on the basis of which they have made themselves

19. Nietzsche, *The Anti-Christ*, 12.

20. Nietzsche, *Jenseits von Gut und Böse*, Fünftes Hauptstück, §191, 5:112 (*Beyond Good and Evil*, 103–4). Cf. Wolfgang Welsch, "Nietzsche über Vernunft—'Meine *wiederhergestellte* Vernunft,'" in *Rationalität und Prärationalität*, ed. J. Beaufort and P. Prechtl (Würzburg: Echter, 1998), 107–15.

21. Friedrich Nietzsche, *Zur Genealogie der Moral*, Dritte Abhandlung, §25, KSA 5:404. English translation: *On the Genealogy of Morals*, trans. W. Kaufmann and R. J. Hollingdale (New York: Vintage Books, 1989), 155.

22. See ibid., Zweite Abhandlung, §3, 5:294 (*Genealogy*, 60).

23. A. Schopenhauer, *Die Welt als Wille und Vorstellung*, Buch 4, §54, in *Zürcher Ausgabe: Werke in 10 Bänden* (Zurich: Diogenes, 1977), 2.1:347.

24. Nietzsche, *Zur Genealogie der Moral*, Dritte Abhandlung, §27 et passim, 5:409 (*Genealogy*, 160).

25. Ibid., 5:412 (*Genealogy*, 162).

26. Ibid. (*Genealogy*, 163).

into rational beings who, in their animal nature, see only what is to be overcome, controlled, and rendered invisible. Human beings are first and foremost animals, and they also are to be understood as such.

Fueled by the successes of evolutionary biology, neuroscience, and neurobiology, this point of view has been reinforced in the current era of scientific naturalism. There is a tendency to reduce reason and spirit to the activity of the brain: "Mind is what the brain does."[27] Admittedly, this formula has been criticized on the grounds that the brain carries out activities over and above those of what is here designated "mind," "spirit," or "reason," or that it is not sufficiently specific,[28] or that reason and spirit cannot be reduced to epiphenomena of brain activity, but are also manifest in social processes and institutions and hence in the realm of the "objective spirit" (thus Hegel). Today there is a distinct tendency to understand human reason and the human spirit naturalistically, whether in terms of a first or biological nature (Pinker, Dennett,[29] Korzeniewski[30]) or in terms of a second, cultural nature (Ricoeur,[31] McDowell,[32] Tomasello[33]).[34] It is no longer the dis-

27. Steven Pinker, *How the Mind Works* (London: W. W. Norton & Co., 1997), 21.

28. See G. Northoff, *Philosophy of the Brain: The Brain Problem* (Amsterdam: John Benjamins, 2004); Northoff, "Sind wir nichts als Gehirn? Das Selbst und sein Gehirn," *Existenzanalyse* 27, no. 2 (2010): 27–31, who attempts to identify, in a more differentiated manner, affective-prereflexive self-referential processing in the cortical midline structures of the brain as being the empirical basis of the phenomenal self. See G. Northoff and J. Panksepp, "The Trans-species Concept of Self and the Subcortical-Cortical Midline System," *Trends in Cognitive Science* 12, no. 7 (2008): 259–64; J. Panksepp and G. Northoff, "The Trans-species Core SELF: The Emergence of Active Cultural and Neuro-ecological Agents through Self-Related Processing within Subcortical-Cortical Midline Networks," *Consciousness and Cognition* 18, no. 1 (2009): 193–215.

29. Daniel C. Dennett, *Consciousness Explained* (Boston: Little, Brown and Co., 1991); Dennett, *Breaking the Spell: Religion as a Natural Phenomenon* (New York: Penguin, 2006).

30. B. Korzeniewski, *From Neurons to Self-Consciousness: How the Brain Generates the Mind* (New York: Humanity Books, 2011).

31. Paul Ricœur, *Soi-même comme un autre* (Paris: Édition du Seuil, 1990).

32. John McDowell, *Mind and World* (Cambridge: Harvard University Press, 1998); McDowell, *Reason and Nature: Lecture and Colloquium in Münster 1999*, ed. Marcus Wollaschek (Münster: LIT, 2000).

33. M. Tomasello, *Die kulturelle Entwicklung des menschlichen Denkens* (Frankfurt am Main: Suhrkamp, 2002).

34. For the history of this concept, see Norbert Rath, *Zweite Natur: Konzepte einer Vermittlung von Natur und Kultur in Anthropologie und Ästhetik um 1800* (Münster: Waxmann, 1996).

tinction between human beings and God that plays a role in directing the attempt to define the humanness of human beings, but purely the distinction between human beings and animals.

5. Explanation and Orientation

There are good grounds for this, insofar as we are dealing with the scientific explanation of phenomena: God is not a phenomenon that can be explained scientifically, and the reference to God is no help where the scientific explanation of phenomena is concerned. Explanations seek to prove that the occurrence of a phenomenon is more likely than it would otherwise have been under the given circumstances. They may do this inductively, abductively, or deductively. In other words, they may deduce the description of a phenomenon ("Socrates is mortal") from a general principle ("All men are mortal") taken together with information regarding a particular set of conditions ("Socrates is a man") (deduction); or they may trace it back reductively to a general principle (induction) or a specific condition (abduction). They must thereby not only distinguish between the universal (principle or law) and the particular (phenomenon), but in the phenomenal realm they must also take into account a distinction between what they explain and what they do not explain. When it is claimed that everything is explained without distinction, the concept of explanation loses its sense; and when, in the realm of experience, it is impossible to demonstrate a distinction in relation to which an explanation can succeed or fail, the effort to explain becomes meaningless.

The philosophical discussion of God does not refer to any such distinction in the realm of experience. God is not an object of experience; rather, God is the precondition for the possibility that anything can be experienced at all—in other words, for the possibility that there is something that can be experienced and someone to experience it. Even in theological terms, one cannot say that there are some things that were created by God and others that were not. Either everything that is distinct from God is God's creation, or there is nothing created. Hence any philosophical reference to God (however it may be described) does not explain what exists; at most, it explains what it means that anything at all exists, and not nothing. Furthermore, theological discussion of God is not a failed attempt to explain the phenomena of the world; rather, it receives its meaning and its profile within the sphere of our human endeavor to orientate ourselves in the confusing world in which we find ourselves. Its purpose is to provide a critical analysis and exposition of the Christian life orientation, as opposed to a pseudoscientific explanation of the world.

Questions of orientation are quite different from questions of explanation, and they call for different answers.[35] Whereas questions of explanation relate to the why ("Why does something occur?") or the how ("Why does something occur in this manner?") of a phenomenon, questions of orientation focus on the conduct of human life when dealing with the phenomena, not on the phenomena themselves. They are not questions of being, but questions of meaning, so they explain what something signifies for us rather than why it is as it is. We do not live in a world of facts and laws, but in the world of everyday life that is structured, from a personal and cultural point of view, more or less meaningfully. It therefore discloses the unstructured and disordered, the inaccessible and confusing, as the permanent reverse side and concomitant of human life. Meaning is not simply given; it must be wrested time and again from the meaningless, nonsensical, and paradoxical. In order to get our bearings in confusing life situations, we need orientation strategies. Those that have stood the test of time in relevant practical situations are core components of our culture. They must serve two purposes: they must *order* the world for us, and they must make it possible for us to *find our place* in this ordered world. In order to orient ourselves in a particular field of practice, we must be in a position to see phenomena in a distinctive context, so that we can relate to them in a distinctive manner (ordering). On the other hand, we need a procedure that will help us to locate ourselves within

35. On the concept of orientation employed here, see Ingolf U. Dalferth, *Die Wirklichkeit des Möglichen: Hermeneutische Religionsphilosophie* (Tübingen: Mohr Siebeck, 2003), part 1; Dalferth, *Malum: Theologische Hermeneutik des Bösen* (Tübingen: Mohr Siebeck, 2008, 1–14 and 519–47; Ingolf U. Dalferth and Stefan Berg, eds., *Gestalteter Klang—gestalteter Sinn: Orientierungsstrategien in Musik und Religion im Wandel der Zeit* (Leipzig: Evangelische Verlagsanstalt, 2011); Werner Stegmaier, ed., *Orientierung: Philosophische Perspektiven* (Frankfurt am Main: Suhrkamp, 2005); Stegmaier, *Philosophie der Orientierung* (Berlin: de Gruyter, 2008).

the orientational order in question (finding our place). This is how we order our practical situation, by setting up or emphasizing relevant distinctions: distinctions of space (in front, behind, above, below, right, left), of time (today, yesterday, tomorrow, previously, afterward), of social context (family relationships such as father, mother, daughter, aunt, grandfather), and of life orientation (good/bad, good/evil, pleasant/unpleasant, pleasure/displeasure, beneficial/harmful, etc.). And we find our place in these contexts by defining ourselves and other persons and things with the aid of these distinctions, so that we are able to set up meaningful relationships with others and what is other.

In Christian faith and thought the distinction between God and humanity is a central element of these orientation strategies. To unfold what they mean by "human," Christians take as a guideline not only the distinction between human and animal, and between one human being and another, but also first and foremost the distinction between God and humanity. Without the distinction between God and humanity, a human being could not be considered as a creature: a creature is that which is not God, but would not exist without God. Without the distinction between human and animal, we are liable to lose sight of the fact that a human being is one creation among others, each of which is to be appreciated for its own distinctiveness and uniqueness. And without the distinction between one human being and another, we are at risk of seeing the fundamental theological issue as the distinction between human and animal life (human and nonhuman) and not as the distinction between humane and inhumane life (humaneness and inhumaneness). Yet the latter is the primary concern of the theological debate over our understanding of the humanness of humans.[36]

6. The Theological Dilemma

Admittedly, if one casts a glance at the current state of the debate, one observes a rather strange state of affairs. Whereas philosophy is

36. Cf. Rebekka A. Klein, *Sozialität als Conditio Humana: Eine interdisziplinäre Untersuchung zur Sozialanthropologie in der experimentellen Ökonomik, Sozialphilosophie und Theologie* (Göttingen: Edition Ruprecht, 2010).

moving further and further away from a virtually unqualified view
of the human person as an *animal rationale* (i.e., a rational being),
theology—or certainly a significant strand in contemporary theology—is insisting more and more doggedly that the human being is
just that and nothing else. Confronted by the developments in the
understanding of what it is to be human that I have outlined above,
theologians of Catholic, Orthodox, and Protestant origin apparently
consider themselves obliged to mount a defense against scientific
progress and current naturalistic anthropology of something that it
was not in any way their task to defend: that a human being is not
merely an animal but a rational animal, an *animal rationale*.

The reason for this strange behavior is clear: from time immemorial
Christian theology has viewed human reason not simply as a distinctive biological feature but as the divine spark within the human person.
It is therefore now defending traditional philosophical-theological anthropology against current naturalistic trends by laying great stress on
human rational activity as that which distinguishes the human being
from all other living beings, as the "finite creator," a moral person, a
being endowed with conscience, and the free and rational designer of
his own life. Reason is what makes human beings human—reason in
the theoretical sense (the capacity to recognize truth), in the practical
sense (the freedom for self-determination), and in the pragmatic sense
(the capacity for intelligent and purposeful behavior). In contrast
to other living beings, guided by reason, humans can align the conduct of their lives with what is true, good, right, and beautiful; and
since they can, they therefore should. For, as rational beings, they
bear a responsibility not just for themselves but also for the whole
of creation, since other living beings can neither have nor perceive
any such overarching responsibility. Only human beings, as rational
beings, are in a position to be aware of the overall context of life as
it extends beyond the here and now of their particular situation and
to comprehend this in all its facets and dimensions as the Creator's
creation. Because of this, human beings, as rational beings, are pro-
nounced creation's spokespersons and are required to be aware that
they are responsible before God and their fellow creatures for the
creation in its entirety. Under these circumstances, it is easy to see
why the naturalization of human reason is perceived as an attack on

their humanity and their special position within creation as a whole. Anyone who questions the idea that human reason is the receptive organ for the divine not only disparages the human but also denies the Creator.

Neither Paul nor John nor the other New Testament authors thought or wrote in those terms. They did not consider human reason to be the one great good by which everything stands or falls from a theological point of view. Paul emphatically contrasted the "word of the cross" with the "wisdom of the world" (1 Cor. 1:17–20 NASB) that perceives in the word of the cross foolishness rather than the power of God. Decisively and uncompromisingly, he placed his confidence not in reason and wisdom but in faith and God's power; not in human insight but in the experience of the gospel brought about by the Spirit; not in philosophical wisdom but in the foolishness of the theology of the cross (1 Cor. 1:22–23). He saw the two only in terms of an either/or—not in terms of any kind of mediation that could open up reason to faith or base faith on reason.[37]

7. Toward a Grammar of "Faith" and "Reason"

Problems always arise when reason and faith are read as nouns (*reason* and *faith*) or as verbs (*think/recognize/acknowledge* and *believe/have faith*) and understood ontologically as descriptive titles or anthropologically as terms for human capabilities or mental processes. As a result, they are interpreted as activities: "reason" as "I think," and "faith" as "I believe." But this is a grammatical illusion. The one who thinks engages in mental activity; the one who believes/has faith can be, but is not necessarily, thus engaged, nor is his mental activity the theological focus when we say that he is justified by faith. The use of the active form of verbs such as *sleep, dream, get angry, feel,* or *believe* is misleading if we are intending to say that an activity was in fact being carried out by the one of whom it is predicated. In each case it is that something is happening with the person involved,

37. Even a nontheological reader such as A. Badiou (*Saint Paul: La fondation de l'universalisme* [Paris: Presses Universitaires de France, 1997], chap. 4) clearly recognizes this.

rather than that he or she is doing something. Nietzsche excluded
this interpretation even from the thought process itself.

> With regard to the superstitions of logicians, I shall never tire of em-
> phasizing a small, terse fact, which these superstitious minds hate to
> concede—namely, that a thought comes when "it" wishes, and not
> when "I" wish, so that it is a falsification of the facts of the case to
> say that the subject "I" is the condition of the predicate "think." *It*
> thinks; but that this "it" is precisely the famous old "ego," is, to put
> it mildly, only a supposition, an assertion, and assuredly not an "im-
> mediate certainty." After all, one has even gone too far with this "it
> thinks"—even the "it" contains an *interpretation* of the process, and
> does not belong to the process itself. One infers here according to the
> grammatical habit: "Thinking is an activity; every activity requires
> an agent; consequently."[38]

If we want to avoid this kind of error, we must read "reason"
and "belief/faith," "think," and "believe/have faith" not as nouns
or verbs, but modally or adverbially. They tell us, not what one is,
but *how* one is; not what one does, but *how* one does it. People live
rationally or irrationally, and they live in faith (having faith) or in
unfaith (not having faith). Neither can be reduced to the other or
derived from the other, but only taken in combination with the other.
One can live rationally in unfaith or rationally in faith, but it is not
irrational to have faith or rational not to have faith; nor is it irrational
not to have faith or rational to have faith. "Unfaith" and "faith" are
human modes of living before God; "reason" and "unreason," in
contrast, are human ways of living in the world. One cannot live in
the world without, in fact, living before God, nor can one live before God without doing it either in an unbelieving way (in unfaith)
or in a believing way (in faith). However, if each human being lives
in the world either rationally or irrationally (sometimes in one way,
sometimes in another), then so does each human being who lives in
unfaith and each one who lives in faith. There are unbelievers who
live rationally and believers who live irrationally. But there also are
believers who live rationally and unbelievers who do not.

38. Nietzsche, *Jenseits von Gut und Böse*, Erstes Hauptstück, "Von den Vorur-
theilen der Philosophen," §17, 5:30–31 (*Beyond Good and Evil*, 24).

Between the qualifications of manner that apply to reason (rational/irrational) and those that apply to faith (in faith/in unfaith), however, there is an asymmetry fraught with implications. How we *live* (whether rationally or irrationally) is a decision we must make for ourselves, and we must make it time and again throughout our lives. In contrast, the decision as to how we exist *before God*, whether in faith or unfaith, is not a matter for us to decide ourselves; it is the consequence of everything that has befallen us before we arrive at any possibility of decision and before any alternative choices whatsoever are opened up. In the state of unfaith in which every human being lives initially, and in which most human beings live permanently, there are neither grounds nor option to decide for or against something. One lives as one lives, and there is nothing further to be said. In faith it is different. In faith one can decide against unfaith, but in a state of unfaith one cannot decide in favor of faith. In a state of unfaith there is nothing to be decided, because one has neither the option nor the grounds to be aware of the difference in meaning between faith and unfaith, nor does one understand it. "Faith" and "unfaith" are not distinctive meanings of reason but rather different orientations within faith.[39] Within faith, however, it is not a question of deciding to choose faith, but only of refusing to fall back into unfaith. As we know, that is not impossible. One can only choose to be what one has not yet become, and if one says that one "chooses" or "decides in favor of" what one is, it means that one is staying as one is, not choosing something different. One can only (a) choose to be what one is not *and* (b) make this choice in the knowledge that it represents a valid mode of existence for oneself. In faith, therefore, it is only unfaith that one can choose or not choose, while in unfaith one cannot choose either.

39. They are not suited to describing particular religious or ideological options viewed from the perspective of the rational observer. When taking a descriptive approach, one cannot classify particular attitudes to life as faith and others as unfaith; one can only describe different (religious) attitudes to life that one considers as to a greater or lesser degree convincing, tenable, or justifiable. The distinction between faith and unfaith is not a descriptive difference arrived at through reason but an orientational difference arrived at in faith: only from the perspective of faith can something be qualified as unfaith, and from the perspective of faith it is the state from which one has come to faith that is defined above all as unfaith.

Hence it is only *in faith* that one can decide for or against unfaith. But one never makes a decision in favor of faith, since in unfaith it is impossible and in faith unnecessary. To decide, in faith, against unfaith and thus in favor of faith is not an option in favor of faith taken from a standpoint outside of faith; rather, it is a way of putting faith into effect in one's life, that is to say, of living one's life in faith. When someone makes a *deliberate* decision in favor of faith, and thus begins to live with conviction in accordance with a position they previously held only formally through baptism, this is sometimes described as new birth; there is indeed a convention identifying the latter as the real change event. But even this does not constitute a decision in favor of faith by which an unbeliever switches from unfaith to faith. A person who is "born again"—as the metaphor expressly puts it—does not accomplish this change by his or her own decision; rather, that person consents to, or says amen to, the change that originates with God.

Just as birth is not the result of a child's own decision to choose life, so too new birth is not the result of a human being's own decision to choose faith. Instead, it is a form in which one chooses, in faith, a mode of life, a mode that can take various guises. One can decide how to live out one's faith, and Christianity recognizes not only one mode for doing this. Whether one lives, can live, or wants to live in faith is not a matter for one's own decision and thus is not to be inferred from whether one lives rationally or irrationally.[40] The whence of faith is always unfaith (no one comes to faith who did not previously live in unfaith), but the how of faith is not reason or unreason; rather, it is the interruption of the rationally or irrationally lived life in the world by what Paul calls δύναμις θεοῦ, the power of the gospel (Rom. 1:16) or the word of the cross (1 Cor. 1:18). Where faith is concerned, reason cannot be the starting point, the arbitrator,

40. Here an important parallel between "life" and "life in faith" becomes apparent. Only if one lives can one live rationally or irrationally. Thus how one lives is a matter for decision; *whether* one lives, in contrast, is not (initially). Only once one is alive can one decide against continuing to live and in favor of ceasing to live. Similarly with faith: the fact that one is living in faith is not a result of one's own decision. In faith, however, one can decide against faith and in favor of unfaith. Whether that is rational or irrational is another question, as are the reasons, motives, or circumstances that lead one to do or not to do it.

or the touchstone; at best, it acts as a secondary and subordinate assistant. It cannot be a neutral court of instance, as Locke, and in fact most philosophers of the modern era, held.[41] It is found only in a specifically qualified form as the reason of unfaith (unfaith lived in a rational way) or as the reason of faith (faith lived in a rational way), but not as something that is a third position vis-à-vis faith and unfaith and by whose judgment this faith stands or falls.[42]

8. Special, General, Individual, Universal

This clear embedding, hermeneutical precision, and theological qualification of every use and understanding of reason was clearly seen and unambiguously presented by the Reformation theology of the sixteenth century. This had far-reaching consequences for the controversial question of the true definition of what it is to be human. Its central negative argument can be summarized as follows: because the traditional use of the term *reason* was so lacking in specificity, neither the reference to reason as *genus proximum* (rational being) nor to it as *differentia specifica* (living being endowed with reason) is

41. According to John Locke, it is reason that has the last word against faith, since although reason is not in a position to pass judgment on revealed truths, it is able to judge whether they have been revealed at all. See John Locke, *An Essay Concerning Human Understanding*, book 4, chap. 18, "Of Faith and Reason, and Their Distinct Provinces," in *The Works of John Locke in Nine Volumes* (London: Rivington, 1824), 2:29.

Yet this is precisely what is debatable if one does not construe "revelation" cognitively and hence understands (better, misunderstands) it as a special source of knowledge. See Ingolf U. Dalferth, *Radical Theology: An Essay on Faith and Theology in the Twenty-First Century* (Minneapolis: Fortress, 2016), chap. 12. It likewise should not be forgotten that neutrality is not an essential feature of reason; it is a particular mode of using reason, one that must always first be striven for, is difficult to achieve, and is not always appropriate. See John Churchill, Ingolf Dalferth, Patrick Horn, and Jeffery Willetts, "How Cool Is the Philosophy of Religion? A Symposium on D. Z. Phillips' *Philosophy's Cool Place* (Cornell University Press 1999)," *International Journal for Philosophy of Religion* 71, no. 1 (2012): 3–19. The effort to achieve neutrality is in fact not restricted to the use of reason outside faith but is just as likely to be a feature of its use within faith.

42. See Ingolf U. Dalferth, "Glaubensvernunft oder Vernunftglauben? Anmerkungen zur Vernunftkritik des Glaubens," in *Kommunikation über Grenzen*, ed. Friedrich Schweitzer (Gütersloh: Gütersloher Verlagshaus, 2009), 612–27.

any help in defining the nature of the human being. Alongside this is a corresponding positive argument that claims to provide the negative argument with its allegedly missing specificity, and that finds its shortest and most succinct expression in Luther's theological definition of the human person: *homo iustificari fide* (humanity justified by faith).[43] The implications of this will be explained. But the conflict between the two definitions patently hinges on what merits the designation "specific," which is why I will take this as my starting point.

From a theological perspective, human beings are viewed correctly when they are conceived of in their relationship to God; in other words, in the way they live their lives before God when dealing with the other (their environment), with others (their social world), and with themselves (their personal world). This expression "before God" does not add a further determination alongside the others; rather, it locates them quite specifically and thus says something about the manner in which they are put into practice and lived out. One does not live one's life—say, as a student, a mother, a daughter of divorced parents, and a violinist in a student orchestra—and then "before God" as well, any more than one lives one's life as all those and then exists as well. What Kant demonstrated concerning the existence predicate (i.e., that it does not describe or determine but rather locates or positions the thing described in the experiential world) applies also to the relational determination "before God": it positions a human as an individual in relation to God rather than describing him as a special being within the world of experience. What "human" means in this context is given substance by whatever can be said concerning an individual that is special, which is different for each human being. To that extent, each individual is a special human being. But the relationship with God is not an addition to

---

43. Martin Luther, *Disputatio de homine* (1536), WA 39/I:176.33–35: "Paulus Rom 3 Arbitramur hominem iustificari fide absque operibus, breviter hominis definitionem colligit dicens: hominem iustificari fide." ("In brief form, what Paul expresses in Rom. 3: 'For we hold that a person is justified by faith apart from the works prescribed by the law' is the definition of the human being, which means that the human being is justified through faith.") The text and German translation (here and in what follows) are from G. Ebeling, *Disputatio de homine*, erster Teil, *Text und Traditionshintergrund* (Tübingen: Mohr Siebeck, 1977), 15–24. However, reference is made to the more accessible edition WA 39/I.

this; rather, it positions the human being, thus identified as special, before God, which is the same for every human being. In their dealings and relationships with the other, others, and themselves, human beings are always *particularized* as special instances of the general, so that they are viewed as particular humans, with specific biographies, among other humans. Through their relationship with God, however, they are *individuated as persons before God*.[44] They are not merely special, but individual, so that they are viewed, not only in the particularizing (and hence also always generalizing) perspective of the general and the particular, but also in the individuating (and hence universalizing in the strictest sense) perspective of the unique and the universal. Only the individual can be universal: only the individual can be determined—not just in relation to changing environments, as one who is special, different, and distinct from others who are special and may thus be determined as one instance of the general, but also in every environment as the same: as *this* human being *before God*. By means of the individuating, universal relationship with God, a human being is individuated to become a unique *person*. This individuation cannot be reduced to a particular modifier that can be added to the other special features of a human being. Rather, it underscores what is already implied in every other description: that it is a description of *this unique person*. Precisely this is what makes it possible and necessary to differentiate systematically between "person" and "work," between the person who is unique (not of himself or herself, but through God alone) and her particular story, which makes her, alongside and among others, a special human person in the world.

This singularizing relationship with God makes humans something that they can neither be nor become of themselves: *persons*. As persons, each a special human being in distinction from others, humans are characterized by their ability to respond to their

---

44. In theological terms, we may not speak of a "person" when the subject is a particular (of whatever sort) from the perspective of the world, but only when we are seeking to express something that is unique from God's perspective. Luther, in his circulated disputation of 1537, *De veste nuptiali* ([On the wedding garment], WA 39/I:283.1), formulates this with precision: "Fides facit personam [Faith makes the person]."

constitutive relationship to God in one of two ways: in faith or in unfaith. Both are ways or modes of existing, and they show in the way in which they live their individual lives as particular human beings in relationship to God. One who lives her life in faith is living as a particular human being among other particular human beings in a way that is her way of actually living as a singular individual before God. By contrast, one who lives his life in unfaith is living as a particular human being among other particular human beings in such a way that he ignores, suppresses, or explicitly disputes that he exists as a singular individual before God.

This is the norm for all human beings. No one is born a believer: everyone begins their life in unfaith, even if this can only be said from the perspective of those whose mode of life is no longer unfaith but faith. There is not a single believer who has not come from unfaith to faith: faith is never the first state, but always the second. There is no one for whom it would be impossible to come from unfaith to faith: no human being is excluded as such from becoming a believer. But nor is there anyone who would or could come of their own accord from unfaith to faith. There is no direct path that leads from unfaith to faith; this change calls for an about-face that can only be described as a radical reorientation of one's life.[45] If one accepts that one cannot live, at the same time and in the same respect, both in faith and in unfaith (one lives either in faith or in unfaith) and that there is no one who does not live either in faith or in unfaith (no one lives neither in faith nor in unfaith), just as there can be no one who neither exists nor does not exist, or who simultaneously both exists and does not exist, then for human beings there are two and only two modes of existence: unfaith and faith. Since no one lives in faith who has not previously lived in unfaith, since not everyone has faith, and since it is only in faith that one can know about unfaith, whereas in unfaith one cannot know about either faith or unfaith, it follows that faith is the atypical mode of existence of some human beings, while unfaith is the typical mode of existence of all human beings, even if this cannot become clear to them as they are, but only from the perspective of faith.

45. See Dalferth, *Radical Theology*, chap. 12.

9. *Animal Rationale* and *Homo Iustificari Fide*

The discussion above provides an outline of the fresh thinking un-
dertaken by the theology of the Reformation regarding the being and
nature of the human person. In attempting to consider and understand human beings in real terms, Reformation theology's conception
of the human being necessarily differed from that of the preceding
philosophical and theological tradition. The ensuing reflections draw
on these resources. In his *Disputatio de homine*, Luther emphatically
counters the philosophical definition of the human being as *animal
rationale*, *sensitivum*, *corporeum* (an animal having reason, sensation, and body)[46] with the theological definition of the human being
that he found in the Pauline writings: The human being is *homo
iustificandus* (or *homo iustificari fide*).[47]

There is a great deal that is significant in these two definitions, both
from a methodological point of view and as regards their content.[48] On
the one hand, Luther quotes the philosophical definition of the human
being in the Aristotelian tradition, which places importance not just
on human reason but also on human sensory perception and physical
nature. Human reason is interwoven with the sensory and physical
dimensions of the human animal and can only be correctly understood
in its interaction with them. Thus the philosophical definition does not
offer an arbitrary definition (a nominal definition); rather, within the
meaning of the Aristotelian theory of science, it offers an essential definition (a real definition) of the human being that claims to capture and
summarize the truth of the human being within the context of the other
cosmic beings. It is intended to offer recognition of the truth and not
merely to provide information about the philosophers' use of language.

46. WA 39/I:175.3–4: "Philosophia, sapientia humana, definit, hominem *esse
animal rationale, sensitivum, corporeum*." ("Philosophy, [that is] human wisdom,
defines the human being as an animal endowed with reason, sensation, and body.")
    47. WA 39/I:176.33–35.
    48. See the detailed commentary by G. Ebeling, *Disputatio de homine*, zweiter Teil,
Die philosophische Definition des Menschen: Kommentar zu These 1–19 (Tübingen:
Mohr Siebeck, 1982); Ebeling, *Disputatio de homine*, dritter Teil, *Die theologische
Definition des Menschen: Kommentar zu These 20–40* (Tübingen: Mohr Siebeck,
1989). In connection with this problem, see Ingolf U. Dalferth, "Homo definiri nequit:
Logisch-philosophische Bemerkungen zur theologischen Bestimmung des Menschen,"
ZThK 76 (1979): 191–224.

On the other hand, Luther makes it clear that neither the philosophical nor the theological definition simply affirms what a human
being is; if that were the case, they would contradict each other. In
fact they are not contradictory, because they arrive at their definitions from different standpoints and perspectives: the first definition
follows Aristotle in defining the human being from the perspective
of *sapientia humana* (human wisdom), whereas the second follows
Paul, finding its basis in Scripture. Both are correct in their respective contexts, but both give rise to problems if one combines their
respective insights in a philosophical-theological jumble, seeking
to give either the theological definition in answer to philosophical
questions or the philosophical definition in answer to theological
questions. Worldly wisdom and scriptural exposition are the two ways
in which one comes to an understanding of the truth about human
beings. But both ways lead to insights limited by their viewpoints
and horizons, which cannot be transferred automatically to other
realms of inquiry or knowledge.

Third, the philosophical definition of the human being is guided
exclusively by the human/animal distinction, or, as Luther says, "haec
definitio tantum mortalem et huius vitae hominem definit."[49] The
theological definition, by contrast, takes into account the "whole
and complete human person": "Theologia vero de plenitudine sapientiae suae hominem totum et perfectum definit."[50] It focuses on the
human being both in this present life ("homo huius vitae"), and also
in the future form that his life will take ("vita futurae formae suae").[51]
Since this flows wholly and exclusively from God, it is impossible to
conceive of the human being in the actual entirety of his present and
future life without allowing oneself to be guided by the fundamental
human-God distinction. A comparison with other living beings makes
it possible to recognize real and important human characteristics.
However, only a comparison with the Creator can open up a full and
complete understanding of the human person; a comparison with

49. WA 39/I:175.7–8: "This definition describes man only as a mortal and in relation to this life."
50. WA 39/I:176.5–6: "Truly, theology from the fullness of its wisdom defines the
human being as complete and perfect."
51. WA 39/I:177.3–9.

other created beings will not accomplish this. Since the Creator is not present in the experiential world of created beings and therefore is not available for comparison, one must beware of (mis)understanding the fundamental human-God distinction in such a way that the meaning of "God" is worked out against a human background. (To do this would result only in a differentiation between the human being and the human image of God.) Rather, one must take the opposite approach and define what "human" means from God's point of view, since it is only thus that both God as Creator and human beings as creatures can be taken into account. In order to speak with any seriousness of created beings, one must also speak of the Creator. But the Creator is not to be discerned within the thinking of the world; at best we find the human idea of a "creator" arrived at by a posteriori reasoning from effect to cause.[52] Even if human reason is "[virtually] divine,"[53] it is still not in a position to know the Creator.[54]

For that to be the case, according to Luther, it would have to be able to reason from the cause to the effect and not just from the effect to the cause. But despite human reason's distinguishing attributes and "maiestas" among all creation, "nec ea ipsa ratio novit a priore, sed tantum a posteriore."[55] One can reformulate Luther's argument as follows: human reason can only ever speak of God *abductively*, that is presumptively,[56] and it can only consider him as first cause, not as Creator. Its "knowledge of God" is at best mere hypothetical conjecture, not assured insight. In order to be able to speak of the Creator, it must have reasons for considering the effects it takes as its starting point as "creation" or "created." But this is impossible, since

52. WA 39/I:175: "10. Tantem talem sese maiestatem esse, nec ea ipsa ratio novit a priore, sed tantum a posteriore." ("10. Even though it has such majesty, this same reason does not know the basis of its cause except by drawing inference from the effects.")

53. Ibid.

54. Ibid.

55. Ibid.: "This same reason does not know the basis of its cause except by drawing inference from the effects."

56. See Charles S. Peirce, "Harvard Lectures on Pragmatism," *Collected Papers of Charles Sanders Peirce*, ed Charles Hartshorne and Paul Weiss, vol. 5: *Pragmatism and Pragmaticism* (Cambridge, MA: Harvard University Press, 1934), 171 (CP 5.171): "Abduction is the process of forming an explanatory hypothesis. It is the only logical operation which introduces any new idea; for induction does nothing but determine a value, and deduction merely evolves the necessary consequences of a pure hypothesis."

then it already would have to know the Creator: only one who knows the Creator can legitimately speak of creation as well. The choice of "image" (thus Wittgenstein) for the thought is crucial: when we speak of creation, the Creator has already come into play, and any kind of "inference" from created effects to a creating cause is nothing more than an explication of the image, not a knowledge-generating deduction. We are not learning anything new, merely developing what we mean when we speak of creation.

As created beings, humans and other living beings therefore can be defined solely from God's perspective (*coram Deo* [before God]) and not from the perspective of the world (*coram mundo* [before the world] or *coram seipsis* [before themselves]). This perspective is not to be found within the world's horizon, and thus it is not a worldly perspective. On the contrary, it encircles the world and its horizon within itself, so that it is a perspective within which the world in its entirety is divinely determined—from God's point of view. Just as humans live their lives *coram mundo* ("I" / "what is not me") and *coram seipso* ("I" / "others") from the perspective of a worldly standpoint, so they also live their lives *coram Deo* ("I together with all that is not me and is not God" / "God") from the perspective of a divine—a nonworldly—standpoint. This standpoint, which theology calls faith, is not circumscribed by worldly horizons (although every human being can be defined on the basis of this standpoint). Rather, it denotes, within a worldly horizon, such a distance from the world that from this standpoint one sees and defines *everything*—the world, God, others, and oneself—in a new and different way, not according to the ways of the world. Access to this new standpoint (faith) and horizon (*coram Deo*) opens up, not as a result of a change of standpoint within the horizon of the world, but only by means of a radical move from within the world's horizon to a position within God's horizon. This move is radical because one cannot accomplish it oneself (this would only ever result in a change of worldly standpoint within the world's horizon) and because one must comprehend not only everything but also first and foremost oneself, in a fundamentally different way: not as an *animal rationale*, but as God's creature—a being who owes its entire existence to God alone and not to itself. Only one who understands himself or herself as a creature can and must[57] also understand everything else as creation. No one can do this unless he or she understands God to be Creator. But it is only where God makes himself comprehensible as Creator that one can understand him as Creator and oneself as his creature. And it is only when one understands God and oneself in this way that one lives in faith.

Hence it is only from God's perspective that it is possible to speak meaningfully and responsibly of Creator and creature. One cannot speak in this way from the world's perspective, even when guided by a concept of God and reason that idealizes the reasoning human as a being open to God, underestimating the fact that human reason is thoroughly written and engraved into the animal aspect of one's life in such a way that it cannot be abstracted from it. What is more, reason passes away with the human body. It is not reason that constitutes a basis for hope, but the Creator alone, "who gives life to the dead and calls into being things that were not" (Rom. 4:17 NIV). Philosophy knows nothing of such a Creator. Its concept of God can perhaps envisage "divine preservation and government" of the world, but not creation ex nihilo.[58] Only theology recognizes creation and a Creator; philosophy does not.[59] Philosophy knows only about the world, and

57. To understand the one as created and the other not is not an option. On the contrary, either everything is God's creation or nothing is: there is no possibility that some things are part of God's creation while others are not. This is part and parcel of the grammar of the Christian idea of creation. For this reason alone, Christians have fundamental questions about the evils of the world. The predicate 'created' does not draw a distinction within the experiential world; instead it relates this world in its entirety to the Creator, whom it does treat as distinct. The idea of creation does not evince any (ontic or experiential) distinction within the world, but rather an (ontological or existential) distinction between the world and God.

58. See Ebeling, *Disputatio de homine*, zweiter Teil, 423: "Ratio [reason] achieves at best a certain knowledge of the gubernatio [government] but not of the creatio mundi [creation of the world] by God." Accordingly, it can to some extent add to humanity's knowledge of its *causa materialis* and *formalis* (material and formal cause), but has nothing to contribute where the questions of its *causa efficiens* (efficient cause) and *causa finalis* (final cause) are concerned. If these questions are valid at all, they are not philosophical or scientific, but theological questions. Cf. ibid., 333–469.

59. WA 39/I:175: "13. Nam philosophia efficientem certe non novit, similiter nec finalem.—14. Quia finalem nullam ponit aliam quam pacem huius vitae et efficientem nescit esse creatorem Deum." ("13. It is certain, however, that philosophy knows neither the efficient cause nor yet the final cause [of the human person]. 14. For, as a final cause, it sets nothing higher than earthly well-being and it does not know that the efficient cause is God the Creator.")

in the world there is no God, merely questionable ideas of God. Even theology is a similarly worldly affair, and even theological ideas can be called into question. But theology can claim with good reason to be able to speak of creation insofar as it is explicating a faith that justifiably confesses that, without any human contribution, it has been called forth from the nothingness of death, from remoteness from God and absence of interest in God. Only a faith that—entirely passively and originating from somewhere entirely other—has given an existential purpose to human life provides sufficient grounds to talk seriously of a creation ex nihilo. No such grounds are provided by a cognitive understanding of faith as the *cum assensione cogitare* of infinite truths that cannot be rationally inferred from the finite but have to be accepted on authority. Faith is viewed as a supernatural virtue that owes its consent to what is believed to the movement of the will by the divine Spirit and not to the insight into its truth. Thus one has faith in what one does not know, since one can do no other, but one does not know what one has faith in, even though one assents to it. That is philosophically unconvincing and theologically unsatisfactory.

10. Deeper Insight into Reality through Change of Perspective

Luther takes a different approach. In no sense does he deny that the philosophical definition captures and communicates what is important and right from the viewpoint of human wisdom (i.e., that it really understands the thing it is referring to). He does not rescind or relativize any of it. "Et sane verum est, quod ratio omnium rerum res et caput et prae ceteribus rebus huius vitae optimum et divinum quiddam sit."[60] But the philosophical definition is not an apt definition of the human being for theological purposes, since it conceals the very reality that is the theological point: the human person lives not just *coram mundo*, in a world structured and made accessible by reason, sensory perception, and physical existence, but *coram Deo*, in relationship with God. This relationship is given existential

60. WA 39/I:175.9–10: "And indeed it is true that reason is the chief cause of everything, the best in comparison with the other things of this life and [nothing less than] divine."

form as faith and unfaith, and it manifests itself in day-to-day living as the mode in which the life of the *animal rationale, sensitivum, corporeum* is lived, either in faith or in unfaith. Since it is concerned with the how of human day-to-day living and not with the what of humanness, this formalization does not incorporate a further characteristic into the philosophical definition of the human person in such a way as to define him as a living being who is not just rational, sensory, and physical but also believing. Even a praying *animal rationale, sensitivum, corporeum* is merely a being who is understood from the perspective of his relationship with the world, not that of his relationship with God.

However, because he is concerned with this change of perspective, Luther cannot expand, clarify, or broaden the philosophical definition; he is compelled to set it aside and adopt a different approach. The philosophical method of defining something by specifying its *genus proximum* and *differentia specifica* produces no result if there are no phenomena within the worldly horizon of experience that belong to the relevant genus and to which the relevant distinctions can be applied. The definitions of the human animal as *rationale, sensitivum*, and *corporeum* take account of such experiential distinctions (rational/nonrational; sensory/nonsensory; physical/nonphysical), whereas his definition in terms of his relationship with God does not. Nothing in the experiential world is antithetical to it, which is why the philosophical method for arriving at a definition, oriented as it is toward experiential distinctions, cannot help us here.

Thus Luther alters the definition of the human person not only in terms of its content but also in terms of the methodological procedure for arriving at the definition, so as to allow the human being to be defined with proper regard to the reality of his relationship with God. Instead of giving a formal definition, he quotes a *Pauline shorthand term for the event, which identifies the human being as the place of God's free self-mediation.* What marks out humans as humans from a theological point of view is not a particular way of being (*animal*) with its specific assets and abilities (*rationale, sensitivum, corporeum*), nor a fundamental focus on God or a rational structure that is open to God and can function as an organ receptive to the divine self-disclosure; rather, it is an event (*iustificari fide*), by which human persons become what they could never become of themselves: righteous before God. If human persons are defined and understood from the perspective of this event, then it becomes plain that it is not on the basis of their *competences and activities*, which mark them out as special living beings among living beings, that they become what they should be. Quite the contrary, it is their *incompetence and passivity* that single them out in God's eyes and make them what they can and should be as humans before God: creatures who live in fellowship with their Creator. From the perspective of their relationship with God, humans look different from the way they look from the perspective of their relationship with the world: not as a bundle of activities and competences, but first and foremost in clear and complete passivity. "The human being is God's work in progress."[61]

This enables us to understand why Luther's Pauline shorthand term for the human person (*homo iustificatur fide*) diverges appreciably from traditional forms of the definition, whether it is taken as a nominal definition (a definition of a concept) or as a real definition (a true description of a reality). It does not tell us what human beings *are*, but rather what *happens* to them. More, in fact: this one concise phrase summarizes in shorthand the whole complex history of God and humanity. If we want to understand this shorthand term, we must not unpack it as if it were the definition of a concept, seeking to determine its subject, predicate, *genus proximum*, and *differentia specifica*. Instead, we must go back to the multiplicity and reality of the life stories of human beings who have lived with, without, in opposition to, through, and because of God—stories such as we find in the Bible, but, equally, stories to be found in the plenitude of human life. The Pauline term for the human being sums up the multiplicity and diversity of stories of human beings with God, and of God with human beings, in a brief, succinct formula. In order to understand these stories, one must interpret them according to the way they characterize the human person, and at the same time according to the way they characterize the one whom they call God. We are not told the details of these life histories, but the fundamental difference

---

61. E. Jüngel, *Indikative der Gnade—Imperative der Freiheit* (Tübingen: Mohr Siebeck, 2000), 114, takes his cue from WA 39/I:177.3–4: "Quare homo huius vitae est pura materia Dei ad futurae suae vitam."

that lies at the heart of them is unmistakably highlighted: when it comes to the way in which God relates to the human person and the human person to God, it is principally the fundamental relationship between Creator and creature that is to be safeguarded, and it is on this that the good order of creation depends overall. It is solely and exclusively God who is *active*; the human being, by contrast, is first and foremost *passive*. In the complex living relationship between God and humans, passivity is the normative human determination, whereas activity is the normative divine determination.

11. Divine Activity and Human Passivity

It makes no difference if this basic allocation of roles between God and his creation gives rise to instances of particularization and progressive determination over the course of history. There are numerous good reasons for speaking not only of human passivity but also of human activity: life consists essentially of both. This becomes apparent not just from the spontaneity and receptivity of human behavior toward what is other, toward others, and toward themselves in the world, but also from the (entirely worldly) activities that human beings have developed and cultivated in relation to the one they consider as God. There are also good reasons for speaking of God in terms not only of activity but also of passivity. Even if one believes that one cannot say that God allows himself to be determined by what takes place in creation, since this would appear to put his divinity at risk (an unnecessary and nonsensical thought), one still cannot dispute that God can determine himself in such a way as to be divinely present in the changing situations of created life in whatever manner is best.[62] Yet even if both poles of the relationship between God and humanity must be conceived of as governed by the opposing tension of activity and passivity, it is essential to preserve the dividing line between the first and the second: with God, activity comes first and passivity second, whereas with human beings, passivity comes first and results in activity. God is the one who builds, and humanity is the one under

---

62. See Ingolf U. Dalferth, *Becoming Present: An Inquiry into the Christian Sense of the Presence of God* (Leuven: Peeters, 2006).

construction. God could be God without human beings, even if, as a result, he were other than he is. But human beings could not exist if God were not who he is: the builder of humans.

Gerhard Ebeling interpreted Luther's distinction between the philosophical and theological definitions as a view of humanity oriented according to the categories of substance and relation: "Here it is not the predicament of substance which is decisive for human determination, but that of relation—what man is deemed to be *coram Deo* and *coram mundo*. This dispenses with the process of definition illustrated by the Porphyrian tree right from the start. Human existence is interpreted here in terms of the tension between being required to respond to a demand and being given as a gift, as that which truly constitutes it."[63] As Ebeling demonstrates, however, it is not the distinction between substance and relation as such that is the decisive factor but rather the distinction between the situation of the being *coram mundo* and *coram Deo, and how this is understood.* And even this distinction finds its real anthropological point not in the separation between these two contexts but rather in the fact that the pure and exclusive *passivity* of human persons within the realm of God's activity is set in opposition to their *activities and passivities* within the realm of the world (their existence as an *animal rationale, sensitivum, corporeum*). The human being is the object of God's action, the one for whom and in whose best interests God acts. God is "semper ubique actuosus [always and everywhere active],"[64] whereas humans, in their relationship to God, are crucially and entirely passive: "*mere passive,*" as Luther never tired of saying. They become what they are through what happens to them. And they understand what happens to them as what God does to them and for them. Hence it is only within the sphere of their absolute passivity that humans can speak meaningfully and intelligibly of God's absolute activity. Here, in fact, they must do so, whereas everywhere else, in their worldly relationships with the other, with others, and with themselves, it is at best possible but for the most part unnecessary and superfluous to speak of God at all. God is the one who is understood anaphorically, from

---

63. G. Ebeling, *Disputatio de homine*, Dritter Teil, 2:409.
64. WA 18:753.14.

a position of faith, as the one to whom one owes the transition from unfaith to faith, and from whom one therefore hopes cataphorically for the same beneficial effect to be brought about in the lives of other human beings. No one has "earned" this in any sense of the word. Whenever and wherever it happens, it happens entirely gratuitously. "*Mere passive*." But what does this mean?

3

Mere Passive

The Passivity of Gift in Luther's Theology

1. The Reciprocity of Giving and Receiving?

> When justification is interpreted one-sidedly as the pure act of receiving a pure gift, a mere passive acceptance of divine activity, so that the divine positive is matched only with a human negative, there is a weakening of the Christological point of the event of grace as it is especially apparent in the "joyful exchange" of attributes between Christ and the sinner. The reciprocity of giving and receiving is indispensable to the understanding of gift, particularly when the exchange is not just of something for something else, but when God and the human being give and receive themselves; this determines not simply their actions, but—first and foremost—their being.[1]

No one who is familiar with Luther's theological concerns will deny that justification is first a matter of how human beings *are* before

1. B. K. Holm and P. Widmann, Invitation to the Word—Gift—Being Conference, Aarhus, September 2006. Cf. B. K. Holm, *Gabe und Geben bei Luther: Das Verhältnis zwischen Reziprozität und reformatorischer Rechtfertigungslehre* (Berlin: de Gruyer, 2006); B. K. Holm and P. Widmann, eds., *Word—Gift—Being: Justification—Economy—Ontology* (Tübingen: Mohr Siebeck, 2009).

God and only then, and from then onward, of how they act as well.[2] Justification is not sanctification, even if there is no sanctification without justification and if justification that does not lead to sanctification is a theological absurdity. There may well be concepts of gift in which the "reciprocity of giving and receiving . . . is indispensable to the understanding of gift." But in that case our understanding of "receiving" and "mere passive acceptance" must differ from what Luther meant by *mere passive* in the context of a theology of justification. But what did he mean? The present chapter aims to discover just this. My intention is simply to outline some of Luther's basic insights—those that ought to constitute key reference points for a debate concerning the Lutheran understanding of faith in terms of gift and passivity.[3] It is not essential that our theological thinking follow this pattern. But if we are attempting to shape our thinking in accordance with Luther's theology, we will have to engage with his arguments and ideas as set out below.[4]

2. Luther's Theological Definition of the Human Being

Luther's well-known theological definition of the human being in the thirty-second thesis of the *Disputatio de homine* (1536) gives a

---

2. Where God is concerned, any differentiation between being and action is pointless, since God's being is action (*esse est operari* [to be is to act]), so that God is what he does and does what he is. It therefore is with good reason that the Christian doctrine of God is the doctrine of the Trinity—in other words, the doctrine of God's life as Father, Son, and Spirit for and with his creatures, and not merely a theistic theory of God's existence and activity.

3. In what follows I will draw on different phases of Luther's theological work in order to show that this is a thought form that was normative for Luther's theology right from the initial crystallization of his Reformation insights, even though the details continued to be thought through in various ways and to receive different emphases.

4. The following reflections owe important ideas to Phillip Stoellger's habilitation thesis, "Passivität aus Passion. Zur Problemgeschichte einer categoria non grata" (University of Zürich, 2010). See also Bernd Wannenwetsch, "Affekt und Gebot: Zur ethischen Bedeutung der Leidenschaften im Licht der Theologie Luthers und Melanchthons," in *Passion, Affekt und Leidenschaft in der Frühen Neuzeit*, ed. Johann Anselm Steiger (Wiesbaden: Harrassowitz, 2005), 1:203–15; Cornelia Richter, "Bodenloses Vertrauen: Humanwissenschaftliche und theologische Erkundungen" (habilitation thesis in systematic theology, University of Marburg, 2010), part 1.

precise statement of the facts to be considered: "Paul, in Romans 3:
'We hold that a man is justified by faith apart from works' briefly
sums up the definition of man, saying, 'Man is justified by faith.'"[5]
The human being is defined in theological terms as *iustificandus,* as
one whose relationship with God must be put right. It is thus assumed that this relationship is not as it could and should be. One can
accentuate this in terms of a theology of gift or grace and give it a
positive emphasis, indicating that the unexpected and unanticipated
irruption of God's inconceivable gifts into a human life shows that
this life can be much more and much better than it is, or could be
and become, of itself: even the good aspects of human life can be im-
measurably improved.[6] However, one can also describe the situation
in negative terms in the traditional hamartiological manner by saying
that human life is in need of improvement and raising to a higher level
because in practice human beings—all human beings!—ignore God
and fail to acknowledge him as their Creator. Given this situation,
however, human beings are not interested in setting to rights their
relationship with God themselves, nor are they in a position to do
so. They do not take the initiative, because they do not know God;
they are not interested in God when they hear about him; they do
nothing to further God's interest in them; and they do not cooperate
with God when God creates them (anew). This is the reason why, for
human beings, the word *iustificandus* implies that their participation
in this event is *mere passive,* whereas, as regards God, it implies that
he alone is actively at work here since, in contrast to his creatures,
he is *semper actuosus.*

The word *fides* (faith), as that by which the human being is justified
(iustificari *fide*), thus has a double perspective:[7] it is to be understood

5. WA 39/I:176: "Paulus Rom. 3: Arbitramur hominem iustificari fide absque
operibus, breviter hominis definitionem colligit, dicens: hominem iustificari fide."
Text and translation in G. Ebeling, *Disputatio de homine,* Erster Teil, *Text und
Traditionshintergrund* (Tübingen: Mohr Siebeck, 1977), 22.

6. See chap. 4 below.

7. Every attempt to attribute faith to the human person alone (i.e., to construe it
as *opus hominis* [the work of the human person]) or to attribute it to God alone (i.e.,
to understand it as *opus Dei* [the work of God]) is thus doomed to failure from the
outset. The word *fides* must be treated as having a double sense, so that it indicates
both the process by which God works in human beings (bringing them into a right

as *mere passive* where the human being is concerned but as wholly and entirely *active* where God is concerned. There is both a grammatical (verbal) and a theological (factual) explanation for this.

Its grammatical explanation is that, although in Christian usage the verb *believe* is predicated of a person or persons ("I believe . . . ," "we believe . . ."), its active form does not imply activity on the part of these persons, but rather a "passivity," a being-affected, an inclusion in the life of God, in that God becomes so present to them that, contrary to their current experience of themselves and the world (*contra experientiam*), they are able to rely on the presence of his love and to direct their lives according to it (assurance of faith that runs contrary to fact). Viewed in this way, to have faith is neither to know, to feel, nor to act. It is not knowing about God, feeling God, or worshiping God, however much all these things can be done in faith—and indeed will be done, in one way or the other. Yet faith itself is neither a cognitive, emotional, nor practical phenomenon; indeed, it is not a phenomenon in any of the usual senses at all. For believers, God often appears just as absent, from a cognitive, emotional, and practical point of view, as he does for other people, but they trust that the truth of God's presence is not measured by how they experience God's presence or absence but by how God himself makes himself present to them. He may seem absent to them because they are unable to experience him in their own way, but as far as he is concerned, he is present with them because he is present in his own way. God's presence with human beings is not disclosed through their going to be where God is; it is the other way around, through God making himself present to human beings where they are. They do not believe because they experience God's presence in their lives; rather, they believe because they live their lives in faith, oriented toward God by God's presence.

Believers do not transport themselves into God's presence by means of their own activity; rather, they become believers by a passive process, in that God makes himself present to them in such a way that they cannot help but radically reorient their lives toward God. This

---

relationship with God) *and* the process by which human beings are worked on by God (being brought into a right relationship with God).

is well illustrated by the Christian use of the verb *believe*. This verb is used diathetically in an active sense, whereas in fact it conveys a passive sense. Just as deponent verbs in Latin are only used in the passive, even though they have an active meaning (*laetari*: to rejoice; *arbitrari*: to think; *loqui*: to speak; *frui*: to enjoy), so the English *believe* is a word that is used actively but in its theological usage has a passive meaning. Anyone who says "I believe" in the Christian sense is talking about what happens to him and not what he does; and anyone who says—in what is, objectively speaking, the only acceptable mode of expression—"I believe in God" is saying that what is happening to him is brought about by God. Faith is not a type of knowledge, feeling, or action, but an ordering of all of a human being's knowledge, feeling, and action by the one who makes himself so present to a human that the latter is able to have faith in him and to live in reliance on the presence of his love. From the perspective of the human being, faith is a purely passive determination of human life; from God's perspective, on the other hand, it is an active determining.

But the point of this double definition of faith is not fully captured yet by distinguishing, in a creation-theological way, between God's activity and human passivity. Both aspects are also qualified in terms of their content. Since human passivity corresponds to the *good gift of God*,[8] the *mere passive* on the human side indicates the state in which human beings, as God's creatures, are in need of the good gift of God and are enriched thereby in a manner unmerited and unanticipated, so that they become better than they are or can become of their own accord. Human passivity is the hamartiological mark of the condition of *sin* in which human beings are less than they could be and, before their Creator, should be. This condition is not overcome soteriologically until God's gift comes into play, so that sinners become what they could never have become of their own accord: *justified* sinners. To that extent the *mere passive* of faith involves *God making human beings new* and transforming the state of human existence before God from the old state of remoteness from and ignorance of God into the new state of life with God.

---

8. As Luther says in his commentary on Ps. 31:1 (1513/15): "Ecce mere passive ponitur, quia 'sine penitentia sunt dona et vocatio dei'" (WA 3:174). ("This verse implies pure passivity, since the gifts and the invitation presuppose no act of repentance.")

Precisely this is the point of the *mere passive* formula, as Luther's reasoning and conclusions show in a number of contexts. In 1537, in a sermon on John 20, he pointed out that the gloria (glory) of the institution of forgiveness of sin consists in its pure passivity, in other words, in the fact that it "refers only to those who allow it to happen to them, that is, sinners."[9] It is available to all those who not merely in fact do nothing about it but in principle are unable to do anything about it themselves. This hamartiological passivity is not seen as a defect; rather, it is expressly perceived as a soteriological benefit. So in a sermon given on November 19, 1531, we read, "The Christian is a purely passive person, not an active one; he does nothing but allow gifts to be given to him. Unless you allow gifts to be given to you, you are not a Christian."[10] Thus Christians are in fact defined by what they *become*, and not by what they do.

> The Christian is a purely passive, not an active, being. If you have ceased to receive, you are not a Christian. You do not become one through praying, fasting, going on pilgrimages or anything else; otherwise, you would be a prayer, a faster, or a pilgrim [but not a Christian]: you only become one through receiving. I have done nothing other than receive. There is no doubt that he [the Christian] discovers how difficult this is. This is why Paul complains in Romans 7[:18], "I know that nothing good dwells in me, that is, in my flesh" [NASB]. Here he is not speaking of concupiscence, but of the impossibility of distinguishing between himself and what he deserves. Isn't that person a rogue who realizes that he has need of something and that Christ wants to give it to him and he is unable to accept it nonetheless? In summary: we must act like a woman; we must prefer to cajole and accept.[11]

9. WA 45:461.30–32: "ad patientes tantum pertinet, id est: peccatores."
10. WA 34/II:414.4–6: "Christianus est homo mere passivus, non activus, der ym nur lesst geben. Si non sinis tibi dari, non es Christianus."
11. WA 34/II:414.19–29:
> Christianus es homo mere passivus, non activus. Wen dw nymmer entpfehest, non es Christianus, Nicht von Bethen, Fasten, Wallen c. sunst werest dw eyn Bether, Faster, Pylgram, sed tantum ex accipiendo, Das ich do nichts gethan habe den entpfangen. Quae res sit quam difficilis quidem, experitur. Ideo Paulus Ro. 7. conqueritur: "Invenio in carne mea non bonum." Non loquitur hic de concupiscencia, sed de illa opinione, quod non potuit separare a se merita. Jst das nicht eyn schalk, qui sentit se egere et Christum velle dare und darffs doch nicht nhemen? Summa: oportet nos facere sicut mulier: Er durch dryngen und nhemen.

Here, therefore, "receiving" is understood precisely *not* as a human activity but, instead, as a passive "doing nothing." One *becomes* a Christian, not through the act of *receiving* something but solely through *what* one receives *from God*: *God's gift*, not the *act of receiving* this gift, is what makes sinners Christians. Far from precluding human beings from engaging in all the activities without which their lives would not be what they are, this gift of God allows such activities to be included within their lives. However, these activities are not what make a human being a *Christian*; rather, it is God's gift alone.

In his exposition of Psalm 90:16 in his second series of lectures on the Psalms (dated 1534/1535), Luther extends this idea into a sequence of steps.

> First of all we ask you to do your work, Lord. We do nothing, but are mere spectators and recipients; we are purely passive. God shows himself to us and makes us whole through his work alone. And this is what comes first, that he himself makes us whole and frees us from this disease with which the devil struck Adam down, that is, eternal sin and eternal death. Afterward we follow with our desire to be righteous, when our Lord God has already made us righteous. But that too is God's grace, proceeding from God's first work, so that it may come only from him and that he may be Lord. "Our Lord God is gracious and kind." May he always be thus and rejoice in us.[12]

As regards God, therefore, Luther emphasizes that in the first and crucial operation (justification) it is God *alone* who is at work, whereas in the second operation (sanctification) God is at work *also* so that in both, God alone is shown to be the *Lord*. As regards human beings, in contrast, Luther stresses that in the second of these works they

---

12. WA 40/III:588.2–10:
   primum petimus opus tuum, Domine. Ibi nos nihil agimus, sed tantum sumus spectatores et receptatores, sumus mere passivi. Deus ostendit nobis se et facit nos salvos suo solius opera. Vnd das mus das erste sein, quod ipse nos salvos faciat et liberet ab isto morbo, quem diabolus inflixit in Adam, scilicet peccatum aeternum et mortem aeternam. Post so wollen wir komen vnd auch from sein, wenn vns vnser Herr Gott vorhin hat from gemacht. Sed tamen haec etiam est gratia dei et procedit ex primo opere dei, Das ers gar allein habe et sit dominus. "Vnser Herr Gott sit iucundus et delectabilis." Ach das er so blieb vnd habe sein freunde an vns.

too are active and at work, since the first operation enables them to participate in the second. In the first operation, on the other hand, they are *mere passive* participants, not as protagonists but merely as *spectator et receptator.* But Luther speaks of *looking on* and *receiving*, not in connection with human beings overall but specifically where *the sinner* is concerned. We are not supposed to interpret this to mean that Luther assumes or accepts that there is some degree of the sinner's own activity—how should sinners participate in their own remaking and new creation, except if it be in a reciprocity of receiving that corresponds to God's activity of giving? Indeed, Luther's reference to sinners as merely looking on and receiving instead emphasizes their total lack of activity where their re-creation is concerned: sinners contribute nothing at all of their own to this operation, and so far there are (as yet) no human beings who are not sinners. Luther's theological statement makes no assumption that sinners possess any anthropological capability of receiving the gift of God. It is a retrospective judgment by those who, as believers, know that not they but God alone has made them what they now are: free from sin in their relationship with God.

However, the emphasis on this fundamental passivity in the first operation is in no way quietistic. Rather, it is a matter of re-creating sinners as human beings who can themselves become active and work for the good of their fellow humans. But the way this takes place makes it clear that it is not sinners themselves who accomplish good things to which they can appeal before God or others, but that all the good they do is attributable to God and not to themselves. Luther defined this more precisely in his exposition of Psalm 90:17: "Here it is certain that the work consists in God's guiding and directing this work in us, a work in which we ourselves cooperate and are not purely passive, as in God's initial work."[13] In the first operation it is the Creator alone who is active: human beings, in contrast, as sinners, are wholly passive. Only once they have been freed from their sin do they become *cooperatores Dei* who work together with God as those who are justified in a passive way and not as sinners. Only

13. WA 40/III:590.29–32: "Hic profecto opus est, ut Deus hoc opus super nos gubernet ac dirigat, ubi nos quoque operamur aliquid nec sumus mere passivi, sicut in primo opere Dei."

as such can they do what is good, and they can only do good because
they have been made good in themselves. Hence when they do what
is good, God is the one who makes good what they do.

Here Luther is describing the justification and sanctification events
using the traditional creation-theological model: in the creation of the
materia prima, it is only God who is active; subsequent processes require
cooperation with the created material, but this is both impossible and
futile unless God is still at work. Luther uses this model again in his
Lectures on Galatians (1531) to describe the problem of sin: "All of this
arises from the fact that damned hypocrisy will not allow itself to be
justified and shaped by God the Creator by means of divine blessings;
it refuses to be purely passive material, but wants to do actively what it
had to suffer from God and had to receive from him."[14] The sinner does
not want to behave passively, as *materia prima*, but actively, as *materia
relativa*, as *materia* relative to *forma*, which is always collaborative and
resistant when it is being molded and shaped into a specific substance.
But this is far removed from the way in which either *becoming a creature* or *becoming a Christian* is to be understood. The right analogy
for re-creation is not the genesis or coming into being of one creation
from another, but the original being-created, the genesis of the *materia
prima*. This *materia prima* becomes what it is completely passively, and
it is only as such that it can be what it is in the actualizing contexts of
forma: potential for the hylomorphic formation of substances.

The guiding model for Luther's argumentation for his theology
of justification is based on the creation-theological *ex nihilo creare*
(to create from nothing) as found in Romans 4:17. Only a work of
creation can be active of itself, but its createdness is not the result of
its own activity. Much more relevant here is what the eleventh-century
Master Guido (Magister Wido) said: *esse* only denotes an action if
it refers to God, whereas when it refers to created substances such
as human beings, it is used in the passive sense.[15] Thus, when we say

14. WA 40/I:407.14–17: "Quae omnia hinc oriuntur, quod maledicta Hypocrisis
non vult benedictione divina iustificari et formari a Deo Creatore, non vult esse materia mere passiva, sed active ea operari vult quae ipsa patiendo debebat Deum sinere
operari et ab eo accipere."

15. Cf. Robert W. Hunt, "Studies on Priscian in the Eleventh and Twelfth Centuries,
I–II," *Medieval and Renaissance Studies* 1, no. 2 (1943): 224; Richard W. Southern, *Saint
Anselm: A Portrait in a Landscape* (Cambridge: Cambridge University Press, 1990), 49.

Deus est, we mean, God is active; in fact, he is pure activity. When, on the other hand, we say *homo est*, we mean, human beings have become what they are by purely passive means. Hence we cannot use the verb *to be* (*esse*) univocally of both God and humans.

This thread follows Luther's argumentation from beginning to end.[16] God is always and inherently active: both in the first operation of *creatio ex nihilo* and in the second of *cooperatio* with created beings. The creature, on the other hand, is always and inherently passive: *mere passive* in the first operation, in dependence on God's corresponding activity, but also in all that follows. This is the theological model that Luther employs to think through and unfold his theme of passivity. Let us take a closer look at some aspects of it.

3. Becoming as Gift

Luther emphasizes the passivity of the human being in the fundamental acts of his life, not primarily in order to stress the antithesis to human activity, but instead to draw attention to the corresponding *activity* and *gift of God*. What the human being becomes and can become comes from God. God, however, *gives only what is good*, that is, only what *makes us good*. Hence God's gift is always a *good gift*. It is never something evil or bad, even if it comes to us in the form of a punishment intended to make us good when we are not good. *Everything God gives us makes us good*—that is the basic rule.

Conversely, this means that all that we are *that is* good, we have received. Those who *are* (even though they could not have been) owe their being wholly and entirely to the one who has called them into being. Similarly, those who *are Christians* owe this wholly and entirely to the one who, by his creative word, has made them Christians. *To be* and *to be a Christian* are not states of affairs that one can attribute to oneself in any way; they must be attributed wholly and entirely to God alone as his good gift. Being and being Christian are thus understood,

16. Sweeping polemics, such as those of the representatives of the Radical Orthodoxy movement, who trace the origins of modernity's theological fall back to Duns Scotus and map Reformed theology wholly from this perspective, should therefore be treated with caution. They cannot be substantiated from the theological content of Luther's argumentation.

from a theological point of view, as divine acts of creation ex nihilo: as *creation* of being and of new being.

In *De servo arbitrio* (1525) Luther makes it unmistakably clear that John 1:12 speaks of the gift of creation.

> John does not speak of any human operation, whether great or small, but rather of the renewing and transformation of the old self, who is a son of the devil, into a new self, who is a son of God. This self behaves purely passively (as we say); it accomplishes nothing at all, but is accomplished, whole and entire. For John is speaking of being created; he says that the sons of God are created by means of a power given to us by God and not through the power of a free will implanted within us.[17]

Even the re-creation of the human being is an act of *creation* and therefore is something that the old self with all its abilities cannot accomplish of itself, but can only *become* and receive as a gift: "It accomplishes nothing at all, but is accomplished, whole and entire [*nec facit quippiam, sed fit totus*]." This is true for us humans as created beings: we cannot create ourselves, nor can we play any part at all, no matter how marginal, in our own creation. It is true also for new human beings as God's new creations. The *homo novus* (new self) comes into being from the *homo vetus* (old self), but the *old* self cannot play even the smallest part in the process of becoming new, not even by *being the one* to *accept* God's gift. The old self can only be replaced by the new when God's gift puts an end to the oldness of one's life and *makes one anew*—into a *creatura* who is no longer *peccator* and thus *homo vetus*, but, as *homo iustificari fide, has become homo novus* living as a Christian.

Only on the basis of and because of this *innovatio* (innovation) and *transmutatio* (transmutation), brought about by the Spirit of Jesus Christ, can the new creature relate to this either by living as *homo novus* or by pretending not to be a *homo novus* or a Christian but

---

17. WA 18:697.25–30: "Iohannes non loquitur de ullo opere hominis, neque magno, neque parvo, sed de ipsa innovatione et transmutatione hominis veteris, qui filius diaboli est, in novum hominem, qui filius Dei est. Hic homo mere passive (ut dicitur) sese habet, nec facit quippiam, sed fit totus. De fieri enim loquitur Iohannes, fieri filios Dei dicit potestate divinitus nobis donata, non vi liberi arbitrii nobis insita."

preferring to stay a sinner ignoring one's createdness. The character of sin thus changes from factual ignorance of God and godlessness to become explicit opposition to, or enmity with, God. But that does not change the sinner's basic situation *coram Deo*. Sinners cannot turn themselves into nonsinners, so for sinners there can only be a new beginning in their relationship with God when God himself thus initiates it. Only creatures (human beings) can be sinners, but no creature (human) must necessarily be a sinner. Rather, any sinners can live as creatures in such a way that they do not ignore their createdness and thus their Creator—can live, in other words, as believers (i.e., as *Christians*). But if they could, then there is no reason why they should not. And if, as sinners, they cannot and will not do what, as God's creatures, they could and should do, then either there is no future for sinners or else the future must be opened up to them *ab extra* (from without) by God himself, who re-creates the sinner as a new creature—a *homo novus*.

Without God's creative gift there could be neither creatures nor sinners nor Christians. For wherever we have creation (that is to say, the making or becoming of something new and not merely the changing or becoming different of something old), it is not the creatures who are the actors, but God alone. Thus in the new creation, too, they do not contribute to what they are becoming, however much they become new in order to work together with God. The *mere passive* that marks out the (new) self, to the extent that it is created, has its import not in excluding the human being's own activity but, on the contrary, in enabling the human being to live not as a sinner but as a nonsinner, whose future consists not of death but of eternal life. The emphasis that the theology of justification attaches to *mere passive* therefore has nothing to do with quietism.

> Thus [it is true] of the new creature, that after the new birth we must practice righteous works. That is what we preach. But those who are converted do nothing toward this, for as creatures, works, created beings, we are created in order that we should then walk the path of good works. It is plainly stated and written. More or less like this: upon emerging from its mother's womb, a child contributes nothing toward becoming a complete creation. Why did God give it limbs? So that, when it is born, it is to move, to walk, stand, eat, drink, work,

rule, because it is born to do these things. If it did nothing, it would be a log, a stone.[18]

The new self is not intended to be a log and a stone. As the old self, however, it was just such a log and a stone as far as God was concerned, even though this did not prevent God from making a new creation of it.[19]

So we have established the following: (1) God's gift is always a *creative* gift. It *makes* what it *gives*, and it gives by making the one to whom it gives into what it gives. (2) God's gift is always a *good* gift. It makes what is good, and it makes what is not good into something good. This is just as true of humans' *being* as of their *being as Christians*. We cannot earn either for ourselves; rather, we owe both to God as gifts that make us human beings what we are before God: living beings (*creaturae* [creatures]) and beings who are living rightly (*iusti*) before God.

4. Becoming and Becoming New

When considering, as we have been above, the way in which human beings become new in terms of the theologies of justification and of sin, then we should not overplay the important difference between *becoming a creature* and *becoming a Christian*. One who *is created* does not exist previously in any sense but comes into being ex nihilo. One who *is created anew*, by contrast, is already in a condition such

18. WA 41:611.23–29:
  Sic de nova creatura, quando renati, debemus vivere in bonis operibus. Nos praedicamus. Sed qui convertuntur, nihil faciunt dazu, cum simus creatura, opus, geschepff, ad hoc creati, ut tum in bonis operibus ambulemus. Es ist deutlich geredt und geschrieben. Similitudo crassa. Puer ab matris utero, ehe es fertig wird, nihil facit ad hoc. Cur data ei membra a deo? Es sol sich regen, natus sols ghen, stehen, essen, trincken, erbeiten, regiern, quia ad hoc natus. Si nihil faceret, esset ein klotz und stein.

19. As Luther explains regarding Abraham and Sarah:
  Was it not an impossible thing that God promised Abraham—that a son would be born to him by his wife Sarah? . . . It was just as impossible that a child should be born from a log or a stone, as from Abraham and Sarah. Yet Abraham did not waver in the face of this impossible thing, since he had God's word and promise. Rather he believed firmly that the promised Son would be born from such an old decaying stump and log. (WA 49:407.21–29)

that this becoming can be described retrospectively as the creation of a "new human being" from an "old human being." The kind of becoming that is meant here is thus not a change from *nihil* to *aliquis* (from nothing to someone; creation), nor from possibility to actuality (actualization), but rather from impossibility to reality, in other words from being as a *peccator* (*homo vetus*) to a new being as a *iustus* (*homo novus*). This becoming is characterized by the fact that the old self is not simply other than the new self, but that the old self *resists and fights against* what it can and should be from God's perspective: God's child. Here there is *enmity against God* and not merely a complete absence of any relationship with God.

When one becomes a Christian what happens is not a mere change from a *malum* (evil) to a *bonum* (good), with the *malum* being what is not good and the *bonum* being what is not evil or wicked. The *malum* to be overcome here is not merely something that is other than the *bonum*; it is resistant and antagonistic to it. Similarly, the *bonum* that is striven for is not merely something that is other than the *malum*; it is something that resists and conflicts with the *malum* and, in a heightened manner, overcomes and eradicates the *malum*— overcomes it in fact, where God is concerned, not with another *malum* but purely with *bonum*, thus overcoming evil with good.

Understood like this, *new creation*, unlike creation, always has two sides. It is a becoming not simply ex nihilo, but *e contrario* (from what is contrary). This is why, on the one hand, it must break the lethargy and resistance of the old, and, on the other hand, it must enable and realize the new. This is what makes it necessary, when we are speaking of humans being made anew, to distinguish between a *resistant passivity* and a *pure passivity*.

As regards the first, the resistance and antagonism of the old must be broken. Here God's coming is experienced as *his wrath*, and God's work is suffered as *destruction and eradication*. Passivity means here that human beings find they are subjected to God's punitive and eradicating treatment,[20] or, as Luther says of Romans 8:26 in the appendix to his *Lectures on Romans*:

20. It is important from a theological point of view, nevertheless, to add immediately that this eradication applies to the sin and not to the sinner, since this destructive and abolishing work of God is only the reverse side of his re-creating work.

> For it is God's nature to destroy completely whatever remains of our
> will and intentions before he establishes in us his will and intentions. In
> 1 Samuel, chapter 2, it says: "The Lord makes poor and rich; He brings
> low, He also exalts" [NASB]. By virtue of this his most holy will he
> makes us capable of receiving his works and his gifts. For we are capable
> of receiving them when we cease from our intentions and rest from
> our works and become purely passive, both inwardly and outwardly.[21]

This resistant "passivity" is the hamartiological passivity of sin as it
is struck by God's work of subjugation. Sin must be restrained, since
humans must be returned to the *nihil* state from which they were
originally before something new can come into being.

It is only from that state that something new can come into being,
something that is not merely an instance or variation of the permanent
change from one event to another in the old. For this new being to
be brought about, however, the creature must be in a state of *pure
passivity, just as it was at its initial creation.* What takes place here
must come *purely from God.* Thus God's coming is experienced as
the creative *love of God,* which makes what it loves. It does not simply
eradicate sinners; it makes them lovable as a result of the good it does
to them by differentiating between themselves as persons and their
works, and by not identifying them with their sin but eradicating it
and saving them from its fatal consequences.

God's activity is enacted here as a sovereign *deliverance, redemption,
and re-creation* that the one who is saved or redeemed cannot match
by accepting or receiving. Even its acceptance can only be secondary—
a response of gratitude (or rejection!) to what one has received and
become. This idea can be paraphrased in numerous different ways:
Only a child can respond to being a child, but this is not what makes
it a child, but merely results in it *living* as a child in a *right* or *wrong*
manner. Only the heir can respond to her inheritance, but this does not

---

21. WA 57:193.1–7:

Quia natura Dei est prius penitus destruere, quicquid in nobis est consilii et
voluntatis, antequam statuat in nobis consilium suum et voluntatem. Sic primo
Regum 2: "Dominus pauperem facit et ditat, deducit ad inferos ac reducit." Eo
enim piissimo consilio capaces nos facit operum et donorum suorum. Capaces
enim tunc sumus, quando nostra consilia cessant et opera quiescunt et efficimur
pure passivi tam interius quam exterius.

make her an heir; rather, she acts as an heir by accepting or rejecting her inheritance. Only the one who has been set free can respond to his freedom, but this is not what *makes* him free; rather, he lives as one who has been set free and who either is grateful for his freedom or is not grateful—with the result that he squanders what he has become.

Of course the process of re-creation cannot move on to this second stage (sanctification or the deliberate avoidance of sanctification) unless the first stage, justification, has already taken place. We first must be returned, so to speak, despite our own resistance, to the state of *nihil* out of which we are to be created anew, and this is only possible by the crushing of the antagonism of the *homo vetus* to God. Consequently, we possess no natural receptivity for the gift of grace as long as we are sinners. Or, to put it another way, not only are we, as sinners, not capable of receiving the gift of grace; in fact, we actively *resist* it. The capacity for receiving and desiring grace must first be *mediated* or *imparted* through our liberation from our state as sinners.[22] Here, therefore, God's gift serves to destroy the sinner's sinfulness.

> Thus he opposes all our ideas, so that it appears that he is even more offended by our petitions and that even fewer of them are granted than previously. He does all this because it is God's nature first to destroy and eradicate what is in us before he gives us what is his. As it is written: "The Lord makes poor and makes rich; he brings low, he also exalts." By virtue of this his most holy will he makes us capable of receiving his works and his gifts. For we are capable of receiving his works and decisions when we cease from our intentions and rest from our works and become purely passive in relation to God as regards both our inner and our outward actions.[23]

22. Indeed, we shouldn't even speak of a "capacity" here because the removal of the obstacle of sin puts human beings in a state in which they live off and enjoy the divine grace. To construe this as the receiving of a special "capacity" only raises the further question of how creatures are able to receive that "capacity." It is easy to see that this leads into an infinite regress of needing a capacity for receiving the capacity for receiving the capacity for receiving the capacity. If this regress can be stopped at any point, it can be stopped at every point and then the best is not to make the first step at all.

23. WA 56:375.15–24:

Sic donat, vt contraveniat omnibus nostris conceptibus i. e. cogitationibus, ita vt appareat nobis post petitiones magis offensum esse et minus fieri ea, que petimus, quam ante. Quod totum ideo facit, Quia Natura Dei est, prius

God makes us, as human beings, recipients of his gift, not simply because he gives this gift but also because he gives the ability to receive the gift: God gives the gift and, in so doing, makes it possible for us to receive it at one and the same time.

We must look for the answer to the question of how it may be possible to receive God's gift, not in the human realm but with God. For humans are not *capax* of grace; instead, the resistance of sin must first be crushed in order to make them *capax*. This takes place through our being returned to the state we were in before we were created: the state of *nihil*. From this state we are created anew, in that we become Christians *mere passive*—Christians, in fact, because this *mere passive* becoming, which Luther illustrates with the metaphor of the happy exchange, is unfolded soteriologically as Christ's intercession for the sinner. Luther understands this in a double sense. On the one hand, Christ freely takes on himself the sinner's sin and its consequences, so that the sinner is wholly passively set free from sin. On the other hand, he freely gives the sinner a share in his own life with God, so that the sinner enters, wholly passively, into the enjoyment of God's life-giving generosity to Jesus Christ. In this sense, in which everything is owed to Christ, becoming a Christian is in the strict sense *re-creation*. It is not that the old becomes different or that the new is merely another instance of the old; rather, there is a completely original new creation, in which, by being drawn into the Christ event, human beings become what they are intended by God to be: the neighbors of all those who, through God's unmerited generosity, become *mere passive* God's neighbors because God makes himself their neighbor.

5. Anthropological Consequences

Luther's eschatological creation-theological thought form, with its Johannine and Pauline models and root metaphors—being born, being

---

destruere et annihilare, quicquid in nobis est, antequam sua donet; sicut Scriptum est: "Dominus pauperem facit et ditat, deducit ad inferos et reducit." Eo enim consilio suo piissimo facit nos capaces donorum suorum et operum suorum. Capaces autem tunc sumus operum et consiliorum eius, Quando nostra consilia cessant et opera quiescunt et efficimur pure passiui respectu Dei, tam quoad interiores quam exteriores actus.

made new, being created, and being made righteous—thus firmly excludes any involvement of natural powers in the re-creation of the human being. Just as it is impossible for the created being to have recourse to itself and its abilities when it is created, so it is equally impossible for the newly re-created being to have recourse to itself and its abilities when it is re-created.

The rightness or righteousness that is attributed to human beings as a result of this coming into being is therefore defined by Luther strictly as *iustitia aliena* (alien righteousness) or *iustitia passiva* (passive righteousness): "*Iustitia passiva* is a kind of righteousness that we cannot create or bring about through our own action, but must allow another to create and bring about in us"[24]—and indeed in such a way, that this "allowing" itself is understood as pure passivity and not as a minimal form of activity. Not only does this alien righteousness accrue to us wholly from another; we "suffer" it, since it is through the activity of another that we *are made righteous* wholly passively. Indeed, it always remains completely passive as far as we are concerned; it never passes across into our own use. Many good things

can be found in our works, where we can bring them forth purely on the basis of our natural abilities (as the sophists say) or even on the basis of the gift of God. (For these types of righteousness acts, too, are given to us by the work of God, as is everything that is ours.) But this most excellent righteousness, the righteousness of faith, which God reckons to us through Christ, is neither political nor cultic, nor is it the righteousness of God's law, nor is it to be found in our works. It is an entirely different righteousness, namely, one that is purely passive (whereas the kinds of righteousness described above are active). For in this righteousness we do nothing and give God nothing in return; we simply receive and allow another to act in us, namely God. This is why we are able to call the righteousness of faith—that is, Christian righteousness—passive. And this is a righteousness shrouded in mystery; the world does not recognize it. Indeed, even Christians do not hold onto it firmly enough, but reach for it only when beset by temptations. One therefore must impress upon oneself the need to school oneself in it diligently. For the one who does not grasp it securely when in afflictions and torments of conscience cannot stand

24. WA 40/I:41.

firm. For nothing is such a safe and sure comfort to the conscience as
that passive righteousness.[25]

The passivity of alien righteousness—which could be called strict
passivity from an anthropological perspective—is not a defect or
a disadvantage; on the contrary, it is its very advantage and merit.
Precisely because it is wholly and entirely passive, *this* righteousness,
and *it alone*, is also *absolutely sure* and dependable and not to be
squandered. We have not acquired it ourselves: we received it as a
gift. We do not own it: it still belongs to the giver. We cannot squan-
der it ourselves, because we do not "have" it; we "are" it. Indeed we
"are" it through the act of another who makes us righteous and not
because we have first made his act effective by receiving it ourselves.
It is not *receiving* the gift of God that makes sinners new; rather,
it is *this gift* that makes them new, by making them receptive to it
and putting them, as justified sinners, in a position to acknowledge
retrospectively and gratefully the gift that justified them.

In their lives, therefore, Christians constantly must differentiate
between the works in which they cooperate (works of love) and the
work that God is doing in and with them (*iustitia aliena*). Wherever, as
a result of this *iustitia*, they live rightly and well, it is not they who are
responsible for this, but the one who makes them righteous. Even the
opera iustitiae (works of righteousness) are *dona Dei* (gifts of God).
But only the *donum Dei* by which sinners become *Christiani, iusti* or
homines novi, is, as God's creation, a gift that always precedes and

25. WA 40/I:41.12–26:

quod versantur in nostris operibus et a nobis fieri possunt sive ex puris naturalibus (ut Sophistae loquuntur) sive etiam ex dono Dei (Sunt enim et hae iustitiae
operum dona Dei, ut omnia nostra). Ista autem excellentissima iustitia, nempe
fidei, quam Deus per Christum nobis absque operibus imputat, nec est politica
nec ceremonialis nec legis divinae iustitia nec versatur in nostris operibus, sed
est plane diversa, hoc est mere passiva iustitia (sicut illae superiores activae).
Ibi enim nihil operamur aut reddimus Deo, sed tantum recipimus et patimur
alium operantem in nobis, scilicet Deum. Ideo libet illam fidei seu Christia-
nam iustitiam appellare passivam. Haecque est iustitia in mysterio abscondita
quam mundus non intelligit, imo Christiani non satis eam tenent et difficulter
in tentationibus apprehendunt. Ideo semper est inculcanda et assiduo usu
exercenda. Et qui eam in afflictionibus et terroribus conscientiae non tenet
aut apprehendit, non potest consistere. Nulla enim alia tam est firma ac certa
consolatio conscientiarum quam illa passiva iustitia.

underlies everything else in which human beings can play any part. The gift is only ever there because and to the extent that *its giver is present in and with it*. It is a gift that is indivisible from the presence of the giver. Hence, it cannot be "received" by us in the sense that *we* accept, receive, or acknowledge it in order to make us so—since, in the sense relevant here, "we" are not, that is to say, without this gift we would not exist as *homines novi*. It makes us, but we do not receive it, because that would be self-contradictory: the *old* self neither can nor will accept it, since that is the essence of its oldness; and the *new* self can accept it, but does not need to, because it is already new. The justification of one who is without God, that is, the regeneration of the old self as a new self, is not a derivative of the being of the old self, nor can it be dissolved into the active sanctification of the one justified and the life of the new human being. The old self only becomes new when it ceases to be old and is made new *mere passive*. And there is no point at which this creative passivity can be represented as an activity carried out by the new self, since it precedes and underlies the new self *as a matter of principle*.

Admittedly, all of this also applies to the process of being created in the first place. But the new creation goes further, in that the new self is made possible and realized in the face of the activity in which the created being is already engaged, and that is directed against God. Here, therefore, *mere passive* is not simply the sign that we originate wholly and entirely from God; it is also the success-word for the fact that our anti-God activity is overcome by God himself.

One way in which Luther conveys this idea is by calling all activities that stem from this success-passivity *mere passiva*. They are passivity-rooted activities not only in the "that" of life (i.e., existence), as are all creaturely activities, but also in the "how" of life (i.e., the mode of existence), as are the activities of the justified sinner.

Thus Luther can describe true knowledge of God as passive knowledge.

> This is why it says, "You are known by God," which means that you have been convicted by the Word; the gift of faith and the Holy Spirit have been poured out upon you, making you new, etc. For this reason he uses the words "You are known by God" to emphasize the righteousness of

the law and rejects the idea that we can earn knowledge of God through our own works. "No one knows the Father except the Son and those to whom the Son chooses to reveal him" [Matt. 11:27 NIV]. Similarly: "By his knowledge my righteous servant will justify many, and he will bear their iniquities" [Isa. 53:11 NIV]. For this reason our knowledge of God is purely passive.[26]

That is to say, it is not that we know God; rather, we are known by God. And to know oneself in the same way as one is known by God means that one knows not only oneself in the passive mode but God as well. Thus we know him as the one who acts on us, in us, and on our behalf.

Accordingly, the *good works of righteousness* are described as works of passivity: "This is why circumcision was effective in bringing about righteousness for Abraham's posterity: not just on the basis of the work, which was purely passive, but on the basis of God's promise, which was linked with this passive work."[27] This means that the activity center and the driving force of these good works is not with those who do the good works themselves, but with God, who works in and through them to make what they do good and righteous: good works remain *God's* works. Hence humans themselves can never take credit for them but can only ever give God the credit for them.

At quite an early stage Luther takes this idea further into a detailed development of the way the human volitional faculty operates. The human volitional faculty, too, is not free as regards God's activity, but is wholly determined by it, and to that extent it is characterized by a fundamental passivity.

The entire activity of the faculty of free decision-making, which is designated "will," is purely passive, and the sophist's distinction that

26. WA 40/I:610.19–25:
Est ergo sententia: "Cogniti estis a Deo," id est, visitati estis per verbum, donati estis fide et Spiritusancto, quo renovati estis etc. Quare et his verbis: "Cogniti estis a Deo" derogat legi iustitiam ac negat propter dignitatem operum nostrorum contingere nobis notitiam Dei. "Nemo enim novit Patrem nisi Filius et cui voluerit Filius revelare.' Item: 'Notitia sui iustificabit multos, quia iniquitates eorum ipse portabit." Idea notitia nostra de Deo est mere passiva.
27. WA 42:621.1–3: "Abrahae fuit efficax, hoc est, attulit iustitiam, non ratione operis tantum, quod mere passivum fuit, sed promissionis Dei, quae cum hoc passivo opere coniuncta fuit."

says that good works are wholly, but not entirely, from God is empty prattle. They are indeed wholly and entirely from God, because the will is only gripped, drawn, and moved by grace. For this drawing, which passes into the members and powers of the soul and the body, is the activity of grace, pure and simple, just as the motion of the saw as it cuts the wood is purely passive in relation to the one sawing. The saw does not cooperate in the sawing process, but when it is drawn, it does nonetheless act upon the wood, albeit more as the one moved than as the mover. This sawing is described simultaneously as the work of the saw and the one sawing, even though the saw is merely suffering it to happen. But I will say more about this some other time.[28]

Strictly speaking, the human volitional faculty is not the place where free, self-induced, and self-determined activity originates; it is an organ of passivity-rooted activity conditioned and determined from outside, and as such is *mere passivum in omni actu suo* (merely passive in all its activity). It is not the sovereign lord in the life of a human being, but the sounding board of the powers, which it seeks to direct in one direction or another. Thus it does not desire what is good of its own accord; it must be gripped, drawn, and moved by God in order actively to desire and do what is good. But this gripping, drawing, and moving to do what is good does not take place in a neutral volitional faculty that has to be moved from indifference to a desire for the good. Rather, it is enacted as a power struggle in which God's will is asserted in opposition to the power of determination of the human will that is already in effect and that allows the human to ignore this God and to live and act as a sinner. Humans never live in an indifferent and neutral manner: whenever they desire or do anything, their volitional faculties are always governed by specific

28. WA 2:421.7–15:

> Liberum arbitrium esse mere passivum in omni actu suo, qui velle vocatur, et frustra garriri distinctionem sophistarum, actum bonum esse totum a deo, sed non totaliter. Est enim totus et totaliter a deo, quia voluntas gratia non nisi rapitur, trahitur, movetur, qui tractus redundans in membra et vires seu animae seu corporis est eius activitas et nulla alia, sicut tractus serrae secantis lignum est serrae mere passivus a sectore nec ad tractum suum quicquam cooperatur, sed tamen tracta iam in lignum operatur, impulsa magis quam impellens, quae serratio opus eius cum serratore dicitur, cum tamen mere patiatur, sed de hoc suo tempore latius.

powers, interests, and forces. This means that even where humans
themselves take action leading to deeds for which they alone are
responsible, the human will is *impulsa magis quam impellens*: in
other words, it desires that to which it is moved—whether good or
evil. Human activity is always a passivity-rooted activity conditioned
from outside.

So on the one hand, Luther uses the distinction between activity
and passivity to characterize the relationship between God (Creator)
and humans (creatures): in both their creational and their redemptive
relationship to God, humans are passive, whereas God is active. On
the other hand, Luther further applies the active/passive distinction
both to humans and to God. Thus human activity is not in dispute
but is understood as one way in which fundamental human passivity
is enacted. Humans can only be active on the basis of their passivity
as God's creatures; they live their lives as a *passivity-rooted activity*.
But even where God is concerned, Luther does not stop at the simple
attribution of activity (*semper actuosus*). The soteriological nub of
God's activity is precisely his making himself passive, his *active passivity of passion* on the cross. God's activity demonstrates its essential
character in his passion, since it is there that it shows and proves
what it truly is: *creative love* that brings forth new life, even out of
death. From now on one can say of human activity that its essential
character lies in its *passive determination*, in the fact that it is determined by God's creative love. The more clearly humans demonstrate
this passivity in everything they do, the more clearly they represent
and bring to effect the good operation of God's love. Only when it
is undisguisedly clear that human activity results entirely from the
work of God, who brings about the good that humans do, is human
life no longer disfigured by sin but sanctified by God.

Thus there can be no sanctification (new life) without justification
(new creation), in which it is God's love alone that is active, while
godless humans are wholly passive. Only in sanctification—not in
justification—does the justified godless human being cooperate with
God's love. But even here it is God's love that sanctifies human life
and activity, so that it is not humans who bring about the good that
they do, but the one who makes them new. They would not be able
to do good without God; they cannot do it without God; and not

only, therefore, do they not do good without God, but it is God who works and brings about good through them.

6. Ontological Interpretation

Gerhard Ebeling has given an ontological interpretation of Luther's outline of the anthropological issues in the generalized statement "that there is a passive process—coming-into-being—that precedes being, and an equivalent passive state that follows being active—completion."[29] He bases this on a gloss of Luther's on Romans 12:1, in which Luther states:

> Up to this point he has been teaching them that a new human has come into being, and he has described a new birth that results in a new being (John 3). But now he is teaching them about the works of the new birth, for which they will hope in vain until they have become new. In other words, being precedes acting, but suffering precedes being. Thus becoming, being, and acting follow one after another.[30]

In the passage on which Luther is commenting, Paul is addressing the congregation, moving from an exposition of his theology of justification to his paraenesis on sanctification. Can one take Paul's words to the Christians and generalize them in an ontological manner, as Ebeling does, so that one no longer speaks in soteriological terms of Christians being made new (new creation), but in creation-theological terms of humans coming into being (creation)? There are good grounds for this.

For one thing, both Luther and Paul speak explicitly of the coming into being of the *homo novus*, not of the human being as such. There is a clear order to the genesis and being of the *homo novus*,

29. G. Ebeling, "Das Leben—Fragment und Vollendung: Luthers Auffassung vom Menschen im Verhältnis zu Scholastik und Renaissance," in *Lutherstudien*, vol. 3, *Begriffsuntersuchungen—Textinterpretation—Wirkungsgeschichtliches* (Tübingen: Mohr Siebeck, 1985), 311–36 (the quotation here appears on 335).

30. "Hucusque docuit nouum hominem fieri et nouam natiuitatem descripsit, que dat nouum esse, Iohann. 3. Nunc vero Noue natiuitatis opera docet, Que frustra presumit nondum nouus homo factus. Prius est enim esse quam operari, prius autem pati quam esse. Ergo fieri, esse, operari se sequuntur."

an order that leads from passive suffering (*pati*) via being (*esse*) to active operation (*operari*). Admittedly, in Luther's reasoning the *pati* is, significantly, replaced by *fieri* (becoming), so that suffering is not understood in terms of a theology of suffering, but rather ontologically, in terms of creation theology, as coming into being. When related to the structure of the Pauline argumentation, this means that justification is understood in the passive mode as *pati* or *fieri*, whereas the life of sanctification is understood in the active mode as *operari*.

It should be pointed out, however, that this *operari* presupposes an *esse* that, in turn, is the result of a *fieri*. The latter is to be read theologically as divine activity and anthropologically as human passivity, and as such it permanently determines the human *esse* and *operari*. Thus one cannot speak of either justification or sanctification without involving God. What is true of God, however, is that his being is intrinsically at work (*esse est operari*) and that he is always active (*semper actuosus*), whereas his creatures have been brought into being (*facta sunt*), if they are, and act because and insofar as they are. The rightness of their work stands and falls therefore with the recognition that it does not originate with them but presupposes an *esse* that is the result of a *fieri*. If humans do not pay heed to this in their activity, they misunderstand their own *esse* since they are ignoring its *fieri* and are therefore living as if they had not been brought into being—in other words, created by God. This misunderstanding of the human existential situation *coram Deo* is a hallmark of the sinner, which faith corrects.

Luther thus does not see sin and faith as elements of the human *operari*, but rather of its underlying *esse*, so that they are not understood as specific operations or modes of action alongside and among others, but as human modes of being or conditions of existence. This has two important implications. On the one hand, sin and faith become fundamental determinants of what it is to be human, rather than two different ways of living the human life: they do not take their place alongside and among other modes of human life, but shape and determine it as a whole. On the other hand, even this implies that they always occur or appear in human activity, since the *operari* is always shaped by the *esse* mode in which it is carried out: one is not a sinner unless one lives in a certain way, nor is one a believer unless one lives in a certain way. In this present world, however, there is no neutral human *esse* that could form the basis of human life and activity. Rather, the human *esse* that has been brought passively into being (created) is always determined as sinful being (being a sinner) or righteous being (being righteous). Hence it is realized and enacted in an alternative theological mode of existence that may be described as follows. Each human being lives as a sinner (*homo vetus*) or as one who is righteous (*homo novus*), and there is no human being who does not live either in the one way or the other. It is not necessary that one be a sinner or that one be righteous, but it is necessary that one be either the one or the other or, in different respects, the one and the other. If this were not the case, then one would not be alive.

For Luther, therefore, there is no *esse* applicable to human beings in this world that could be differentiated from these determinate characteristics and posited of them in a neutral manner. Some allege that this is Schleiermacher's contention when he finds the consciousness of absolute dependence posited in the consciousness of the distinction between sin and grace in such a way that it can be considered and analyzed in isolation, albeit not lived as such. In any case, it is Luther's view, on the one hand, that creation must be treated as clearly distinct from sin so that there is no confusion between the two and, on the other hand, that human beings are not first created and born *and then* live either as sinners or believers, as if *being created* were to precede *being a sinner* or *being a believer* either chronologically or ontologically. Rather, in this world every human is a sinner or a believer (justified sinner) and lives accordingly in this condition and never simply as a creature. Being a sinner and being a believer are the two fundamental modes of humanness, which determine all human life from start to finish. After all, other beings besides human beings are included in the category of creatures. But only human beings are sinners or believers, since only they are created in such a way that they can live out or fail to live out their relationship to God and therefore can live their lives in such a way that they do one or the other.

Where the two human modes of existence are concerned, it is possible to differentiate between the "what" and the "that," between *what* one is and the fact *that* one is, something that is not true of God. This points to an important asymmetry between the status of the sinner and that of the believer. *What* we are as sinners—namely, those who ignore the fact that we owe our *esse* to God—is something we have become of ourselves through the way in which we live in practice. We ourselves therefore are responsible for our status as sinners: no one has to be a sinner. However, *that* one exists as a sinner, rather than not existing—in other words, one's existence as sinner—is grounded in the fact that even as a sinner one remains *creatura*: even sinners owe the fact that they exist, and have not forfeited their existence, to God alone. But this is different where faith is concerned. *What* one is as a believer—namely, one who has faith—one is through God alone. Sinners cannot have faith of their own accord (no one has faith on one's own initiative and in one's own strength), but any sinner can come to have faith through God (there is no one whom God could not bring to faith), and anyone who has faith has received it from God alone (anyone who believes owes this to God himself).[31] Further-more, *that* one exists as a believer rather than not existing—in other words, one's *existence* as a believer—is due to God alone. In contrast to one's existence as sinner, therefore, the fact *that* one is (*creatura*), as well as the fact of *what* one is (*Christianus*), is due to God alone.

The anthropological consequence of this asymmetry becomes evident in the activity (*operari*) of sinner and believer. In the *operari* of sinners, God's work finds expression only in the fact *that* these sinners exist, rather than not existing (in their *esse*, in other words). *How* such sinners are and act (their existence and life as *peccatores*), on the other hand, is attributable to the sinners themselves. In the *operari* of believ-ers, in contrast, the work of God manifests itself both in the "that" and in the "what": what believers are and do, they are and do (where God

31. It is important that in this context we speak specifically of sinners and not, unspecifically, of human beings. It is possible for every human being to have faith, but this is not possible for a sinner. It is not a contradiction in terms to say that someone is a human being and has faith, but it is a contradiction in terms to say that a sinner has faith. It is a fact that there is no human being who is not a sinner (leaving aside Jesus Christ), which is why there are in fact no human beings who have faith unless God has changed them from being sinners to being justified sinners. A human being *as such* may be able to have faith, but there is no such person. The fact that a human being does indeed have faith, so that such a one lives as a believer and not as a sinner, is to be attributed not to the believer but to the one in whom faith is placed. For it is not the believer who turns the possibility of faith into a reality, but God alone.

is concerned) as an effect of *God's activity* and (where they themselves are concerned) as an expression of their *pure passivity*. Hence they cannot ascribe either what they are as believers or what they do as believers to themselves. For sinners, as for believers, the divine activity manifests itself anthropologically in their original passivity. Sinners ignore this by living as if their *esse* did not result from a divine *fieri*, and in that respect they live their lives in an activity that ignores or disputes their passivity. Believers on the other hand live their *esse* in such a way that their divine *fieri* becomes the distinguishing feature of their whole life and activity so that they carry out every aspect of their activity as a *passivity-rooted activity owed to God*.

Using Luther's Aristotelian-school terminology of the period, this can also be expressed as follows. If the *anima* (soul) is the human *forma corporis* (substantial form) that defines human reality, then, in the case of sinners, this whole hylomorphic complex is corrupted by the fact that the *anima* shuts itself up against God (in unfaith) and is therefore a *forma corporis* that is depraved and, in turn, depraves the human body and the reality of its life. As believers, however, humans become new, in the sense that this corruption is removed by God himself. This takes place as he presents himself to the human *anima* by the working of his Spirit, opening it up to himself in such a way that the *anima* orients itself by and clings wholly to the one toward whom it is directed in faith, namely, God in Christ. But once humans are determined (shaped) by a faith directed toward God in Christ, they receive a new *forma* and become a new reality, one that Luther can formulate succinctly: "Let Christ be my form."[32] That is to say, believers no longer have their own corrupted *anima*; instead, Christ has become the *forma hominis* (human form), which is why the new human being is called *Christianus*. This *forma Christi* (form of Christ) affects and determines them *entirely passively*: it is not that the *homo* chooses Christ as *sua forma*, but that Christ becomes and makes himself the definition of human reality. This is what is contained in the idea of *iustitia aliena*. And this is why everything that the believer does is a working out of this Christ reality, a passivity-rooted activity grounded in God's passion in Christ.

32. WA 40/I:283: "Christus sit mea forma."

This new anthropological reality (*homo novus*) is the result of the divine vanquishing of the *homo vetus* and therefore can always be considered from two points of view: first, what has *actually* come into being thereby (the righteousness of Christ); and second, to whom this has happened and *from what it has come into being* (the reality of the sinner). Given the above, what is said in the doctoral disputation of Joachim Mörlin (1540) is true.

> Christians must be considered from two points of view: in the categories of relation and of quality. When they are considered in the category of relation, they are as holy as angels; that means, on the basis of what is reckoned to them through Christ, since God says that he does not see sin, on account of his only begotten Son who is the veil of Moses, that is, the law. But considered in the category of quality, Christians are full of sin.[33]

This means that, in relation to what constitutes their reality, Christians are righteous, whereas in relation to the one who becomes the newly formed reality, they must be termed, in contrast, not just *creatura* but more precisely and specifically *homo peccator*. Sinners are justified in that their sin is taken away; the one who has committed the sin is formed anew, receiving a new *forma*, namely the *forma* of Christ, and thereby becomes a new reality. This is described in theological terms by stating that Christ freely took human sin on himself and freely allows those who have sinned to share, by faith, in his uncorrupted *esse* as *filius Dei*. He changes places with sinners by differentiating between them and their sin, allowing God to make him liable for their sin and giving those who have been freed from their sin a share in his own inheritance as *filius Dei*.

In each of these respects it is only God in Christ who is at work: any human involvement is wholly passive. When human beings are thus made new, they experience a fundamental change of position *coram Deo*. Their *esse* is reshaped *ab extra* in a manner quite beyond

---

33. WA 39/II:141.1–6: "Christianus est dupliciter considerandus, in praedicamento relationis et qualitatis. Si consideratur in relatione, tam sanctus est, quam angelus, id est, imputatione per Christum, quia Deus dicit, se non videre peccatum propter filium suum unigenitum, qui est velamen Mosi, id est, legis. Sed christianus consideratus in qualitate est plenus peccato."

their own resources, so that they are transplanted by the Spirit of Christ from their position as sinners into Christ's own position. One could say that God constantly creates circumstances and we as human beings always inhabit circumstances—constellations of ourselves and others, of that which is other and God. As sinners, however, we fail to recognize the fundamental nature of our condition and live our lives ignoring the God to whom we owe the fact that there are any life conditions at all and that, even as sinners, we can and do live out our lives in these conditions. In so doing, we obstruct our access to a condition in which this is not ignored, in which creatures live in dialogue with their Creator, just as Jesus Christ clearly did. As sinners, we can only experience such a life if we are transplanted from our sinful condition into this other condition, not of ourselves but by another who brings forth from our *homo vetus* a *homo novus*. We will then live *coram Deo* in such a way that our lives will be shaped and determined by the fact that they are lived out *coram Deo*.

Humans, therefore, are only believers during the transition from the status of sinner to the status of Christian, a transition to which they themselves can contribute nothing, and which they can only ever suffer *mere passive*. This transition leads them across the chasm of their nonbeing, the withering away of the old self and the coming into being of the new self. This coming into being has no substrate in a neutral humanness that was old and has now become new: there is in fact no such neutral humanness. Rather, its continuity is to be found only in the one who reduces the old *in nihilum* (to nothing) and produces the new *ex nihilo*: in the eradication of the old and the creation of the new by God himself. It is therefore not just once, at the beginning, that believers are reliant on being made new by God, but permanently and constantly; they are the location of this transition, but they are not the ones who put it into effect.

The ontological consequence of these considerations is that *relation* becomes the decisive theological reality category, albeit not formally in distinction to the category of substance, but rather in the sense that it denotes the activity of God in bringing forth the new from the old and in putting an end to the old through the new. This is what lies behind the truth of "with respect to God relation is the *res*, that is, the hypostasis

and subsistence."[34] Here it is the *res* because it holds together, across
the chasm of nonbeing, what from a human point of view is at risk of
falling apart: the old self, the sinner, and the new self, the justified sinner.

7. Coming from Nothing and Being Perfected

Luther describes the consequences of this in his lecture on the Epistle
to the Romans in the Scholia on Romans 12:2.

> For just as, according to Aristotle, there are five levels of natural things:
> nonbeing, coming into being, being, activity, suffering (i.e., want, ma-
> terial, form, action, suffering), thus it is also in the spirit: nonbeing is
> a nameless state in which the human being is in sin; coming into being
> is justification; being is righteousness; work is righteous activity and
> life; suffering is being made perfect and complete. And these five are
> always on the move within the human being.[35]

In other words, the following equivalents are established:

In naturalibus:

non esse	fieri	esse	actio	passio
privatio	materia	forma	operatio	passio secundum Aristotelem

In spiritu:

res sine nomine et homo in peccatis	iustificatio	iustitia	iuste agere et vivere	perfici et consummari

The differentiation between *in naturalibus* and *in spiritu* does not
merely indicate a distinction between theological and nontheological
perspectives; it highlights the *theological* distinction, meaning that
from a theological point of view the reality of human life can only be

34. WA 39/II:340: "In divinis relatio est res, id est, hypostasis et subsistentia."
35. WA 56:441.23–442.5: "Nam Sicut In Naturalibus rebus quinque sunt gradus:
Non esse, fieri, Esse, Actio, passio, i.e. priuatio, Materia, forma, operatio, passio,
secundum Aristotelem, Ita et Spiritu: Non Esse Est res sine nomine et homo in peccatis;
fieri Est Iustificatio; Esse est Iustitia; opus Est Iuste agere et viuere; pati est perfici et
consummari. Et hec quinque semper velut in motu sunt in homine."

described and analyzed by bringing the theological and nontheological aspects into a relationship of mutual critical interpretation. The instructive nature of this becomes especially clear where it gives rise to points of friction that draw attention to problems.

Thus in the first section (*in naturalibus*) it is worth noting that Luther interprets the *non esse* as *privatio*. Yet nonbeing is not a lack of being but the nonexistence of the situation in which one could lack or not lack something, and *creatio* is not *creatio ex privatione*, but *creatio ex nihilo*. Perhaps one could be tempted to describe new creation as the removal of *privatio*: as the realization, in a human life, of the correct relation to God, a relation that did not exist in that life even though it could or should have existed. But this only works if new creation is conceived of in relation to a *creatio* that precedes and underlies it and that is the source of the human destiny to a specific relationship with God, a destiny that in fact had been missed but is now realized. It only works, in fact, if new creation is understood as the renewing of and giving of tangible form to God's *creatio ex nihilo* and the gifting of human beings with the *imago Dei*. New creation is not a second attempt at creation, with the world now containing both old and new created beings, nor is it the replacement of the present world, the old creation, with another world, the new creation. The differentiation between old and new does not relate to creation (and hence to what God has done) but rather to the *perverseness* of the creation (and thus of the behavior of the created being): what is overcome in the new creation is not the creation but its perverseness. It follows that this is not another creation; rather, it affirms and brings to effect the *ex nihilo* of the original *creatio* and the special gifting and honor bestowed on human beings in making them, in the face of their ignorance of creation and their godlessness, the *imago Dei*. It does this in such a way that these creatures, who, contrary to their destiny and gifting, ignore their Creator and their createdness, thus fundamentally misunderstanding themselves and their world and living far below their potential, are made new creatures and rendered capable of a life in keeping with their gifting.[36] And this renewal and

36. This calls for a critical correction and reformulation of the definition of the human being in its traditional understanding of *imago Dei*. See chap. 6 below.

enabling are brought about as follows: their *esse* and their *operari* are permanently governed by the *solo Deo* of their having been brought from the *non esse* to the *esse* in such a way that the fundamental nature of the "that" of their beings (their passivity) also constantly shapes and characterizes the "how" of their lives (their activity). As a result, humans become what they can be by virtue of their having been marked out by God: *homo novus*, whose gifting—being made in the image of God—is realized as they focus the activities of their lives on the creative passivity of having been created by God (that is, live as creatures), differentiate in a self-critical way between what they do and what God does (that is, give God the glory), and place their trust in the passive completion of their fragmentary lives by God in fellowship with their fellow creatures (that is, look to God for all that is good).

The second section (*in spiritu*) speaks of human movement from sin to grace. But this still does not mean that the first row *non esse, fieri, esse, actio, passio* speaks of the sinner. Rather, it speaks—with the aid of Aristotle!—of all creation. However, the use of *privatio* in the second row shows that here Luther is already thinking hamartiologically and not purely in terms of creation theology. This is underlined in the third row, which speaks of the *res sine nomine*, that is, the *materia nuda* (in other words, the *apeiron*), and parallels it with the sinner (*homo in peccatis*). But being a sinner is somewhat different from nonbeing: the sinner is not merely *nihil*, but one who is in conflict with God, that is, a creature who works against God and not just one that has not been created. Here passivity is not experienced as privation or as lack, but as opposition, as an *overwhelming deluge of God's wrath*. Luther's recourse to the ontological category of *privatio* is therefore questionable, both soteriologically and in terms of creation theology.

But in the second column it is different. Here *iustificatio* corresponds, in the realm of spiritual being (*in spiritu*), to the passivity of becoming (*fieri*) and, in the realm of earthly being (*in naturalibus*), to *materia*. Here humans are *pura materia* of God's new creation, not collaborative and certainly not antagonistic. In the third column the *forma* (second row) of the *esse* (first row) of the new humanity is the *forma Christi*. It is Christ's righteousness and hence his *iustitia aliena* that makes sinners righteous before God and determines their reality *coram Deo* as *iustitia* (third row). The *iuste agere et vivere* in the fourth column (third row), accordingly, is an *actio* (first row) and *operatio* (second row) of this new reality *(forma)*—in other words, of Christ, that is, God himself. It is not the sinner who does what is righteous and good, but the one who makes him righteous and good: Christ. Again, in perfection (fifth column, third row: *perfici et consummari*) only God is active, while *in naturalibus* it is only possible to speak of *passio*. From *iustificatio* right through to *perfectio*, therefore, everything in the spiritual realm is described as being carried out by divine activity and human passivity: humans do not do and bring about what is good, but God does so in them and through them. The entire Christian life is presented as a life in progress from sin to perfection. At every point in this life, the working of what is good is God's activity, and the object of this good work is the sinner's anti-God activity, which needs to be overcome, or the righteous person's activity, which cooperates with God. This is why, before *perfectio*, Christians are to be addressed as both: as *iustus et peccator*—as *iustus* in respect of *what* God makes of them (new human beings), and as *peccator* in respect of *from what* God makes these new human beings.

Luther is unambiguous in drawing this anthropological conclusion when he describes the being and life of the new human being.

> This is the reason humans are always really and truly in want, always in the process of becoming, or in potentiality and the material realm, and simultaneously always in reality as well. This is how Aristotle philosophizes about things, and indeed rightly, but they do not understand him thus. Humans are always in a state of nonbeing, of coming into being, of being, always in want, potentiality, reality, always in sin, justification, righteousness, which is to say that they are always sinners, always penitents, always righteous. For it is through repentance that the unrighteous becomes righteous. Repentance is thus a middle ground between unrighteousness and righteousness. And thus he finds himself in a state of sin as regards the starting point and in a state of righteousness as regards the goal. If we are always penitent, then we are always sinners, yet it is precisely because of this that we are also righteous and justified: part sinner, part righteous, we are thus nothing but penitents. Similarly, but in reverse, the godless who turn away from righteousness take the middle ground between sin and righteousness, but they go in

the opposite direction. Hence this life is the path to heaven and to hell. None is so good that he could not become better, and none is so bad that he could not become worse, until we reach one extreme or the other.[37]

However, the only aspects that are explicitly adopted are the first three: nonbeing, coming into being, and being. They are simultaneously true, always and for each of us, but they do not represent "stages on the path of life" (thus Kierkegaard), but rather *aspects of the life of all Christians and non-Christians*. Humans live constantly with nonbeing behind them, and they live constantly as *semper ubique passivus*. It follows that they are not established living beings; rather, they live in the precarious dynamic of those who could always be better, but also much worse, than they are. There is no rule or limitation on their beings that would prevent them from escalating even further their most barbaric actions and their most inhuman manner of life: the human is the being whose depravity can always surpass itself. But conversely, there is no circumstance in this life in which humans cannot profit from God's generosity to become better than they are.

Christians who know that live their lives as *penitents*, as Luther's first thesis on indulgences stresses.[38] It underscores both possibilities: "None is so good that he could not become better, and none is so bad that he could not become worse, until we reach one extreme or the other."[39] In this life there is no boundary to what is worse that humans

---

37. WA 56:442.12–26:

> Quare Verissime homo semper est in priuatione, semper in fieri seu potentia et materia et semper in actu. Sic enim de rebus philosophatur Aristoteles et Bene, Sed non ita ipsum intelligunt. Semper homo Est in Non Esse, In fieri, In esse, Semper in priuatione, in potentia, in actu, Semper in peccato, in Iustificatione, In Iustitia, i.e., Semper peccator, semper penitens, semper Iustus. Quod enim penitet, hoc fit de non Iusto Iustus. Ergo penitentia Est medium inter Iniustitiam et Iustitiam. Et sic est in peccato quoad terminum a quo et in Iustitia quoad terminum ad quem. Si ergo semper penitemus, semper peccatores sumus, et tamen eoipso et Iusti sumus ac Iustificamur, partim peccatores, partim Iusti i.e., nihil nisi penitentes. Sicut econtra Impii, Qui recedunt a Iustitia, medium tenent inter peccatum et Iustitiam contrario motu. Quare hec Vita Est via ad celum et infernum. Nemo ita bonus, vt non fiat melior, nemo ita malus, vt non fiat peior, vsque dum ad extremam formam perueniamus.

38. WA 1:233.

39. "Nemo ita bonus, vt non fiat melior, nemo ita malus, vt non fiat peior, vsque dum ad extremam formam perueniamus."

could not actively overstep, and no boundary to what is better that would make it unnecessary or impossible for them to be passively gifted and enriched by God. Their potential for activity makes humans a constant and incalculable source of danger to themselves. But Christians know that their activity is of secondary and not primary importance. The first and fundamental reality is their passivity. This is expressed in the Christian life in terms of *penitentia* (penitence), which is lived out as turning away from sin and turning toward God. This double movement means that in practice believers are *cooperatores Dei* (coworkers with God). They are his coworkers only for as long as and to the extent that they move out from their passivity to become *active* while their activity is still rooted in their *passivity*. This is the guarantee that in this life human beings can never have it so bad that things cannot get better. With all their activities, as Luther says in thesis 35 of *De homine*, they are no more and no less than "the pure material of God for life in its future form"[40]—*pura materia*, not material working together with form and dependent on it. For only this makes it clear that the future of human beings will not be decided on the basis of their own activity, with its limitless tendency to perversion, but wholly and exclusively by the unambiguous, unstinting, and unequivocally positive activity of God's creative love. It is precisely—and only—because they are not at the mercy of their own activity, but are *mere passive*, that human beings have grounds for hope.

Luther's conception of the fundamental importance of existential passivity for the active shaping of human life leaves little room for misunderstanding. But it does throw up questions. The assertion that life is first and last a gift would have no consequences if it did not lead to a specific view and practice of life. This in turn would shed no light on anything if it were not given tangible form in a specific experience (distinguishable from other experiences), understanding, and form of life. What then is the nature of life if it is understood, first and last, as gift? What does it mean to live life as gift? And how is "gift" to be understood if life is experienced, lived, and understood as gift? These are questions that cannot be answered without taking a closer look at the phenomenon of gift.

---

40. WA 39/1:177: "pura materia Dei ad futurae formae suae vitam."

4

All for Nothing

On the Art of Giving and the Limitations of Gift

"To be obliged to decline a gift simply because it was not offered in
the proper way incenses one against the giver," commented Nietzsche
in 1878.[1] But since Nietzsche's day we have learned that the "art of
giving"[2] can miss its target in an even more fundamental way. Anyone
who expects a gift to have a giver,[3] a recipient,[4] or an object[5] has already

---

1. Friedrich Nietzsche, *Menschliches, Allzumenschliches: Ein Buch für freie Geister*,
§297, KSA 2:240. English translation: *Human, All-Too-Human: A Book for Free
Spirits,* trans. R. J. Hollingdale (Cambridge: Cambridge University Press, 1996), 136.
2. Ibid. Here we would simply call to mind that "gifts" are not the same as "presents"
and that there is an even greater distinction between "giving" and "presenting." See
R. Comay, "Gifts without Presents: Economics of 'Experience' in Bataille and Heidegger,"
Yale French Studies 78 (1990): 66–89; G. Dressel and G. Hopf, eds., *Von Geschenken und
anderen Gaben: Annäherungen an eine historische Anthropologie des Gebens* (Frankfurt
am Main: Peter Lang, 2000).
3. Jean-Luc Marion, "La raison du don," *Philosophie* 78 (2003): 3–32: only where
"le donateur manque . . . le don s'accomplit parfaitement" (14).
4. Ibid., 15: "Le don peut aussi s'accomplir comme un don sans le moindre dona-
taire," such as when the gift is to an aid organization or an enemy: "Qui donne à son
enemi donne . . . sans retour, sans revenu et sans raison suffisante—incontestablement."
5. Ibid.: "Le don peut s'accomplir enfin sans donner aucun objet susceptible de
revenir à une valeur d'échange."

missed the target. The truth is that there is a real gift only where no one gives, no one receives, and nothing is given and received. But in that case, what do we have here? Gifts, it would appear, are highly endangered phenomena—if they are phenomena at all.

1. The Impossibility of Gift

That they are not is a view that no one has defended more decisively than Derrida in recent years.[6] *Nothing is gift*, not because there is no giving or making of presents among human beings, but because there is no such phenomenon as a gift. It is not just that the art of giving rarely meets its target in practice; it cannot meet its target in principle, since it attempts the impossible. Those who give in order to make a gift cancel out what they are doing in the doing thereof. The same applies to the recipient and the object of a gift. The making of a gift destroys it, since the conditions that make it possible are simultaneously those that make it impossible.[7] If the *giver* gives something *as a gift* and expects an appropriate reaction, then he perverts his gift into an object of exchange. If the *recipient* receives something *as a gift*, he has already reacted in such a way that the gift is understood from the perspective of an exchange economy with the result that the gift is destroyed. If the *gift* is something that is perceived *as a gift*, it ceases to be a gift and becomes something that places the recipient in a position of indebtedness toward the giver, burdening the recipient with a debt that arguably can never be repaid: the greater the gift the greater the guilt.

Thus, for Derrida, gift-giving (someone gives a gift to another) has the structure of an *aporia*:[8] only where something is given and received as a gift, it seems, is there a gift. But where something is

6. Jacques Derrida, *Donner le temps*, vol. 1, *La fausse monnaie* (Paris: Éditions Galilée, 1991); Derrida, *Sauf le nom (post-scriptum)* (Paris: Éditions Galilée, 1993). Cf. Hans-Dieter Gondek and Bernhard Waldenfels, eds., *Einsätze des Denkens: Zur Philosophie von Jacques Derrida* (Frankfurt am Main: Suhrkamp, 1997); R. Hoerner, *Rethinking God as Gift: Marion, Derrida, and the Limits of Phenomenology* (New York: Fordham University Press, 2001), esp. chaps. 1, 7, and 8.
7. Derrida, *La fausse monnaie*, 22–25.
8. Ibid., 42.

given and received *as a gift*, it has already ceased to be a gift: "The truth of the gift is equivalent to the nongift or to the nontruth of the gift."[9] Or to put it another way: "*Gift as gift* should *ultimately not appear to be a gift*: *neither to the recipient of the gift, nor to its giver*."[10] But that is strictly aporetic, and "it is perhaps in this sense that the gift is the impossible. Not impossible, but *the* impossible, the very figure of the impossible."[11]

2. The Unavoidability of Gift

But what exactly is declared to be impossible here? Not the possibility of the gift, but of it *appearing to be a gift*. What is disputed is gift *as phenomenon*. This allows for a number of reactions. Some agree with Derrida's conclusion and bury the subject of gift phenomenologically: gifts are not phenomena. Others criticize it and argue that gifts are phenomena. Some, like Marion, accept the phenomenology of gift but do so on their own premises, rejecting the whole approach by offering a different understanding of gifts or phenomena or both.[12]

Whereas Derrida holds that no gift is a phenomenon, Marion argues that every phenomenon is gift. To see this, we have to concentrate our analysis on the horizon in which the gift appears. If we analyze gifts in the horizon of economy and exchange or of causality and intention, they will not appear as gifts; they appear in fact in the horizon of giving (that is to say, of *givenness*). Gifts bring their own horizon

9. Jacques Derrida, *Falschgeld: Zeit geben I*, trans. A. Knap and M. Wetzel (Munich: Wilhelm Fink, 1993), 40. Cf. Derrida, *La fausse monnaie*, 42.

10. Derrida, *Falschgeld*, 25; cf. Derrida, *La fausse monnaie*, 26 (emphasis in original).

11. Ibid., 17; cf. Derrida, *La fausse monnaie*, 19. On this subject, see also L. D'Isanto, "Theology's Gift and the Hermeneutics of the Trace," in *The Return of God: Theological Perspectives in Contemporary Philosophy*, ed. N. Grønkjaer (Odense: Odense University Press, 1998), 113–32, esp. 114–17; J. D. Caputo, "Apôtre de l'impossible: Sur Dieu et le don chez Derrida et Marion," *Philosophie* 78 (2003): 33–51.

12. See Jean-Luc Marion, *Réduction et donation: Recherches sur Husserl, Heidegger et la phénoménologie* (Paris: Presses Universitaires de France, 1989); Marion, *Étant donné: Essai d'une phénoménologie de la donation* (Paris: Presses Universitaires de France, ⁴2013); "On the Gift: A discussion between Jacques Derrida and Jean-Luc Marion, moderated by Richard Kearney," in *God, the Gift, and Postmodernism*, ed. John D. Caputo and Michael J. Scanlon (Bloomington: Indiana University Press, 1999), 54–78.

with them, that of *givenness*. In this horizon nothing appears that is not *given*. And since there is nothing that could not appear in this horizon, not only is gift a phenomenon, but every phenomenon is gift.

But everything has its price. If all phenomena are gift, then gifts are not special phenomena. Where specific situations are concerned, Derrida's thesis and Marion's counterthesis run the risk of amounting to the same thing. There can be no distinction between "Gifts are not phenomena" and "All phenomena are gifts" *in phenomenal terms* (i.e., with reference to specific phenomena), but only *in phenomenological terms* (i.e., in terms of the debate about correct phenomenological methods). If all that appears to us as givenness—and only that—is gift, then "gift" does not constitute a particular phenomenal field, and it is impossible to establish a phenomenal distinction between the giving of gifts and other processes of social interaction and communication. The phenomenon of gift is saved, so to speak, by allowing its phenomenological disappearance into the givenness of phenomena and thus into the phenomenological method.

Yet this means that the whole endeavor was all for nothing. Phenomena may perhaps be understood like this, but not gifts. Neither approach describes gifts as they appear to us in actual interactions in the life-world,[13] but as that which a particular type of phenomenological reduction makes of them.[14] Derrida's analysis leads to the annihilation of the gift and thus results in the aporia that a social reality nobody disputes has to be disputed as a phenomenon on phenomenological grounds. There can only be said to be "pure gift" if one disregards everything that makes the gift a gift (the giver, the recipient, the object that is the gift). What is left of the gift, though,

13. "Life-world" is Edmund Husserl's term for the universe of self-evident and meaningful phenomena disclosed to persons in and through their concrete practices in the world. In *The Crisis of European Sciences and Transcendental Phenomenology: An Introduction to Phenomenological Philosophy*, trans. David Carr (Evanston: Northwestern University Press, 1970), Husserl introduces the term in the following way:

> In whatever way we may be conscious of the world as universal horizon, as coherent universe of existing objects, we, each "I-the-man" and all of us together, belong to the world as living with one another in the world; and the world is our world, valid for our consciousness as existing precisely through this "living together." We, as living in wakeful world-consciousness, are constantly active on the basis of our passive having of the world. (108–9)

14. See Marion, *Étant donné*, 161–65.

once we have allowed it to die the death of a thousand qualifications by negating everything that comes to mind when we use the word *gift*? Derrida's view is that *nothing* is left, so he denies the existence of gift as phenomenon. Marion then retaliates that without the given, such qualification and negation processes would not be possible at all, so that in fact exactly the opposite is true: *everything* given phenomenally is self-giving and therefore gift.

3. Save the Phenomena—or Phenomenology?

Both positions use figures of thought with which theology is all too familiar: how we approach something (i.e., the mode and the horizon in which we explore it) decides to a large extent how and as what we perceive it and speak about it. Neither of them is concerned purely with gift: they make reference to gift in exploring the relationship between a phenomenon and the method of approach. In that case, perhaps Derrida's argument is not really against the phenomenon of gift, but rather against the intentional-analytical phenomenology he criticizes and dismantles. And perhaps Marion's argument is not really an argument in favor of gift as a phenomenon, but rather an indication of his premise—the phenomenological method he promulgates. Both instances appear to be less about gift and its limits and more about the limits of phenomenology and how they may be overcome: the debate about gift as a phenomenon is in essence a dispute about phenomenological method.

The central focus of this dispute is the method of phenomenological reduction.[15] Ever since it was invented by Husserl, phenomenology has been disturbed by the fact that the world exists. Blumenberg is correct to say that "the phenomenologist" is defined "by a fearlessness of infinite regress,"[16] but he feels himself permanently "harassed by the fact that there is a world as the totality of all that is the case, and that this bars him from having direct access to his essences."[17] This demands of the philosopher the ability "to inspect an object

15. See Marion, *Réduction et donation*; Marion, *Étant donné*, 108–12.
16. H. Blumenberg, *Lebenszeit und Weltzeit* (Frankfurt am Main: Suhrkamp, [2]1986), 374.
17. H. Blumenberg, *Zu den Sachen und zurück* (Frankfurt am Main: Suhrkamp, 2002), 241.

independently of its existence in nature, in the world, in time. Essence is always what is left over when existence has been subtracted from an object."[18] Thus phenomenological reduction is based on an "elementary indifference to the existence of objects." In Husserl's case this may be due to his background in mathematics, since the mathematician "is indifferent to the existence of his objects, even when he speaks about it as significant in one way or another."[19] The whole point of phenomenological reduction is to isolate the essence of a phenomenon by disregarding its existence.

The fact that this was "fostering a methodological illusion" is borne out by the whole "history of Husserl's difficulties with his method of reduction and its multiple alterations."[20] But not only that. Even a form of phenomenological reduction that does not follow the guidelines of mathematical *Wesensschau* (eidetic intuition) but, like Blumenberg, makes use of free variation to delineate the essence of what is under examination by exploring the possibilities of a phenomenon in the history of language and culture does not in fact describe what is but explores what might have been the case. As a result it concentrates on the possibilities, not the reality, of the real.

In the case of the gift, this is precisely what leads to insoluble aporias. One option is to seek to explore the essence of the gift, as Derrida does, purely from the point of view of its possibilities; he discovers that what is left after the bracketing of the existential realities of giving (giver, recipient, thing given) is not a purified essence of the gift for phenomenological intuition, but simply nothing at all that could be inspected. The reduction sheds light, not on a phenomenon, but only on the trace, the absence, the disappearance of a phenomenon.

The other option is to seek to avoid this, as Marion does, by declaring the very thing that disappears with this bracketing to be the essence of the phenomenon under examination: gift is *what makes phenomenological reduction possible in the first place*, that is to say, whatever is phenomenologically assumed as given is gift.

18. Ibid., 240.
19. Ibid., 243.
20. Ibid., 240–41.

Whereas for Derrida the phenomenological method annuls the phenomenon of gift, Marion makes the gift an essential part of the phenomenological method itself. The one holds that gifts are not phenomena, since they appear only to disappear; the other holds that all phenomena are gifts, since they only exist by giving themselves.[21] They are plainly at loggerheads, but all for nothing. For they are both making the same point that there is more than there appears to be.

4. Essence and Existence: The Interference of the World

Now, phenomenologists have always known that phenomena are not all there is and that not everything is a phenomenon: for example, *horizons*, without which there would be no phenomena, are not themselves phenomena. One cannot isolate and inspect them "as such," by "bracketing" everything of which they are a horizon, since one loses the horizon in the process as well. Horizons limit perspectives, in which phenomena appear to us, but even *perspectives* are not phenomena. And that may in fact apply to a great deal that appears to us in perspectives: is a rainbow, for example, a phenomenon? Or isn't it actually the water molecules and the refraction of the sunlight reflected by them that are phenomena?

The same would seem to apply to the gift. Derrida, on the one hand, follows Husserl in pushing the phenomenological reduction to its aporetic limit, namely, that if one seeks to formulate the *essence* of gift while disregarding its *existence*, there is nothing left for inspection. Marion, on the other hand, seems to opt for identifying the essence of gift with its very existence, with its *givenness*, so that he treats *existence as such*, the *existence of anything at all*, as gift. As a result of the phenomenological reduction, the one is left with no phenomenon of gift at all, whereas for the other all phenomena are turned into gifts.

Both are reacting to the interference of the world in such a way that, in order to be able to differentiate methodologically between the phenomenological illusions of "essence" and "existence," they push them to one of two extremes. If reduction means "abandoning *existence* in

21. Marion, *Étant donné*, 100–112.

order to keep the *essence*,"[22] then reduction results either in the loss of the gift as a phenomenon (Derrida's aporetic phenomenology of negation) or in the phenomenological act of despair that identifies *essence* with *existence* so as not to lose the phenomenon, reducing the essence of gift to the existence of givenness (Marion's universalizing phenomenology of existence). The first position reacts to the interference of the world by limiting the world of phenomena and by opening it toward something beyond itself: there is more to the world than what appears or what can appear. The second position reacts to this interference by describing phenomena as such as the interruption of consciousness by something other than itself: there is more to the world than what appears or can appear, because whatever appears must be given, but its givenness is nothing that either could or could not appear.

5. Saying and Showing: The Surplus of the World

Viewed this way, it becomes clear that the annihilation of gift resulting from the phenomenology of negation, no less than the universalization that results from a phenomenology of being, is ontologically motivated. The one scenario seeks to show that there is more than appears to us since not everything that is appears: the world is more than what appears and can appear to us. The other scenario in contrast argues that what appears is not all that there is, since in what appears more is being shown to us than appears: that is to say that what shows itself to *us* shows *itself* to us. If, in the one scenario, it is wholly in vain to want to show that which does *not show* but rather *withdraws* itself and only appears in other respects as a withdrawal, an absence, a nonpresence, then in the other scenario it is wholly in vain to want to show what cannot there be shown, namely, that what shows itself *shows itself*. The same question concerning the "more" of the world, as compared with phenomena, thus results in two fundamentally different ontological orientations: the openness of the world, in principle, to a "phenomenal beyond," and a givenness of the world, also and equally understood in principle, in the self-giving of phenomena.

22. Blumenberg, *Zu den Sachen und zurück*, 254.

Derrida's annihilation of the gift thus turns out to be a committed plea for an ontological surplus of our world over and above that
which appears or can appear to us as phenomenon. Gifts cannot appear
as phenomena without disappearing as gifts. For that which appears
enters the horizon of exchange and cannot appear there as gift. It is
only possible, at best, to speak of gifts with reference to what does not
show itself but is only there inasmuch as it withdraws itself: gifts do not
show themselves, yet they are not simply nothing. Rather, they appear
in a different way as *withdrawal*, as *absence*, as *nonpresence*. Hence
they cannot be shown, but only disclosed in words. This makes them
ontologically precarious. For on the one hand, they do not belong to
the world of phenomena. Rather, they mark something that occurs only
in and with it: gifts are not phenomena in the world; they mark the
boundaries of the phenomenal world. On the other hand, what becomes
plain is that the world is more than what appears. It is not unveiled in
what shows itself, but has a "before," a "behind," and a "beyond" that
cannot be represented referentially or descriptively. Thus one can speak
of gifts, but one cannot show them. This arouses the suspicion that
they are fictitious and illusory, since one can never display them visibly
but can only ever assert, discuss, proclaim, and promise them, speaking
of them with gratitude and remembrance. It is the boundaries of our
language, not the boundaries of phenomena, that are the boundaries
of our world. The world is more than is manifest. It is also more than
can manifest itself. Its life is dependent on enabling conditions that are
only visible as impossibilities. It has an open horizon.

This is where Marion comes aboard. For him, too, the world is more
than what appears and can appear to us. But for him the decisive proof
of this is not what does *not* show itself, but the very thing that *does*
show itself. The ontological point of the gift is not that it appears only
to disappear. This is at best an indicator that here gifts are being considered within the horizon of exchange. But within their own horizon,
that of givenness, they have another point: they show that, for us, only
what gives itself can appear, in that it shows itself to us. However, that in
itself cannot appear as a distinctive phenomenon. The transphenomenal
openness of the world is not denied but is said to depend on something
more fundamental: that in what appears the world already proves to be
more than what appears, since every appearance is a self-showing. Yet

this is exactly what cannot show itself. The fact that there are phenomena shows that there is more than phenomenon: what there is gives itself. This is not a phenomenon, but phenomena only exist because of it.

Both analyses outlined above attempt to use the paradigm of gift to deal with the interference of the world with phenomenological consideration by working out—in different ways—the methodological and ontological implications for a philosophically tenable phenomenology. Derrida identifies the surplus of the world as its *ontological openness* by pointing to that which can be said but not shown, since in its self-showing it does not show itself but is only there inasmuch as it withdraws itself; Marion, however, does the very opposite, identifying it as its ontological givenness, which he describes as giving of oneself. It is not even what does *not* show itself that is more than what appears, but what does *show* itself: it *shows itself*. That which is *more* than the world of phenomena is not just the indirect and negative trace of that which withdraws itself; it is positively and paradoxically the structure of that which appears: *it gives itself*.

That is more than anything phenomena or phenomenologists can show. A hermeneutics of suspicion will always be able to destroy this and dismiss it as inadmissible metaphysics. Yet both scenarios, whether rooted in a phenomenology of being or of negation, are seeking to come to terms phenomenologically with the disruptive, resistant, interrupting surplus of the world. The world is more than what is or can be, because in every appearance there is something that is only there inasmuch as it withdraws itself (thus Derrida), or because every appearance depends on something that does not appear: the fact that what is *gives itself* (thus Marion).

6. From Exchanging to Giving: Gift as a Universal Phenomenon

At this point it is worth returning to the gift. Both approaches are united in holding that something is only a *gift* when it can be clearly distinguished from an *exchange*.[23] Since Marcel Mauss it has become

---

23. In connection with what follows, see Philip Stoellger, "Gabe und Tausch als Antinomie religiöser Kommunikation," in *Religion und symbolische Kommunikation*, ed. K. Tanner (Leipzig: EVA, 2004), 185–222.

accepted practice, from an anthropological, ethnological, and sociological perspective, to identify a certain class of gift as *gift exchange*.
Here, however, according to Derrida's analysis, the gift disappears
in the exchange. By the same token, however, this particular type
of gift can only be defined against the backdrop of a developed exchange economy in the first place. Whereas an exchange is normally
reciprocal, symmetrical, and equivalent, a gift is strictly distinguished
from an exchange by the very fact that it is not equivalent, not symmetrical, and not reciprocal. These negations are illustrative of the
fact that here gift is understood wholly against the background of
the exchange economy and the three basic obligations set out by
Mauss: the obligation to give, to accept, and to reciprocate, or pass
on.[24] But against this background gift can be formulated only in
negative terms and therefore cannot be formulated at all, as Derrida's analyses show. The exchange economy offers an unworkable
context if gift is to appear as gift.

There is a range of possible reactions to this. One can *universalize*
gift, in contradistinction to exchange, so that it becomes something
that exists structurally everywhere. This would then mean that it is
only because gifts exist that exchange can exist as well. One can differentiate between gift and exchange in such a way that the former
is understood differently from the latter: if gift is understood as gift,
it proves to be something other than exchange. Or one can focus on
the actual practices in the life-world where gifts are distinguished
from exchange processes: not every instance of giving is an element
of an exchange.

Marion pursues the first of these courses: he replaces the horizon
of understanding with the gift. Only within the horizon of givenness,
and not within the horizon of exchange, can gift be comprehended as
gift. Within the horizon of exchange it can only ever be defined negatively as that which cannot be exchanged. That is far from negligible,
but it is not sufficient. For gift is neither an instance of exchange nor
an alternative to exchange; it cannot be defined only negatively. Gift

24. A fourth obligation, namely, the human being's obligation to God or the
gods, is mentioned only marginally. See M. Mauss, *Die Gabe: Form und Funktion
des Austausches in archaischen Gesellschaften* (Frankfurt am Main: Suhrkamp,
⁴1999), 39–42.

is givenness; it is that without which nothing is that is, since only as givenness is it anything for someone.[25] What is is gift, and only that which is gift is anything at all.

The end result is a radical phenomenology that no longer seeks to comprehend the *essence* of gift while eliminating its *being*, but instead sees the essence of gift precisely in its being: *Gifts are phenomena because phenomena are gifts*. But what if that were wrong, and phenomena were not gifts? Here everything hinges on which proposition, "phenomena are gifts" or "gifts are phenomena," expresses the more fundamental insight. The first is a proposition concerning the phenomenality of phenomena and, as such, is a questionable universalization of a correct view of the character of gift. The second is a proposition concerning the gift character of gifts, one that makes a critical point: in actual practices in the life-world, a gift can only be something that is there *for me*, but not *from me* or *through my agency*; in other words, it is something *given to me*. There can be no gifts unless there are recipients, and there can only be recipients because gifts make them recipients.

A phenomenology of gift must therefore become a hermeneutical phenomenology of the life-world. For if *gift* appears as gift only in the horizon of givenness, then *givenness* is the being of something for someone (i.e., not necessarily the being of something *as something* for someone, but its mere *being for . . .*). Furthermore, if a *horizon* is nothing but the free play of possibilities in which something is there for someone, then this horizon is also that in which the something that is there for someone can be understood by him or her. This is the reason there is no gift unless something that is there for someone can be understood by the one for whom it is there as "It is given to me." Wherever there is a gift, it is to be understood in this way; the one for whom it is there must understand that it is there for him. Hence, not everything that exists is gift. What is merely possible is not gift, but what is merely real is not gift either, since what is merely there but is not there *for me* is not a gift *for me*, and what I cannot understand as given for me is not a gift for me.

25. See Marion, *Réduction et donation*; Marion, *Étant donné*.

7. From Intention to Interpretation: Gifts as Hermeneutical Phenomena

For me to be there in such a way that I can perceive something as being there for me, and can perceive myself, correspondingly, as the one for whom the something is there in the way it is, is a hallmark of *hermeneutical phenomena*. They are not only *really* there for me; they are there in such a way that I can perceive them as being there for me, and I can correspondingly perceive myself as the one for whom they are there in that way. Where exchange is concerned, anyone can participate if they know the value of the object of exchange and the rules of the exchange of values. By contrast, no one receives a gift without becoming a recipient and being able to perceive oneself as the recipient of a gift.

This is why gifts are hermeneutical phenomena—not because they have to be perceived *as gift* in order to be gifts, but because they would not be gifts if they could not be perceived in the life-world as being there *for me*, but neither *from me* nor *through my agency*. It is not understanding that makes the gift; rather, the gift makes itself comprehensible by eliciting an understanding of myself as recipient and of itself as that which is given to me.

This has methodological consequences. If gifts are hermeneutical phenomena, they must be considered not just phenomenologically but also hermeneutically. In contrast to phenomenology, hermeneutics considers its subjects using hermeneutical interpretation rather than phenomenological reduction. It does not reduce phenomena to an essential structure that fulfills an intention by exercising a methodological *epoche* (suspension of judgment) in respect of the characteristics of its being and reality. In fact, it does quite the opposite, taking their situatedness in reality as the starting point and considering them in their interconnectedness with the other, in their interwovenness with changing realities, and thus in the characteristics of their possibilities. So it understands phenomena to be always, to a certain extent, both understood and misunderstood; accordingly, it seeks to shed light on what they are from the point of view of how they have been understood from time immemorial and how, from now on, they could be understood against the backdrop of what is possible at any given time.

The methods of phenomenological reduction idealize phenomena by using abstractive oversimplification to separate and isolate them from the life processes within which they function. By contrast, the point of hermeneutical methods is to consider phenomena in their changing forms and modes of understanding, within the processes of life and against the backdrop of their unexploited possibilities. In this way, in contrast to isolating misunderstandings, they are understood on the basis of their concrete contexts and changing situations, within the horizons of possibility that the latter offer.

8. Concrete Communication: Gifts as Phenomena of the Social Life-World

To understand gift, therefore, one must change style. In other words, rather than beginning from an essential structure postulated using the guidelines for phenomenological reduction, with its aporetic borderline cases and exclusions, cancellations, and self-cancellations, one must begin from the giving and receiving of gifts in specific life-world contexts. Only from such contexts, and with them in mind, is it possible to show borderline cases for what they are; and only from such contexts is it possible to highlight the features that differentiate between gifts and other social interactions and those they have in common. In the life-world, gifts always function as part of the processes of interaction and communication in the realm of social practice. In disregarding this aspect, one loses sight of them completely. But from this life-world perspective it also becomes evident that not everything is gift.

Both phenomenologically and from the point of view of the logic of the language, therefore, the abstract question as to the nature of gift as gift is the wrong question to ask. It is no accident that gift disintegrates when subjected to phenomenological reduction, since the code word *gift* does not denote *something*, neither an object nor a thing, but rather a *particular social use* of objects or things: in other words, a particular way of communicating.

This is more than an indication of the multiple meanings of the word *gift*, which can mean both what is given and also the act of giving; it also goes beyond Levinas's emphasis on the primacy of the saying (*dire*) over the said (*dit*). It is a criticism of a phenomenology that dissects its phenomena outside of actual life contexts, disregarding their pragmatic impurities and idealizing them eidetically as pure phenomenon. If a gift is something that is only given in and as part of its communicative usage, then one cannot disregard this usage without losing everything. If gift is to be brought to mind or implied, not just in terms of a phenomenology of negation as the other of exchange, then one must take into consideration the social locations and practices in which giving takes place as the giving and receiving of gifts. If that is excluded, one is not left with "pure gift" but quite simply "no gift." The route to life-world actualization of the practice of giving is thus the reaction offered to the loss of gift in the horizon of the exchange economy.

These actualizations are many and varied. However, they are always *enactments of personal communication*, which are not means but ends in themselves, not associated with specific expectations of the other but overstepping the bounds of predefined rules. The how of such communications is more important than the what and the why, since they enact personal relationships in friendship, family, and community. One of these enactments is the making of presents.[26] "A giving that confounds the laws of exchange is an *anomalous giving* that oversteps the bounds of the established order. The making of a present as an emphatic form of giving is the *overflow of giving beyond what is given*."[27] Examples of such giving include acts of communication such as forgiveness, giving one's life for someone else, gifts of charity, and similar acts "of personal relationship, located

26. See Gisela Clausen, *Schenken und Unterstützen in Primärbeziehungen: Materialen zu einer Soziologie des Schenkens* (Frankfurt am Main: Peter Lang, 1991); Friedrich Rost, *Theorien des Schenkens: Zur kultur- und humanwissenschaftlichen Bearbeitung eines anthropologischen Phänomens* (Essen: Die blaue Eule, 1994); Helmuth Berking, *Schenken: Zur Anthropologie des Gebens* (Frankfurt am Main: Campus, 1996); Gerhard Schmied, *Schenken: Über eine Form sozialen Handelns* (Opladen: Leske und Budrich, 1996); Gert Dressel and Gudrun Hopf, eds., *Von Geschenken und anderen Gaben* (Frankfurt am Main: Peter Lang, 2000); Beate Wagner-Hasel, *Der Stoff der Gaben: Kultur und Politik des Schenkens und Tauschens im archaischen Griechenland* (Frankfurt am Main: Campus, 2000).

27. Bernhard Waldenfels, "Das Un-ding der Gabe," in Gondek and Waldenfels, *Einsätze des Denkens*, 385–409 (the quotation here appears on 399).

beyond the boundaries of the market and the state."[28] It is in such relationships that we *become* who we are for others, able at last to live our lives as such. In the life-world the giving of gifts, in contrast to exchange, is always about personal acts of communication that precede and underlie all economic and political orders because they first and foremost establish and preserve that without which those orders would not and could not function: the symbolic identity of the social actors (i.e., individuals, socialities). Through giving we become what we cannot make ourselves into: recipients.

9. From the What to the How: Receiving as Getting

Now one is never simply a recipient; one is always a recipient *of something*, and what is received is the *gift* that makes the recipient what he is. The one to whom attention is given becomes someone who is heeded. The one who is addressed is being treated as a person. The one to whom something is bequeathed becomes an heir. The one who is forgiven becomes free from guilt.

One becomes a recipient *completely passively* by *getting something*. This changes the recipient, who now confronts the unavoidable decision as to how to respond—by accepting or refusing it. But it changes him positively, since he gets opportunities and possibilities that he would not have had of his own accord.[29] Unlike punishments, gifts can be refused, but only because they have changed us merely as a result of our getting them: now one can and must take decisions that were not possible before. Accordingly, a gift is something someone gets (from someone or something) with the result that life opportunities accrue to him that he would not have had of himself and to which he must respond. Gifts are not gifts because they are given, but because they

---

28. Maurice Godelier, *Das Rätsel der Gabe: Geld, Geschenke, heilige Objekte* (Munich: Beck, 1999), 291.

29. One may get punishments too, but these are not gifts in the sense relevant here, because they do not feed one new and positive possibilities; instead, they actually restrict the available life options in certain respects. Admittedly, this does not mean that gifts cannot remove some possibilities or that punishments cannot open some up. These ambivalences are rather the presuppositions for the fact that gifts can be understood and assessed in more than one way, and punishments can be perceived not merely as restrictions but also as pointers to potential orders of events.

are *received*—or, in the Kierkegaardian sense, *appropriated*. In appropriation the subject does not act; instead, one becomes the subject in that the conduct of another toward one is such that one cannot fail to respond. But paradoxically, one does not become a subject by free self-determination but only through absolute heteronomy—as a result of someone who is a subject conducting themselves toward one as a subject and making it necessary for one to conduct oneself thus toward them—in other words, by acting as a subject or by failing to do so. The same applies to getting something: from the point of view that is relevant here, someone who gets something is not the one who does something but is in fact the very one who does *not* do something, the one who *becomes* what befalls him, who *obtains* what he gets, but who is also required to respond to it since not to do so becomes a reaction in itself.

What is decisive if something is to be defined as a gift, therefore, is not the what, the from whom, and the for whom, but the how, the mode of receiving in which and through which something becomes a gift.[30] There are no gifts as such: in the life-world a gift must involve a situation of receiving, in which people become recipients of something new, of life opportunities not previously available to them. Leaving aside this situation of receiving, there perhaps may be subjects who give each other something, or there may be an exchange of objects (e.g., things, feelings, values) that are handed over by one subject to another, but there is no longer a gift. The situation of receiving sets the boundary on gift. What is decisive is not who is giving, or what or to whom it is given, but the mode of being provided with something, the fact that the flow of life is interrupted by something that

30. This does not allude to one mode of getting among others, but to getting as a specific mode of acceptance or receiving. I therefore distinguish between different modes of acceptance, one of which is getting. With acceptance as a mode of reception or taking or appropriating, the emphasis lies (or appears to lie) on the fact that one *does something* in taking, receiving, or appropriating something. When one *gets something*, in contrast, the emphasis lies precisely on the fact that one *does nothing* in respect of what one receives, but rather that something befalls, accrues to, or is presented to one, that it falls to one's lot or comes one's way. The recipient who *gets* something is not considered to be the subject but rather the one on the receiving end of an event. He is in the dative: something happens *to him* that makes him into a particular kind of subject. He becomes the recipient of a gift, which makes him in a very specific way a "gifted one."

comes our way from somewhere entirely other, the fact that we are being determined by something that we are not giving to ourselves but that we come by. Neither the intention of the giver ("I am giving that *as* a gift"), nor the thing that is being given ("*This* is a gift"), nor the intention or activity of the recipient ("I *consider* this *to be a gift*") makes the gift a gift, but the fact *that one receives it*. That alone makes one a recipient and the thing received a gift.

The fact that one is or has been provided with something precedes any decision to accept or reject it. Indeed, this very fact makes it necessary for one to decide one way or the other, since in such a situation one cannot not respond to what one has been provided with. It is not the recipient who makes the gift a gift; rather, the gift makes the recipients recipients—only because of this can they perceive it as a gift and themselves as its recipients. To put it another way, a gift makes the addressee a passive recipient. He does not accept it, but is provided with it; it is not presented to the recipient as to a subject, but places him in the dative, making him into what he becomes thereby: a recipient. The abbreviated formula appropriate to the social grammar of gifts is therefore not "I accept," but "*To me* it is given."

In fact, the "art of giving" consists in giving in such a way that the gift does not have to be rejected because it was "not offered in the proper way."[31] But this is not decided by reference to the giver; instead, it is decided on the basis of the fact that the gift makes the addressee into a recipient. Anyone who does not just want to give but wants to give *gifts* must recognize that there will be circumstances where the giver does not come into the picture, but where the whole weight of significance lies instead in the gift. One can make oneself into a *giver*, but one *is made*—by the recipient—into a *giver of gifts*; and one *becomes* a recipient solely *through the gift*.

It follows that one can give without giving a gift. One can also take something given without receiving it, or without receiving it *as* a gift. Something does not principally become a *gift* by being understood *as a gift*; it becomes a gift when it is received as something one comes by (all for free or passively), that is, as a life opportunity that comes one's

31. See Friedrich Nietzsche, *Menschliches, Allzumenschliches: Ein Buch für freie Geister*, §297, KSA 2:240 (*Human, All-Too-Human*, 136).

way and to which one can and must respond. Anyone who is given a
gift becomes a recipient before she can perceive herself as a recipient
or what she receives as a gift, or before she accepts or rejects this gift.
Gifts, in turn, are creative hermeneutical phenomena—not because
only what can be perceived *as a* gift is gift, but because gifts enable
and provoke a particular understanding and self-understanding, that
is to say, the understanding of oneself *as a recipient* and of that which
is received *as a gift*.

10. Constitutive Passivity

If the life-world location of the gift is in its reception; if receiving
is what takes place at the point where one gets something, but before one can decide for or against it; and if it is precisely this that
makes one what one cannot make oneself, then from the point of
view of the recipient, gift is characterized in practice by passivity—not the passivity of passion in the sense of suffering, but the
passivity *of becoming*. One who receives gifts is *in the process of
becoming*, with the result that, regardless of all his physical and
psychological life activities, he is completely passively determined:
he becomes what the gift makes of him. A gift is first and foremost
a gifting, and only as such can it also turn out to be a given task.
Three comments must suffice:

1. Gifts *make* something of us that we could not make of ourselves. They break the circle of self-reference and the subject logic
of human knowledge and activity and thus reveal, quite apart from
any subject-object or subject-subject connections, something that
one could term the dative structure of human existence: *to us is
given*, and *we are those to whom (something) is given*. From the
perspective of gift, human beings are not subjects, observers, or
doers, but rather recipients, those affected, addressees. They become
what the gift makes them—donees (in the case of a donation), those
who are freed from debt (in the case of forgiveness), rescuees (in the
case of help), those who are reconciled (in the case of atonement),
pardoned ones (in the case of a penal system), beloved (in the case of
loving).

In each case, however, the opposite is not a gift. For those affected, gifts are something positive; they are giftings, not deprivations. They put possibilities our way that we would not have of ourselves and that broaden, rather than narrow, our horizon of possibilities.

2. What this means in practice varies according to our life situation. Something given is not necessarily the same gift for each person. In a situation of guilt, for example, a glance, a handshake, or a word can convey the gift of *forgiveness* if it offers us the possibility of a new beginning. This only holds good for the guilty one, who cannot give it to herself: she can only receive it from the one against whom she has incurred guilt. Someone who is not guilty is not forgiven for anything by this. Someone who is guilty, however, cannot forgive herself, nor can anyone forgive her except the one against whom she has incurred guilt. The latter does not have to forgive her, nor does anyone have an entitlement or a right to forgiveness. Forgiveness is always a free gift—both for the one who practices it and for the one who receives it. It cannot be demanded or forced, only requested and received. If it is granted, it does not remove the guilt: one is still guilty, even if one has been forgiven. The guilt is not undone, and the memory of it cannot be expunged. In fact, a situation where guilt is forgiven is fundamentally different from a situation where there is no guilt. But forgiveness would not be forgiveness if there still were guilt between the other and me. It is not the guilt of the doer but the *situation* between the doer and the victim that has changed, without the guilty one being able to achieve this of his own accord.

3. The fact that duties and obligations can arise from gifts is thereby included, not excluded. These are not a kind of "guilt" imposed by the gift. Nor are they an abstract "ought," from which one cannot extricate oneself. In fact, gifts are more likely to give rise to *duties* if one cannot accept them without practicing them, and to *obligations* if one cannot realize the possibilities that have been put our way unless one brings them to fruition for others and with others. A gift of friendship cannot be cultivated on one's own. It requires one to have fellowship with others. Quite unspectacularly, that applies to many gifts and giftings. Einstein put his finger on the nub of the matter

when he said, in the course of conversation, "I just find more joy in giving than in receiving, in every sense."[32] Gifts place one under an obligation because it often is only together with others that one can live out what they make one.

11. Passivity as Debt?

On the one hand, therefore, gifts change our life before we ever reach the moment of choice or decision. On the other hand, it is only this decision and its practical consequences for our lives that show us the nature of the gift we have been provided. Gifts make one a recipient before one can respond to them (either positively or negatively) or act out and communicate the response in one's life. But it is only as one does this that what one has been provided becomes evident and understandable.

Therefore it is not the absence but the very presence of certain life consequences that indicates the reality of a gift (e.g., thanks or joy, shame or guilt). So recipients owe everything to the gift that makes them its recipients with the result that they become what they are: someone who is gifted musically would not be who he is without the gift. But this gifting does not impose debt on him, nor does it place him in debt to another; one can be thankful for one's musical gift without being thankful *to someone*.

The language game of "indebtedness" and "thankfulness" leads us astray if it is misunderstood from a moral point of view. For the one who *owes everything* to the gift that makes him what he is (gifted, a donee, liberated, pardoned, etc.), it is thanks to the gift that he is all that he is. Thanks to the gift, he is what he owes to the gift. But that does not mean that he is in debt to another or that it is thanks to another that he is what he is. One is thankful *for something*, but not necessarily *to someone*. By the same token one does not thank the gift. Rather, one is thankful—if one is thankful at all—*for* the gift, to the one to whom one owes the gift.

---

32. According to an account by H. Born, "Einstein ganz privat," in *Weltwoche*, August 26, 1955, reprinted in *Jubiläum: 70 Jahre Weltwoche*, November 17, 2003, 68–69.

12. The Ambivalence of Passivity: Deficiency or Enabling?

The problem presented in linguistic terms here is not merely the human tendency to transfer behavior patterns achieved in personal situations to impersonal phenomena and situations. Rather, it is the fundamental polysemy of the passive structure of the gift situation. This passivity is established with the very getting of the gift and thus precedes, as an enabling condition, every concrete antithesis of activity and passivity, spontaneity and receptivity as regards what is provided. Precisely because of this, time and again it is interpreted and symbolized in the light of the structure that this condition presupposes and enables.

Thus Schleiermacher describes it as dependence, distinguishing it, as *absolute* dependence, from a dependence that, in contrast to freedom, is only relative. Leibniz, on the other hand, construes it as the *finite* in contrast to the infinite, interpreting it, in the light of the associated restrictions, as a *metaphysical evil*. Again, in life-world contexts it is described as the *unavailable*, distinguished from the available as that which is disordered, chaotic, uncontrollable, dangerous, and endangering. In every case the symbolization follows the strategy of interpreting the fundamental passivity in the light of one side of the polar contrast subordinated to it and enabled by it: as *dependence* instead of freedom, *finitude* instead of infinitude, *unavailability* instead of availability.

But this means that a one-sided negativity is imposed on the chain of interpretation. For what figures as dependence can be understood both negatively as un- or nonfreedom and also positively as gifting and the enabling of a relative freedom and dependence. Similarly, finitude can be understood not only negatively as the restricted other of infinitude and hence as a metaphysical evil, but also as the other of the infinite Creator and hence as creatureliness, which indeed is not evil, since it does not separate the creature from the Creator but relates it as a creature to him, allowing it to live and have its being from him. And finally the inaccessible, too, which irrupts uncontrollably into the human life, can be experienced either as an unanticipated happiness or as something impenetrably meaningless. One way or another, humans find themselves passively exposed to it. But that does not mean that it has to be interpreted or symbolized negatively.

13. Religious Interpretations of Passivity

This is particularly clear when it comes to religious symbolization, which understands the *familiar* against the background of the basically *unfamiliar*, so that *transcendence*, for instance, reminds us of the permanent reverse side of *immanence*. Religions use symbols to present "what is not shown when something shows itself," while every self-showing is undeniably accompanied and determined by something as a background, even if it "is only there inasmuch as it withdraws itself."[33]

This has consequences for religious symbolization. Since that which is there with everything does not appear alongside the other as something remarkable, special events are needed to make us aware of the presence of that which does not show itself. These events can be nonrecurring and remembered (revelation), they can be recurring phenomena (myth and ritual), or they can be tied to specific times and places (sacral phenomena). All religions recognize events when the presence of what does not show itself is revealed more clearly than usual, and they hold these in remembrance in rituals and doctrine as their fundamental insight, revelation, or original foundation.

Because the background that accompanies everything that shows itself does not appear as such, but only as part of or along with the other, it cannot be considered directly, in the same way as that which shows itself; it can be considered only indirectly, by being expressed as what is different from that which shows itself. In a religious context, therefore, it is indirect modes of thematization that dominate, since the nondeterminable can be considered only by reference to the determinate and determinable.

For the same reason there ultimately is no religion that is not attended by challenge, skepticism, and doubt on the part of those who are not (not yet, no longer, or not at the moment) able to perceive what this religion considers to be the nonperceivable reverse side of the perceivable. Conversely, religions are reliant on the process of

33. Bernhard Waldenfels, "Phänomenologie der Erfahrung und das Dilemma einer Religionsphänomenologie," in *Religion als Phänomen: Sozialwissenschaftliche, theologische und philosophische Erkundungen in der Lebenswelt*, ed. Wolf-Eckart Failing et al. (Berlin: Töpelmann, 2001), 63–84 (the quotations here appear on 75 and 84).

actualizing this difference symbolically over and over again—indeed, of thematizing and communicating it incessantly—since what "is only there inasmuch as it withdraws itself" becomes noticeable only to the extent that it is thematized. That of which religions speak is "not there," but they do not speak of it unless there exists, at the very least, an awareness of this fact.

Religions adopt different ways of attempting to tie the realms of the indefinable, the chaotic, the meaningless, the unavailable, and the uncontrollable back into the realms of rationally established rules and meaningfully understandable structures so that they are thematized as the Other and as the reverse side, incomprehensible in itself, of the meaningful, the available, and controllable. From a cultural point of view and from the perspective of the philosophy of religion, religions are continuous social experiments in living life together in a controllable way with the uncontrollable.

That does not necessarily mean that we want to make the inaccessible accessible. We are on the wrong religious track if we try to remove the inaccessibility of the inaccessible through magical, cultic, or intellectual practices, discovering necessities where none exist and seeking meaning where there is only meaninglessness. Yet religions per se are not irrational superstitions; rather, they are thoroughly rational attempts to lead a life of human dignity in the very face of what is absolutely meaningless and of the inescapability of the inaccessible (e.g., in giving thanks for what is good as a gift of God and in asking God for help, comfort, and deliverance when confronted by what is evil).

This is quite different from interpreting *everything* from the perspective of givenness as a gift. Here it is a matter of failing to understand oneself if one does not understand oneself from the perspective of the specific gift one has been given, so that one ignores what the gift enables one to do. A musical gift that one does not use is an unredeemed promise, and a gift for friendship that one does not live out is a lost opportunity.

That applies similarly to the shared life of human beings. Typically, it is precisely these religious gift situations that are community situations in which one remembers how one came to be and becomes what one jointly is (commemorative situations), in which one is giving thanks for something (thanksgiving situations) or is asking for something (petition

situations). Thus *commemorative situations* are not merely the individual and collective recollection of what has been, but the shared
realization of the origin of our own identities from what has come our
way within the order of what is available and can be experienced, but as
something inaccessible and new that surpasses experience and cannot
be limited to any such order. Similarly, *thanksgiving situations* are an
expression of having been surprised and overwhelmed by something
positive. One is speechless with happiness. One stammers because one
does not know how to thank and requires aids to articulation so as
to be able to give thanks. And *petition situations* express the fact that
one cannot help oneself, no longer has any idea what to do, and needs
outside help: one is helpless with anxiety, often incapable of making a
request on one's own behalf, and reliant on the intercession of others.

Remembrance, petition, and thanksgiving are familiar phenomena
of life and are also central to religion. But they are not simply parallel situations. Only one who remembers can request and be thankful, and only one who knows how to be thankful can also make a
request. One must remember that there can be ways out of aporetic
situations, even if one cannot see them or carry them out oneself.
Sometimes one must know exactly whom to thank for something in
order to turn to the right person with a specific request. If we do not
make this distinction, requesting and thanking lose their meaning.

Even from a religious viewpoint, not *everything* can be lumped
together as a reason for thankfulness.[34] Life is too merciless for that,
and evil is ever-present. But gifts are always a reason for thankfulness,
which is why one cannot declare everything that exists to be a gift.
Evil challenges us to protest and to resist; gifts challenge us to give
thanks. This distinction is important and should be borne in mind
where thanksgiving is concerned as well.

One who thanks is reacting to a positive experience. This experience can be the remedy for a lack, but it also can be the surprise
of abundance. In both cases thanks is given for something positive,
but not every positive is an answer to a request for the removal of a
lack, nor can it be construed as such. If religions were to dismiss the

---

34. This is why the thesis "everything is gift" is much too sweeping to be theologically apposite. See Martin Bieler, *Freiheit als Gabe: Ein schöpfungstheologischer
Entwurf* (Freiburg im Breisgau: Herder, 1991), 501–4.

ambivalence of passivity in such a one-sided way, they would lose touch with the reality of life.

14. Gift as an Indicator of Lack? On the Questionableness of an Anthropology of Deficiency

Religious practice—in the Jewish and Christian tradition, at any rate— shows evidence to the contrary. With its topological differentiation between situations of commemoration, thanksgiving, and petition, it takes account of the ambivalence of the passivity of receiving that makes human beings what they are. It thus contradicts a view that understands human beings in their fundamental dependence, finitude, and passivity, not merely biologically, but anthropologically, as *deficient beings*, interpreting their absolute dependence as absolute neediness, their finitude as a metaphysical evil, and their experience of the in- accessible as the threat of fundamental meaninglessness. Where this takes place, the understanding of gift is blocked and obstructed, not by the *exchange economy* but by the *anthropology of deficiency*. This may take the form of the modern biological-anthropological view that human beings are characterized, in comparison with other living be- ings, by basic deficiencies. Or it may take the form of the traditional biblical-theological view that human beings are the divine answer to a basic deficiency in creation and that woman, similarly, is the answer to a basic deficiency in the life of the man (or, put more precisely, to a basic deficiency in human life when it is lived without being determined by gender difference). For only in this way did reproduction, tradition, history, and culture become possible, turning what was merely a po- tential human world into a real one—for better or for worse.

Yet to construct all of that from a deficiency and a lack is errone- ous even so, if one in no way disputes the phenomena put forward as evidence. Along with the genesis of humans in the course of biological evolution, there came into being in the world something that certainly was not there before. But was the former state of the world therefore "lacking," "deficient," or "in need of human beings"? Did the world need us? Did it lack something when we did not yet exist? Anyone who takes this view is measuring the former state of the world against its present state, making us the yardstick by which the goodness of the world is defined. Even so, this is wrong if one has good reason to be convinced that it is better that we exist than that we do not. The world could exist without us, but we could not exist without the world. That is no lack either for it or for us: neither for the world, since even without us it would exist—albeit not as this world, but as a different one—nor for us, since without the world we would not be anything at all that could either lack or not lack something.

The idea that our existence presupposes something without which it would not exist and has a prehistory out of which it originates does not reveal a deficiency that we should remedy; nor does it sketch a deficiency into our existence as something that renders us lacking. All humans become human through what they receive, through what comes their way, so that the things that are sent their way, the processes that are constantly unrolling in their lives, are interrupted and opened up to something new. They evolved from primates into humans as a result of their biological growth process being interrupted by others. And they have evolved from humans to fellow humans because over and over again their social growth process has been opened up by others to others, and to what is other. Humans are humans not just *with* others but *through* others—namely, through what is meted out to them by way of life opportunities and life-changing gifts. It would be quite in vain to want to live as a human without others: even someone who retreats to a desert island like Robinson Crusoe, or to a pillar like the Stylites, draws on the otherness of others. Even he remains, in memory and imagination, reliant on the otherness of others as the bringing into play other life opportunities.

The problem is to be found elsewhere, in the semantics of symbolization. If fundamental reliance on others is defined as absolute dependence, then the freedom to self-determination forms the counterfoil against which this reliance is described, and the idea of dependence is developed philosophically and theologically. But if human reliance on the allocation of gifts is understood from the perspective of the freedom to individual self-formation, then it almost inevitably becomes a dependence with negative undertones and overtones, so that it is perceived precisely *not* as a fundamental openness to others (or what is other) and the enabling of something new.

The philosophical and theological consequences are disastrous. Philosophically the human being is then understood as a deficient being who is seeking, by means of his sociality, his reason, and his cultural activities, to compensate in a rough-and-ready way for the deficiencies of his biological basic endowment. And theologically one must similarly construct corrective theologies in order to show why and to what extent religious faith is possible, necessary, desirable, ponderable, rational or at any rate not wholly irrational. It is insisted that "the human experience of suffering . . . [is] . . . universal—and the need for comfort, hope, redemption no less so,"[35] and faith and religion are presented as satisfying these needs and offering the sought-for answers to these existential questions. Religion and faith, it is said, are not relics of early human cultural history but are what human life clamors for in the face of its biological deficiencies. It is to them that we owe the evolutionary advantage that allows us to survive in a hostile and dangerous environment. But this anthropological match reduces the gift of faith to the overcoming of an evolutionary threat, the compensation for an anthropological deficiency, or the satisfaction of an existential need.

Alternatively, one can attempt, as Ebeling does, to prove that faith is necessary by pointing out the need that faith meets. Ebeling is speaking particularly of Christian faith. But what kind of faith has a "basis" that depends on a need being demonstrated to humans—a need that they do not recognize and from which faith will free them without their even being aware of it? This is a time-honored thought pattern that makes sense to many people, but from a theological point of view it has just one serious flaw: it is not talking about what the New Testament presents as faith.

15. More Than Necessary and All for Nothing: Toward a Theology of Gift

What is being discussed and considered under this heading is not the remedy of a deficiency but a *phenomenon of excess*. It is not, or at any

35. H. Maier, "Die Überwindung der Welt: Auf dem Christentum liegt kein Fluch; Eine Antwort auf Herbert Schnädelbachs Polemik," *Die Zeit* 27 (2000), http://www.zeit.de/2000/27/200027.replik_.xml.

rate not primarily, about the answer to questions that human life poses
and leaves open; rather, it is about the calling to mind of astonishing
and overwhelming experiences of abundance, of the unanticipated,
the new, the unimaginable, that which never has been dreamed of, that
remodel one's life in faith and redefine it from the ground up. Faith,
as an abbreviated formula for being determined by the good that God
accomplishes in the human life, is not so much the overcoming of a
deficiency or the removal of a lack as it is a being overwhelmed by a
surprising irruption and unanticipated occurrence of undreamed-of
life opportunities, a being caught up into the abundance of grace.

To be sure, faith also provides answers to human needs, though this
is not its only or primary function. But it does so without allowing the
needs to define what the answers could and should be. On the contrary, faith stands for quite the opposite, a being overwhelmed by the
occurrence of unanticipated chances and possibilities, unpredictable
bright prospects, and unhoped-for life opportunities. Anthropological deficiency does not define what faith is. Rather, this deficiency
responds to a gift that one had neither needed nor expected, since it
is more than all that one could have dreamed of, hoped for, wished
for, regretted the absence of, or craved. Faith is always *more than
was anthropologically necessary*: it does not merely fulfill a lack; it
manifests abundance.

It is mistaken to seek to demonstrate that this abundance is necessary by portraying it as the answer to what humans have always sought
for, whether they knew it or not. This is not so, and it is misleading
to pass off as anthropologically necessary something that humans do
not actually need in order to live good, human, and contented lives.
From a basic theological perspective one instead must trace God's
actual incursion back into the human life, as an event that hands us
more than we would ever have expected, hoped for, or needed. God's
grace is *all for nothing*, not because one cannot either earn it or pay
for it (true as this is), but because one did not need it and had no idea
what one could be missing without it.

After all, not everything one *does not have* is a deficiency; not
everything one *becomes* realizes a predisposition that one always had;
not everything that one *is provided with* satisfies a need, so that it can
be said to be that need's fulfillment; nor can one be said previously

to have lacked everything that is *given* to one. Who would want to try to prove that human beings have a predisposition or a need to experience the music of Mozart, or at least to experience music, or to live and experience anything at all, and so on, wherever this more and more tenuous mode of foundational thinking may lead us. But who, on the other hand, would want to dispute that the music of Mozart has introduced into human life something that has made it better, more beautiful, more worthwhile, more hopeful, more relaxed, exciting, and human?

We distort our view of the phenomenon of gift in our life-world practice, and even more so in the religious aspects of our life, if we fail to be aware of the one-sidedness of this viewpoint, which considers the relationship between recipient and received in one way only, or uses images that are sometimes but not always appropriate. Wittgenstein's philosophy has repeatedly highlighted the danger of the "bewitchment of our understanding" by means of oversimplifying images. In his theology of the prevenient grace of God, Barth has expounded the experience of the presence of divine grace in the human life in theological terms as being focused on abundance and not lack. And phenomenologically, Levinas is another who has observed and heeded the necessity of considering the basic structure of human life not solely from the perspective of deficiency.

As he states in *Totalité et infini*, the "*désir* d'Autrui"—the desire and need for the absolute Other—is not a lack or need (*besoin*) of something missing, not "like a hunger to be satisfied or a thirst to be quenched," but a "*désir sans satisfaction*," a desire that is strengthened with each fulfillment, that cannot be exhausted or allayed because it does not originate from the desirer but rather from the desired.[36] We need the Other not just because without it we are missing something or someone, but because without it *we ourselves* would be missing. "On s'amuse mieux à deux"[37] not just because one enjoys oneself *more* as part of a couple than on one's own, but because without

36. E. Levinas, *Totalité et infini: Essai sur l'extériorité* (Paris: Livre de Poche, 1971), 21–24.302.

37. Richard A. Cohen, ed., *Face to Face with Levinas* (New York: SUNY Press, 1986), 22. Cf. Ingolf U. Dalferth, "Mehr als Zwei: Von der Logik der Relation zur Hermeneutik des Dritten," *Archivio di Filosofia* 74 (2006): 123–37.

the Other one would not be on one's own: one would *not be at all*, so that neither enjoyment nor the absence of enjoyment would be a possibility.

Viewed in this way, the need of the Other is not a deficiency but a good, not a lack but a mark of distinction. That we are and what we are and can be we owe crucially not to ourselves but to others and, according to Levinas, to *the* Other, the Highest One. In practice it is with the finite other, but in, with, and as part of this always also with the *infinite Other*, that we must deal; and because he unreservedly turns his face toward us, we cannot guiltlessly turn away from the face of this specific Other. Behind every finite other stand other finite others, who—like us—are others of the infinite Other. Only thus are we who we are. And it is only when we live like this that we live humanly.

We can put this the other way around: one who *is not* is not *missing* something; rather, he *is* not. And one who *is* is not in need of the other because she is missing something, but because she is *precisely who and what she is*: one who needs the other because it is only through and as a result of the other that she is. It is not need that defines the other; rather, the other is the one to whom the one in need owes herself and her need. This is why, in the course of a lifetime, this need cannot be removed or canceled by any fulfillment. On the contrary, every fulfillment confirms, renews, and reinforces it.

The gift of grace, too, through which and as the result of which the Christian faith understands itself, is not the end of the search but the beginning of hope. We receive it, but not just as something inaccessible and unexpected. Indeed, it is precisely by giving new form to life as faith, love, and hope, that the gift of grace makes clear what we could have known but have ignored (in the form of faith); what we should have done; what ought now to be done, but also what in fact need no longer be done since it has been done by God (in the form of love); and that, when confronted by all this, we have more to hope for than we ever could have dared to hope (in the form of hope). So the gift of grace does not remove a deficiency that has long oppressed the human life; rather, it results in human life, with all its faults and merits, being redefined, realigned, and reorientated through faith, love, and hope.

Here the crucial point is that the gift determines the life and not the other way around. This becomes evident in that it does not just appear *in one's life* as something new, but makes *the whole of one's life* new. Through it, everything that was and is and will be becomes the place of God's presence and therefore is transparent to what it truly is *coram Deo*. Accordingly, no phenomenon of life can be understood theologically unless it is critically understood afresh in the light of the differentiation between the new, which is willed by God, and the old, which is in opposition to God. Hence the gift not only establishes a fundamental temporal distinction between *then* and *now*: it requires us to integrate this with the eschatological distinction between *old* and *new*. In the light of these distinctions, every point of the human life story can be critically viewed according to which aspects or parts of it deserve to be designated as old or new and therefore ought to be either rejected and dismantled or retained and developed.

Theology thus becomes a redefinition of human life that is not self-evident. It starts from a position of faith, which itself is to be understood as a gift of grace. It is not something that one has always sought and at last has now found. Quite the opposite: one was wholly unaware that one should have been seeking it until it came one's way. This, at any rate, is how it is presented by Jesus's "logic of the *more than necessary*" or the similar Pauline logic of grace as alone and unconditional.[38]

One need think only of the miracles of the feeding of the multitudes in the Gospels: not only was hunger satisfied, but also there was such lavish provision that no one knew what to do with this abundance of good gifts.

Turning to the calling of the disciples: those whom Jesus called to discipleship were not people who were exhausted by the hardship of their daily lives and frustrated by their occupations, even though this frequently is read into the texts: it is no accident that their call

38. For what follows I am indebted to H. Weder, "Komparative und ein parataktisches καί: Eine neutestamentlich orientierte Skizze zur transzendierten Notwendigkeit," in *Denkwürdiges Geheimnis: Beiträge zur Gotteslehre; Festschrift für Eberhard Jüngel zum 70. Geburtstag*, ed. Ingolf U. Dalferth, Johannes Fischer, and Hans-Peter Grosshans (Tübingen: Mohr Siebeck, 2004), 557–81.

is presented as a new creation rather than as a better offer of jobs as fishers of people—for example in Caravaggio's *The Calling of Matthew the Tax Collector* in the Capella Contarelli in San Luigi dei Francesi, with its subtle but apposite reference to Michelangelo's *Creation of Adam* in the Sistine Chapel.

Turning to other miracle stories, Jesus's "miracles" are not responses to requests or an expression of the uncontrolled human wishful thinking of the early Christian communities, but quite the reverse: the evangelists tell of the invasion of grace into the lives of human beings by describing the wholly extraordinary nature of this surprise as an overwhelming inundation of the miraculous.

Again, one thinks of the prologue to John's Gospel and the incarnation of the Logos: it was not as if the world had been waiting for this moment for a long time. On the contrary, it did not even notice what had happened, since—as far as it was concerned—it was not lacking anything and since it was far too preoccupied with itself to notice that it might have been deficient in any way that ought to be remedied and satisfied.

Or one thinks of the Pauline doctrine of sin, which does not in fact argue that all human beings are sinners, and redemption through Jesus Christ is therefore relevant and important for all. It argues precisely the opposite: In and through Jesus Christ something has happened simply because God willed it and not because there was any necessity for it, something that is so incredible and overwhelming that no one and nothing in the world remains unaffected by it.

Or one thinks of the incorporation of this experience in the third article of the Apostles' Creed, which does not speak of *sin*, but only of the *forgiveness* of sins and *eternal life*.

Or one thinks of the dogmatic development of the idea of creation, which understands everything created as the expression of God's love that freely ordains itself to be the enabling and realization of the freedom of others.

Or one thinks of the dogmatic formulation of the idea of redemption, which does not view it as the removal of a lack, but rather as the unimaginable "more" of each of our potential life goals, so that their hoped-for fulfillment cannot be envisaged and heaven is therefore unimaginable.

Wherever one looks in the New Testament and in its theological continuation and adoption, one finds this logic of abundance, of the more than necessary, of the all for nothing, of something that comes our way and is discovered, not of possibilities sought after and longed for.[39] This is what one must explicate if one wants to explain the ground of faith and make it comprehensible. This is why one must begin *here* and not with any kind of conditions, structures, or dispositions of those whom this abundance of grace takes by surprise, creates anew, and sets in a realm of undreamed-of possibilities. Grace does not just uncover what is buried; it creates something genuinely new. It brings forth needs that we not only did not have before, but of whose possibility we were not even aware. It awakens a longing for God that leaves us restless until we find our rest in God. Grace is not the answer to the restlessness of the human heart; rather, *cor nostrum inquietum donec requiescat in te* (the heart is restless until it rests in you), as Augustine put it. It makes us sensitive to God and is not simply the answer to our search. Only afterward do we know what has happened, and even then we know only that it is *maius quam cogitari possit* (greater than could ever have been thought), as Anselm said. Beforehand we neither dreamed of it nor desired it. As Kierkegaard's Climacus realized, one can never "quantify" oneself in advance into what comes afterward. Only from the perspective of the afterward does one realize not only what was already present in the beforehand in hints that can now be picked up on, but also what can be forgotten of the beforehand, since the afterward has already completed and surmounted it. Only from the perspective of the afterward, therefore, does one become *difference-sensitive* with regard to the beforehand—so that one learns to differentiate where once one saw no reason to differentiate since one neither noticed nor missed anything. Only a posteriori does the ground of faith become clear, and only *post festum* (after the fact) does it dawn on one—if at all.

It follows that in all models the New Testament logic of the more than necessary and the all for nothing has the same point. Whether the emphasis is on the chronological *ante* or the logical *pre*, on the

39. "I do not seek; I find," said Picasso. "I have been found, though I did not even know that someone was seeking me," says faith more precisely, going beyond Picasso, who is not able to imply an ongoing "I" in the exchange of the old for the new.

gratis of a theology of grace or the *maius* of an escalatory logic, the superfluous of an anthropology of deficiency, the *sola fide* of a theology of justification, or the self-giving of a theory of gift that is not absorbed into a giving and that exceeds every gift—always it is about the inexhaustible surplus of gift beyond everything received. The one who is given *this* gift obtains more than he ever can receive. Its only boundaries are the limitations of the one on the receiving end. But its precise point is also the breaking down of these boundaries so as to ensure that the gift is not defined by its *modus recipiendi*, but that the gift creates its own mode of reception and that its recipients are redefined by the gift. They are what they *become* through the gift; each one becomes what the gift given specifically to them makes of them.

It would be quite in vain to want to decide or discover what this is in advance with regard to others or even to everyone else. What each one becomes happens freely, *extra ordinem* (outside the normal course of events), and cannot be subsumed under any reliable rule. To state the matter both with and against Nietzsche: in contrast to the mania for rules and frenzy of reasoning of the metaphysical "albinos of the intellect" with their "monotono theism,"[40] the gift of faith comes as pure anarchy, not because God gives what he does not have, but because we get what we do not need. This generates hope—not just in the victory of the better over the good, but even more in the victory of the good over the better.

---

40. Friedrich Nietzsche, *Der Antichrist*, §§17 and 19, KSA 6:184–85 (*Anti-Christ*, 14–16).

5

Self-Offering

From the Act of Violence to the Passion of Love

1. The Threefold Paradox of Sacrifice

"Is a religion imaginable without sacrifice and without prayer?" asks Derrida in *Foi et savoir*.[1] He answers this in his usual paradoxical manner. Since religion demands both an "absolute respect of life" and an unrestricted willingness to sacrifice or a "universal sacrificial vocation,"[2] it "*both requires and excludes sacrifice*."[3] In order to retain the inviolability of life, life must be violated. And in order not to need sacrifice any longer, one must perform sacrifice. It is only in "the sacrifice of sacrifice"[4] that religion comes into its own. The conditions of its possibility are also the conditions of its impossibility.

Derrida's remarks on (self-)sacrifice in *Foi et savoir* (translated into English as "Faith and Knowledge") must be understood in the

1. Jacques Derrida, *Foi et savoir* (Paris: Seuil, 2001); translated into English as "Faith and Knowledge: The Two Sources of 'Religion' at the Limits of Reason Alone," in Jacques Derrida, *Acts of Religion*, ed. Gil Anidjar (New York: Routledge, 2002), 40–101, here 88.
2. Derrida, "Faith and Knowledge," 86.
3. Ibid., 88 (emphasis in original).
4. Ibid.

context of his other writings on giving, gift, and sacrifice, especially *Donner le temps, 1. La fausse monnaie* (Paris: Galilée, 1991), and *Donner la mort* (Paris: Galilée, 1992). The essence of his reflections can be summarized as follows: in view of what is termed "the return of the gods" and the deep ambiguity of religions, which can bring out both the worst and the best in humankind, Derrida asks whether there is a future for religion, and if so, in what form. In order to answer this question he asks, from a hermeneutical point of view, what the question is to which religion is the answer. His answer refers to two sources of religion: faith and knowledge, both of which are ambiguous. Thus faith, or lived religion, appears to be both a reaction to violence and based on violence. There is no religion without sacrifice, but sacrifice is deeply paradoxical. Since in sacrificing, religions use violence to overcome violence, they can overcome violence only by using violence against themselves (i.e., by sacrificing themselves). This amounts to saying that the future of religion lies in religion's making itself superfluous, which can be achieved only by overcoming the violence to which religions react by sacrificing religion itself.

This paradox of sacrifice manifests itself in three tangible respects. On the one hand, according to Derrida, sacrifice is "the price to pay for not injuring or wronging the absolute other."[5] On the other hand, the use of violence "in the name of non-violence" is preposterous.[6] This is the first paradox of sacrifice: one must use *violence* in the name of nonviolence in order to avoid doing violence to the nonviolent other.

5. Ibid. Where Derrida is concerned, these critical premises remain wholly un-substantiated.
6. Ibid. This is an old criticism. See Heraclitus DK 22 B 5 (*Aristocritus Theosophia* 681): "They vainly purify themselves by defiling themselves with blood, just as if one who had stepped into the mud were to wash his feet in mud." Montaigne restates the argument in creation-theological terms by pointing out that a corrupted creation cannot be corrected by sacrifices that are themselves a corruption of God's creation (*Essais* 2, §12, ed. Albert Thibaudet and Maurice Rat [Paris: Gallimard, 1962], 502). And Nietzsche uses it to bring a charge of self-contradiction against the gospel: "God gave his son to forgive sins, as a *sacrifice*. This brought the evangel to an end in one fell swoop. The *guilt* sacrifice, and in fact in its most revolting, barbaric form, the sacrifice of the *innocent* . . . for the sins of the guilty! What gruesome paganism!" (Friedrich Nietzsche, *Der Antichrist: Versuch einer Kritik des Christentums*, §41, KSA 6:214–15. English translation: *The Anti-Christ, Ecce Homo, Twilight of the Idols, and Other Writings*, ed. Aaron Ridley and Judith Norman, trans. Judith Norman [2005; repr., Cambridge: Cambridge University Press, 2006], 37).

But there is more to it than that. Even if the violence of sacrifice is unavoidable in order not to violate the absolute other, it is unacceptable to subject other life to this kind of violence. "Absolute respect" therefore "enjoins first and foremost sacrifice of self," namely, giving up "one's most precious interest": one's own life. Only those who sacrifice themselves are truly sacrificing. "Self-sacrifice thus sacrifices the most proper in the service of the most proper." This is the second paradox of sacrifice: one must use violence *against oneself* in order not to subject others to violence.

But there is a third point. Whoever sacrifices himself has sacrificed once and for all. His sacrifice becomes—for him!—"the sacrifice of sacrifice." This is the only "pure" sacrifice (if there is such a thing as a pure sacrifice at all)—and is at the same time the exposure of its fundamental ambiguity: to demand what is strictly excluded is to demand self-annihilation in order to preserve the inviolability of the other. Whoever does not sacrifice himself does violence to the other, and whoever sacrifices himself avoids doing violence to others by doing violence to himself. This is the third paradox of sacrifice: by sacrificing oneself, *the sacrifice is abolished*. Others need not fear from me any further violence, the avoidance of which would give occasion for sacrifice. Self-sacrifice ends the occasion and necessity for sacrifice: it is the end of sacrifice.

Derrida hence grounds sacrifice within self-sacrifice and proves this to be paradoxical. His (implicit) argument unfolds in three steps: (1) from the supposed necessity of sacrifice as a means of avoiding violence against the other, to (2) the unavoidability of self-sacrifice and, at the same time, the impossibility of avoiding violence against oneself, to (3) the *Aufhebung* or abolition and sublation of sacrifice in self-sacrifice, which does away with the need for sacrifice by bringing about the needlessness of sacrifice, insofar as violence against oneself excludes violence against others.

The basis of this entire argument rests on situating the theme of sacrifice in the paradigm of violence: it is always a question of avoiding violence against the Other through violence either against others (sacrifice) or against oneself (self-sacrifice). The possibility that sacrifice could also be something other than acts of violence is never considered. This constitutes the fundamental weakness of the analysis: it reduces sacrifice to an act of violent killing, which is the least important feature of the symbolic universe of the sacrifice and does not stand at its center. The majority of religious sacrifices are not blood sacrifices but food offerings (grain, butter, fruit, flowers), drink offerings, burnt offerings, offerings of money, weapons, household goods, jewelry, statues, and such. This is true of ancient Judaism as well. The Torah is familiar not only with blood sacrifices such as the *'olah* (Heb: whole burnt offering, holocaust), the *zevakh shelamim* (peace offering), the *khatta't* (sin offering, purification offering), and the *'asham* (guilt offering), but also the *minkhah* (meal offering), the presentation of a cake of unleavened bread made from flour, salt, oil, and frankincense. But even in the case of blood sacrifices, the killing of the sacrificial animal is not the central act. Instead, this is the festive meal (*zevakh shelamim*) partaken of by those bringing the sacrifice or—in the case of sin offerings (*khatta't*) and guilt offerings (*'asham*)—the transfer of the transgression from the human being to the animal (a goat) and the sprinkling of its blood on the altar and on the curtain that separates the holy place, the inner sanctuary of the temple, from the most holy place, the place where the ark of the covenant was kept. For example, the symbolic action of the Jewish sin or guilt sacrifice is carried out as a *consecration* (i.e., the identification of the one offering the sacrifice with the sacrificial animal, which then becomes a symbol for the one offering the sacrifice) and as an *incorporation into the holy* (which "through the offering of the blood of the sacrificial animal" effects "the symbolic giving of the life of the sacrificer"[7]), while the killing of the sacrificial animal plays only a subordinate role in the procurement of blood for effecting the incorporation.[8] The religious elements that matter here are not the act of killing but the transfer of identity in the consecration and the self-surrender to the holy in the incorporation.

But even within Derrida's myopic view, one of the key points retains a significant ambivalence. Does self-sacrifice sacrifice "the most proper

---

7. H. Gese, "Die Sühne," in *Zur biblischen Theologie: Alttestamentliche Vorträge* (Munich: Kaiser, 1977), 85–106 (the quotation here appears on 98).

8. For a more detailed treatment of this subject, see Ingolf U. Dalferth, "Atoning Sacrifice: The Salvific Significance of the Death of Jesus," in *Crucified and Resurrected* (Grand Rapids: Baker Academic, 2015), 235–313.

in the service of the most proper" (that is, in the service of one's own self) or in the service of the other? Or does this difference play no role because both converge in self-sacrifice toward the avoidance of violence against others? Since Derrida leaves this in the dark, his argument exposes a weak spot at its most important juncture: it is blind to the difference between *egotistical* and *altruistic* self-sacrifice, between self-sacrifice in the service of one's own well-being and self-sacrifice in the service of the well-being of others.

Both may be described as the end of sacrifice, but only the latter, not the former, can be understood as an act of love. But such an understanding "explodes" (in Blumenberg's sense[9]) the reductive paradigm of violence and opens up a new and different perspective. If the altruistic loss of one's own life for the sake of the other is an avoidable act of violence against oneself—that is, an act of violence that one commits against oneself without having necessarily had to commit it—then it is a self-sacrifice, but it is not an act of love. If, on the other hand, it is an act of love, then one's own avoidable death—that is, the death that one could have avoided—is no act of violence against oneself and, as such, no self-sacrifice but the result of a passion of unselfish love that will allow nothing, not even one's own impending death, to stop one from living one's life on the basis of one's love for others for the sake of others, rather than for one's own sake. It is not the distinction between sacrifice and self-sacrifice, but the distinction between egotistic and altruistic self-sacrifice that opens one's eyes to understand the avoidable loss of one's own life for the sake of the other, not under the paradigm of violence but under the paradigm of love. However, to understand it as an act of love is not to understand it as an act of violence, and hence not even as altruistic self-sacrifice, but rather in a different category altogether. For love exists only where love is lived and practiced. But the practice of love overcomes both sacrifice and self-sacrifice by reacting to violence,

9. See H. Blumenberg, *Paradigmen zu einer Metaphorologie* (Frankfurt am Main: Suhrkamp, 1998), 179–80, describes the phenomenon using *Sprengmetaphorik* (explosive metaphorics): "What we would call 'explosive metaphorics' . . . draws concretization into a *process*, in which it is at first able to follow along (e.g., conceiving a circle's radius doubled and ever further increased) but finally reaches a point (e.g., conceiving the greatest possible, that is, infinite, radius of a circle) where it has to give up—and this is understood as 'giving itself up' as well."

not with violence but with nonviolent love even at the cost of losing one's life. To show this, I first will argue for the need to distinguish between egotistic and altruistic self-sacrifice, since the avoidable (that is to say, unnecessary) loss of one's own life for the sake of another is more appropriately perceived as an act of love toward the other and not as an act of violence against oneself.

2. Egotistic and Altruistic Self-Sacrifice

To see this, we first need to establish the basis for the distinction between egotistic and altruistic self-sacrifice. A classical exposition of this distinction can be found in Schiller's "Theosophie des Julius,"[10] which identifies precisely this difference as the crucial point in the problematic of sacrifice. However, Schiller's argument does not begin with sacrifice; it begins with the reality of love. As Julius, Schiller's alter ego, impresses on his friend Raphael: "I admit freely that I believe in the existence of a disinterested love."[11] "But love has produced effects that seem to contradict its nature. It can be conceived that I increase my own happiness by a sacrifice which I offer for the happiness of others; but suppose this sacrifice is my life? . . . How is it possible that we can hold death to be a means of increasing the sum of our enjoyments? How can the cessation of my being be reconciled with the enriching of my being?"[12] What appears conceivable with sacrifice becomes paradoxical with self-sacrifice: the one for whom it could and should bring an improvement of life no longer lives.

A possible answer may be found in the reference to immortality: "The assumption of immortality removes this contradiction." But Julius sees correctly that love is thereby also lifted: "The consideration of a future reward excludes love."[13] "I grant it is ennobling to the human soul to sacrifice present enjoyment for a future eternal good;

10. Friedrich Schiller, "Theosophie des Julius," in *Sämtliche Werke*, vol. 5, *Philosophisch-Ästhetische Schriften* (Munich: Hanser, 1975), 344–58. References are given to the German text. Translations are taken from http://www.gutenberg.org/files/6799/6799-h/6799-h.htm.

11. Ibid., 351.

12. Ibid.

13. Ibid.

it is the noblest degree of egotism; but egotism and love separate humanity into two very unlike races, whose limits are never confounded. Egotism erects its center in itself; love places it out of itself in the axis of the universal whole. Love aims at unity, egotism at solitude. Love is the citizen ruler of a flourishing republic, egotism is a despot in a devastated creation. Egotism sows for gratitude, love for the ungrateful. Love gives, egotism lends; and love does this before the throne of judicial truth, indifferent if for the enjoyment of the following moment, or with the view to a martyr's crown—indifferent whether the reward is in this life or in the next."[14]

Hence an egotism nurtured by the hope for immortality is also the opposite of love. The question raised must therefore be answered another way: "Think, O Raphael, of a truth that benefits the whole human race to remote ages; add that this truth condemns its confessor to death; that this truth can only be proved and believed if he dies."[15] Then conceive a man who wants to realize this very truth: "Does this man need to be referred to a future life?"[16] The answer, which Julius suggests, is clearly no. Only the one who acts in this way does not act egotistically when he sacrifices himself.

Schiller thus distinguishes between an *egotistical* self-sacrifice, which is carried out in hope of an eternal remuneration[17] and an *altruistic* self-sacrifice, which is carried out for the sake of others—of *all* others and therefore for the sake of the whole of humankind—and alone deserves to be called a sacrifice of love. Only the latter is "a virtue which even without the belief in immortality, even at the peril of annihilation, suffices to carry out this sacrifice."[18] Only someone who sacrifices himself or herself *solely for the sake of others—all others!*—acts truly out of unselfish love.

14. Ibid., 351–52.
15. Ibid., 352.
16. Ibid. (slightly altered).
17. See the rational-choice theory of martyrdom precisely as propounded by Rodney Stark, *The Rise of Christianity: A Sociologist Reconsiders History* (Princeton: Princeton University Press, 1996). Terrorist suicide attacks sometimes function in accordance with the same principle, although they can take place for other reasons as well. See B. Janowski, *Ecce Homo: Stellvertretung und Lebenshingabe als Themen Biblischer Theologie* (Neukirchen-Vluyn: Neukirchener, 2007), 9–13.
18. Schiller, "Theosophie des Julius," 351.

Altruistic self-sacrifice in Schiller's sense of unselfish love therefore distinguishes itself in two ways. On the one hand, it is not motivated by an attitude of egotistical value maximization beyond the boundary of transcendence: it is fundamentally *altruistic*, not egotistic. On the other hand, it is not restricted, particular, or abstract, but *unrestricted*, *universal*, and *concrete*: it is based neither on family relationships, which privilege genetic closeness (i.e., blood or kinship ties) and thus do not include all;[19] nor is it based on bonds of friendship, which do not exist without local proximity or personal acquaintance and therefore are also restricted;[20] nor is it based in an abstract moral maxim that under certain circumstances one must sacrifice oneself for all those who fall under a specific rule. Unconditional, unselfish, and thus universally inclusive love is but a concrete form of love of one's neighbor, which is not a version of the rule of prudence, to do unto others what one expects from others or (in its negative form) not to do unto others as one would not do unto oneself. If that were the case, one would treat others as neighbors because one expects the same from them. *Concrete* love of one's neighbor is precisely not attached to that kind of expectation, but sees and treats the other as a neighbor even when those expectations are unrealistic or thwarted. It is not founded in the reciprocity of like for like but in the experience of having become God's freely chosen neighbor without having a right or entitlement to it; and since God also relates to all others as his freely chosen neighbors, one can rely on God in every situation, for people do not choose God; God chooses people. Everyone therefore has a

19. In this sense the pelican, which tears open her breast to feed her own blood to her young, has long been a symbol of self-sacrificing love.

20. In his major work, *The Imperative of Responsibility* (Chicago: University of Chicago Press, 1985), Hans Jonas criticizes the Christian law of love as inadequate because it is confined to the immediate setting of the action: "Note that in all these maxims the agent and the 'other' of his action are sharers of a common present. It is those who are alive now and in some relationship with me" (5). He believes that this is utterly insufficient as a maxim for action in view of the ecological crisis and humanity's technological capability for permanent self-destruction. Technological changes mean that this ethic must be extended from love of one's neighbor to *love of those most distant from one*. With this in mind, Jonas formulated the ecological imperative: "Act so that the effects of your action are compatible with the permanence of genuine human life on earth." But it is a mistake to place love of one's neighbor in opposition to love of those most distant from one or love of one's enemy. Rightly understood, it includes them.

right to be seen and treated as God's neighbor just as much as oneself. Seen in this light, love of one's neighbor becomes a reorientation of one's life by God. It does not result from a moral self-determination of one's own conduct toward others, but rather manifests the fact that one has become the neighbor of the one who has made all other people his neighbors as well, so that everyone under all circumstances and without exception is to be seen and treated as God's neighbor.

If altruistic self-sacrifice is understood from this perspective, then one cannot stop with Schiller either. If love of one's neighbor leads to death, then this is not a *substitutional self-sacrifice* by which someone goes to his or her death in the place of another in order to save or avoid the death of that other person. On the contrary, it is a question of stepping in for another at the cost of one's own self-preservation, of being present to the other in that person's needs even at the cost of one's own life. Furthermore, such a death is not a sacrifice made out of pity or compassion, in which one gives up one's own life in solidarity with the suffering of another, but is rather a love of one's neighbor that is lived even to death. Something is done *for* others (and not *in place of* others or *in solidarity with* others) that leads to the loss of one's own life. And it is not only done for them, it would be done for all others in a similar situation because not doing so would be incompatible with how one is supposed to conduct oneself toward those who are God's neighbors. In such a case it is a question of living and dying *for the sake of* others and *for* others. One does not intentionally seek out one's own death even though that may be the consequence, but accepts even death because anything else would make one's life, lived in orientation to the law of love, a fundamental self-contradiction. One who dies out of love of one's neighbor does not kill oneself but rather loves the person whom God loves, even if it results in losing one's life.

For Derrida, the paradox in the basic structure of sacrifice is most obvious in the phenomenon of self-sacrifice. According to Schiller, this needs to be differentiated either as an act of violence against oneself (egotistical self-sacrifice) or as an act of love (altruistic self-sacrifice). To distinguish between these two kinds of sacrifice is correct and important, but it does not go far enough. As soon as one understands altruistic self-sacrifice as an act of love, an idea is introduced that breaks the paradigm of sacrifice apart: a death resulting from unconditional, unselfish love does not have to be self-sacrifice; it can also be the consequence of a passion of love.

3. Altruistic Self-Sacrifice and Unselfish Love

Egotistical self-sacrifice is a particular kind of sacrifice—its paradoxical limit case: one does not give up another's life but *one's own life*. This renunciation of life can result from egotistical or altruistic motives. However—and this is what Schiller makes clear—anyone who gives his life in order to save it will lose it: surrender of one's life is not a means of securing one's self-preservation across the boundary of death. Moreover, whoever gives his own life for the benefit of others uses it as a means to an end and therefore remains caught in the paradigm of egotistical self-sacrifice by using his own life as a means to reach an extrinsic goal. By surrendering *one's own* life as a means to an end, one chooses death, but in doing so, one remains the master of one's own self insofar as one chooses *for oneself* one's own death and in this very act gives one's *self* meaning. Surrendering one's life for the sake of others thus can be a subtle expression of an egotistical attitude toward life, which subjects even one's own death to one's own power of action and one's own endowment of something with meaning: one gives oneself death in order to be the one who gives one's own death an altruistic meaning. Even in death one thus is still the master of one's own actions. The sacrifice of one's own life becomes a vehicle to achieve a goal.

Death as a result of unconditional, unselfish love is something else. In this case, one gives up neither the life of another nor one's own life, but *nothing at all*: one *suffers* death in loving advocacy for others. One's own death is in this sense not a gift to anyone, not an act of violence against oneself, and therefore not a sacrifice in the sense outlined: one does not give up one's life but lives it in such a way that it exhausts itself in the love of others. One loves so unconditionally and so unrestrictedly that even one's own self-preservation does not present itself as an obstacle or limit to this love. Thus, what constitutes the horizon in which the sense of one's own death is disclosed is not self-sacrifice (and, as such, sacrifice itself) but love of one's neighbor (and, as such, love itself).

Hence death as a result of love of one's neighbor is distinct from altruistic self-sacrifice in that it is not an act of violence against oneself but involves *suffering in one's own life the consequences of an entirely unselfish love*. Such a death is not a sacrifice in the sense of giving up something, even one's own life, in order to achieve or avoid something. Acts of unselfish love are carried out without a because or a why. They are directed so wholly toward others that one does not make use of one's own life, even as the means to their end. Their point is solely to do something out of love for others even if one loses one's life in the process. When Maximilian Kolbe voluntarily took the place of Franciszek Gajowniczek in Auschwitz–Birkenau, he did not sacrifice himself or use his life as the ultimate means to save the other. Rather, he acted out of love of his neighbor in such a way that he accepted death because practicing unconditional love was a higher goal for him than saving his own life. His death was not the end or means of his love but its consequence. In practicing love, his concern was not his own death but the life of the other.[21] The goal and purpose of acting out of love of one's neighbor is what is best for the other's life, not one's own death. Nor is one's own death employed as the means of achieving this goal, but is rather taken as unavoidable collateral damage, so to speak, sustained in abiding under all circumstances by the love of one's neighbor. It would not be an unrestricted, unselfish love if one were dissuaded by one's own impending death. One who is not thus dissuaded from losing his life does not employ his own death as the means to an end, but suffers death as a result of his unconditional love of his neighbor.

This is why such acts are not sacrifices. Where life is lost out of love, sacrifice ends. No one is giving anything to anybody, whether the life of another or one's own life, in order to reach a goal. If others

---

21. Obviously, this is not necessarily the correct interpretation. But that applies equally to the view that it was an act of self-sacrifice and therefore an act of violence against himself. If it was the latter, there would have been no grounds for the Roman Catholic Church to canonize him. Suicide is no ground for canonization. And all the known facts suggest that this was not an act of suicide but one of manifest love for his neighbor in his direst need.

achieve or receive anything by it, then it is not given to them by the one who lost his (or her) life, even if they could not—or would not—achieve or receive it without this person's death. "Sacrifices of love" are not sacrifices but acts of love. As acts of love they are directed toward the other, but they do not intend the death of the one who loves, least of all as a means to an end. Rather, if the loving one suffers death, then it is because he cannot be dissuaded from living his life for the love of others. His death is a consequence of living a life that is oriented toward the well-being of the other, not the ultimate meaning of that life.

4. The Passion of Love

For precisely this reason one must argue in opposition to Derrida that a religion can neither expect nor exclude the willingness to die for love. Moreover, loss of life out of unselfish love goes beyond Schiller's altruistic self-sacrifice. It is not an act of violence, either against oneself or against others. It is not an act of any kind that the one who dies would carry out in order to end his life; rather, it is a loss of life that is neither sought nor intended, but is suffered—be it in the conscious risk of one's life for others or with actual consequences for others that may not even have been intended. The fact that loss of life out of love results from an intentional activity does not constitute it as a gift for others. One who loses his life out of love does not give it up for others, whether selfishly or unselfishly. He loves the other—even to death. But the motive and goal of his love is life, not death, and that his love leads to death is not the result of an act of violence against himself but a consequence of the actual situation in which he practices his love, which induces the suffering that turns his love into passion.

The decisive difference between sacrifice and self-sacrifice therefore is not that sacrifice surrenders another's life while self-sacrifice surrenders one's own. In the case of the former, the identity of the sacrificer is symbolically transferred to the sacrificial animal, which suffers death in the place of the sacrificer in order to preserve his life; by contrast, self-sacrifice involves giving up one's own life in order to preserve the lives of others. The crucial point is rather that one's own death becomes an expression and execution of unselfish love only when it is no longer the limit case of sacrifice, in which it is not someone else's life but one's own life that is sacrificed, but where nothing, not even one's own suffering or impending death, keeps someone from pursuing unwaveringly what is good for others. The objective of such an act of love is always the preservation and betterment of the life of someone else, and if it leads to one's own suffering or death, then one has not actively aspired to this but rather suffers it as a passion of a love that does not give up on its commitment to others.

It is not self-evident that such an unselfish love exists—a love that does not let itself be held back from living for the sake of others, even if the price is one's own suffering and death. Religions had to go through a long process to discover the reality of such a love, particularly where God is concerned. Biblical tradition documents this impressively, especially where it shows, within the very paradigm of sacrifice, the change from understanding something as an act of violence to understanding it as an act of love. In the process it makes the discovery that sacrifice has no future, but an end: the crucial insight about sacrifice is not that it is religiously necessary, even if impossible to realize, but that it is possible but no longer necessary. One can sacrifice, even oneself, but one does not need to, because what one is trying to accomplish cannot be reached through sacrifice and has long since been reached through the reality of unselfish love.

Important strands in the biblical tradition substantiate this transition from the paradigm of sacrifice to the paradigm of a completely different form of life and thought, most impressively the stories of Abraham's trial and Jesus's crucifixion. The former demonstrates that God's promises are infallibly trustworthy under all circumstances; the latter, that God's power does not reside in violence but in love. Taken together, they prove through exemplary stories of real-life experiments that God is love—a love that does not want sacrifice but a life lived in unconditional commitment to others.[22]

22. For a more extensive account of what follows, cf. Ingolf U. Dalferth, *Malum: Theologische Hermeneutik des Bösen* (Tübingen: Mohr Siebeck, 2008), 449–500.

5. Abraham's Silence: The Ambivalence of God

The story of Abraham's trial in Genesis 22 is found in the cycle of
Abraham narratives that stretches from Genesis 11:27 through Genesis 22 to the account of Abraham's death in Genesis 25. The central
theological motif of this cycle is God's promise that he would give
Abraham the land, bless him, and make him the father of a great
nation (Gen. 12:1–3; 13:14–17). The fact that these promises are emphasized in this way indicates how seriously they had been called into
question in Israel's experience of exile since 587/586 BC, the most
likely time of the origin of this cycle.

If we read Genesis 22 as part of the cycle of Abraham narratives as
it has been handed down, then it does not deal with a drama between
Abraham and Isaac but between *Israel*, for whom Abraham functions
as the progenitor, and *God*.[23] The dynamic of the narrative unfolds
within the context of the programmatic promise and blessing given
to Abraham at the beginning of the cycle: "I will make you into a
great nation, and I will bless you; I will make your name great, and

23. It is remarkable what the story does *not* narrate: Abraham does not speak,
Isaac does not protest, Sarah does not appear at all, Ishmael is not mentioned either,
Abraham shows no ambivalent feelings toward Isaac, and Isaac does not comment
on anything that goes on. He remains a very shadowy figure in the narrative and
disappears completely from the scene after the ram has been sacrificed and Abraham
returns to Beersheba with his servants. All this has again and again given rise to
multiple interpretations and fanciful elaborations. Abraham's silence is eloquently
explained, Sarah's death is depicted as being caused by the shock of hearing about
the intended or actual killing of Isaac, Isaac's role in the story is extensively expanded
by presenting him not as a silent sufferer but as longing and pleading explicitly for his
own binding and sacrificial offering, etc. Many of these interpretations and redac-
tions go back to pre-Christian times and show how unfixed and versatile the textual
history of this narrative was for a long time. But they have little or no basis in the
biblical version of the story. They fill in what readers experienced as missing because
it is not contained in the biblical narrative. But if one sticks to the actual narrative
in Genesis 22, then one may doubt whether it really is a story about Abraham *and*
Isaac rather than one about *Abraham* in which also Isaac appears—just as the Swiss
legend of Wilhelm Tell, in which Tell is ordered to shoot an apple off his son's head
with his crossbow, is not a story about Tell's son, or about the relationship between
father and son, but about the Swiss struggle for independence from the Habsburg
Empire. The figurative inventory of the story and the potential relations between its
characters do not provide an adequate key to a proper understanding of the story.
This will only be possible by sticking to the actual narrative and by interpreting its
point in the context of the dynamics of the actual drama as related.

you will be a blessing" (Gen. 12:2 NIV). This is then explicitly geared to Isaac at the beginning of the Akedah story in Genesis 21:12: not through Ishmael but "through Isaac your descendants shall be named" (NASB), as God assures Abraham.

The critical conflict in the narrative therefore is not between Abraham and Isaac but between the God who promises Abraham great things in and through Isaac, and the *same* God who instructs Abraham to perform a deed directed at Isaac, the realization of which would make this promise completely impossible. What governs the narrative is the tension between God's promise and his own order to kill, which renders the promise impossible: Is God giving to Israel with one hand what he takes back from it with the other? Can one rely on a God who retracts everything promised at any time and without reason? Can one still count on God's fidelity? Can one count on God at all?

Both the promise and the directive that makes this promise impossible are attributed to the *same God*, so that it is impossible to resort to attributing the promise to God and the questioning of this promise to someone other than God, as has been attempted by versions of the Akedah story influenced by the prologue to the book of Job.[24] Rather, Abraham is placed in a dilemma in which there literally is nothing else for him to say since God seems to be caught in a contradiction. Talking to others about God will not get him any further, and talking to God himself has become impossible because God has become so contradictory that he can no longer be addressed definitively as "my God."

6. Abraham's Action Puts God to the Test

Where nothing more can be said, life will decide. This conflict cannot be decided by argument, because God has become incomprehensible and inaccessible as a dialogue partner. It can only be brought to a conclusion by Abraham taking one side of God's paradoxical and self-contradictory will at his word and acting on it to the point where

24. See the versions of the story that were found in Qumran, in which Prince Mastemah and his evil angels machinate against Abraham before God (4Q225, frag. 2, cols. 1–2).

the question of God takes care of itself or where God himself—and this in fact is how the story is resolved—removes the ambivalence in his Abraham/Israel relationship and owns up to his promises. To put it in a nutshell: Abraham is not being tested by God; rather, by abandoning speech in favor of action, Abraham puts God to the test. Abraham virtually compels God either to take leave of his people as God or to prove himself to be God and to stand by his promises to his people. He dares to challenge God, and he wins—not only clarity (this he would have won even if the outcome of the test had been negative) but certainty that God stands by his promises.

Why is this testing of God—this resolution of the conflict within Israel's relationship to and understanding of God—depicted theologically by means of this particular story of Abraham's offering of his beloved son? Because it lends itself excellently to demonstrating the conflict in Abraham's/Israel's relationship to and trust in God. The decisive point of the story is not that Abraham should kill *his beloved son* but that his beloved son is *the only reliable pledge of God's promise*. The existentially extreme situation in which Israel in exile finds itself vis-à-vis God is made apparent here in that Abraham is prepared, upon God's order, to destroy the very pledge of God's promise: either this is the end of all Israel's dealings with God, or God must surrender his ambivalence with respect to Israel once and for all.

It is precisely in order to depict this trial of God that the ancient cult legend of the replacement of child sacrifice by animal sacrifice is taken up here in the Abrahamic cycle and told anew with God, Abraham, and Isaac as protagonists. The story cannot be used to draw conclusions about the arbitrary will of God or about the blind faith that supposedly demands obedience even to the extent of the moral degradation of the believer. It is not about any of this, only about disambiguating a God who in his turning toward and away from his people is experienced as pure paradox, useless when it comes to the direction of one's life.[25] One cannot trust such a God. He has rendered himself superfluous as a point of reference or orientation.

25. This is clearly expressed in the twin parables of *Genesis Rabbah* 56:11, which interpret Gen. 22:15–16. It is Abraham whose strength of faith saves God from becoming enmeshed in a fatal self-contradiction and rendering his own promise void. And in the second parable it is again Abraham who makes God swear never to do anything

The narrative clarification in Genesis 22 results in a more precise understanding of God and of Israel's relationship to God, one that accepts and lives by the understanding that God is not to be found in everything without distinction but only in certain experiences, and that only certain ways of life and action correspond to God's will while others do not. This is the basic insight and starting point of Jewish ethics, culminating in the Torah, and of Christian ethics as concentrated in the commandment of love: one can now say with certainty that nothing can be attributed to God or God's will that contradicts God's promises or would bring human beings into contradiction with God's will as expressed in his promises.

This is not self-evident, for why should a promise given freely not also be taken back freely? Precisely this possibility is excluded in the Akedah story, where its realization is heightened to the point that it would result in God's self-contradiction and self-annihilation and is thus declared a factual impossibility. God's promises are certain, even if one cannot fathom from one's own experiences how one stands with God. This is how one could summarize the practical point of this story.

However, if God can no longer be distinguished from his promises or be thought of as free from capriciousness in relation to them, then he also can no longer be utilized for everything indiscriminately, only for certain things and in very specific respects.

Seen in this way, Genesis 22 recounts by way of an old legend (the replacement of child sacrifice with animal sacrifice) a new story, extremely significant for the religious life and thought of Israel: the story of the verification of the trustworthiness of God's promises through Abraham's trial of God. By taking God, whom Israel no longer understands, at his word and by acting out what cannot be argued out, Abraham brings about a situation in which God must prove himself either to be entirely superfluous to human requirements or to be the one who can revoke his promises only at the cost

---

like this again: "Swear to me that you will never test me again." By divine oath God is now tied to his promise and can henceforth be trusted. See Clemens Thoma and Simon Lauer, *Die Gleichnisse der Rabbinen*, vol. 2, *Von der Entstehung der Welt bis zum Tod Abrahams: Bereschit Rabba 1–63*, Judaica et Christiana 13 (Bern: Peter Lang, 1991), 308–10.

of self-annihilation. God strictly excludes as impossible what human experience seemed to suggest as not merely possible, but as having indeed happened, thus putting human experience as a reliable judge of God firmly in its place: either there is no God, or God's promises cannot be revoked even by God himself. *Tertium non datur!* (There is no third option!) That is the emphasis of the story.

With the conclusion of Abraham's God experiment, the promise is reliably inscribed into the very idea of God; that is, God is no longer separable from what he has promised Israel. God no longer can be played off against his promises. Anyone who says "God" is speaking of the one who stands by his promises.

7. God's Silence: Jesus Puts God Unsuccessfully to the Test

The same applies to Christian faith in God, which is intrinsically related to Jesus's life, work, suffering, and death. However, it is not readily apparent that God's will for humankind is manifested in Jesus. It is true that, according to the Gospels, Jesus directly connected the dawn of God's benevolent kingdom with his person and ministry (Matt. 11:5–6), and during his brief active life he was able to convince a number of people of this connection, to which his band of disciples is testimony. But at the end of his life, he no longer was even sure of this connection himself. According to the oldest Gospels, Mark and Matthew, Jesus died on the cross with a loud cry of God forsakenness: "My God, my God, why have you forsaken me?" (Mark 15:34; Matt. 27:46 NIV). The citation from Psalm 22 here is not a disguised sign of hope in God but rather an expression of despair. It is a lamentation and an accusation by someone who finds himself unjustly and unreasonably abandoned by God, whom God has not stood by or assisted in his need, who dies deserted by God and the world—without the trust in God that Luke has him articulate (Luke 23:46) and without the confidence that John attributes to him for having fulfilled the charge laid on him by God (John 19:30).

According to Mark, God himself has become the reason for Jesus's despair on the cross. There is no question that God is still the one to whom Jesus addresses his accusation. He is not plagued by modernity's intellectual doubt as to God's existence but by practical despair because God has concealed and withdrawn himself and has failed to act in the hour of his greatest need. God, who had been the most intimate center of his life ("Abba, Father," Mark 14:36 NIV), no longer offers him either help or direction.

This contradicts everything the New Testament tells us about what Jesus proclaimed through his teachings, life, and parabolic actions as "the gospel of God":[26] God's time of salvation is at hand and is ending the suffering of all those who change their lives and believe in the gospel (Mark 1:15). As far as we know, Jesus lived in the conviction that through his life and teaching he actually was accomplishing God's will. This is the very reason why, for Jesus, God's silence on the cross is a breaking of his word, unjust and merciless toward the one who has placed all of his hope in God's compassion and righteousness; a willful default of God to render assistance to one of his creatures; the failure of a father to be true to his son; a contradiction of everything he had preached and acted out as God's goodwill for humankind in the parables of the prodigal son, of the good Samaritan, in the healing of the sick, and in the symbolic actions of forgiving of sins. It seems that on the cross the God proclaimed by Jesus has become untrue to himself, and it is in this despair, according to the oldest testimony of the Gospels, that Jesus died.

The story of Abraham in Genesis 22 and the story of Jesus in Mark's Gospel thus both present a God experiment by their respective protagonists that concerns God's trustworthiness and the reliability of his promises. But they do so with strikingly different narrative trajectories and outcomes. In the Akedah story Abraham tests God when, in the face of God's contradictory promises and directions, he no longer knows what his relationship to God is. By the end of the story, God has proved himself to be inseparable from his promises because he has committed himself to them: God is the God of promises, and because God can and will not be otherwise, his promises for Israel are reliable even where this is not recognizable in a real-life circumstance. The gospel story shows that Jesus, on the other hand, dedicated his entire "career" to God's promise and counted on his faithfulness and trustworthiness all the way to the cross, but in the end he was disappointed by God and died in despair.

On a narrative level the first story ends positively, the second negatively. The narrative logic of the Akedah story focuses on the withdrawal of God's ambivalence toward Abraham himself, who through his action puts God in a position in which he must decide for or against himself and thus is forced to commit himself to what he wants to be as God for Israel: in the narrative of the story, the question of God's Godhead is decided in terms of its bearing on Abraham himself and is presented as such. Mark's Gospel, by contrast, pushes the ambivalence of Jesus's God forsakenness on the cross to its extreme, and here there is no narrative resolution for him. The narrative logic of Mark's Gospel lets Jesus end on the cross in contradistinction to everything that, according to Mark 1:15, is contained in the gospel and unfolded in the gospel narrative of Jesus's life and activity. Hence the one story results in a clarified idea of God, and the other leads to the point where the meaning of the term *God* has become completely unclear. While the narrative trajectory in the Abraham story leads its protagonists from uncertainty to certainty about God, the narrative trajectory of the Gospel account leads from certainty about God to the loss of God.

8. The Third View: Autobiographical and Biographical Perspectives

But this is the case only if one reads these stories in isolation and ignores their wider contexts. In the story of Abraham, everything that needs to be said is said *in* the story. In Mark's story of Jesus, on the other hand, a dramatic conflict is built up between Jesus's understanding of God as proclaimed in the gospel and the loss of God by the proclaimer of that gospel as he dies on the cross. This conflict is not resolved either narratively or semantically in the account of his own life; it finds resolution only in the lives of those to whom this story is told and who experience the crucified as the resurrected one, as both the account of the empty grave (Mark 16:1–8) and the secondary ending of Mark (Mark 16:9–20) substantiate. The darkness into which the understanding of God falls on the cross is lifted and removed, not in the life story of Jesus and therefore for Jesus himself, but in the life story of those who believe in him as Christ and therefore for others. The other Gospels corroborate this too, in that they do not conclude the story of Jesus's life experiment with the cross but rather continue it with their accounts of the Easter discovery of his resurrection, the appearances of the resurrected one, and his ascension to God in heaven. God's activity, which is seen in this story and is confessed in the recounting of it, is not presented as occurring in the life, suffering, and death of Jesus but rather in the lives of those who believe in him. And no one is excluded from the possibility of being numbered among them. The theological point of the story of Jesus does not lie in his story itself but in the lives of those who confess him as Christ, and only by including those lives can his story be properly represented.

According to Mark, from the autobiographical perspective of *Jesus himself*, his life story with God ends with his cry that God has abandoned him. It is only with the biographical perspective of *others* on the Jesus story that it becomes apparent that this is not the last word on God's Godhead. For them, the ostensible ambivalence of God on the cross is overcome as a result of their understanding of God being shaped wholly by the Jesus story. To do so, they had to inscribe the unfathomable aporia between Jesus's proclamation of God and the way his life ended into their very idea of God as a dialectic, thereby creating a *Christian* understanding of God that goes beyond Jesus's own understanding.

9. God as Love: From Jesus's Understanding to a Christian Understanding of God

As a result, certain traits of Jesus's idea of God are intensified and deepened while new ones are added. Thus it is God himself, and he alone, who removes the ambivalence manifest on the cross by moving people through the working of the Spirit to believe in Jesus as the Christ. For precisely this reason, the reference to Jesus's story culminating on the cross, told as his life experiment with God, is inscribed into the Christian understanding of God as an indelible element of it. This happens discursively in the narrative unfolding of the metaphors of Jesus's resurrection, his ascension to heaven, and his seat on the right hand of God, all of which establish in their own way that God is no longer to be understood apart from the life story of Jesus and the life story of those who believe and profess that Jesus is the Christ.

The dramatic, theological point of the life experiment of Jesus is not to be found in his own story but in the life story of those who proclaim him to be Christ, and it is this fact that links Jesus's life story with the life stories of believers, not just externally but through the ongoing and determinative image of the same God. This runs as a thread through a process of interpretation that can be traced from the Jewish understanding of God to Jesus's understanding and on to that of Christianity.[27] The Christian understanding of God grew out of the Jewish tradition, building on Jesus's individual focus and continuously deepening and revising this understanding, applying a Christian interpretation to Jesus's crisis on the cross, one that cannot be ascribed to its own powers of interpretation but to the eye-opening work of the Spirit of God.

10. The Creative Passion of Love

The condensation of this complex process in the Christian concept of God as love generates the idea of an unlimited and unselfish love that establishes in Israel's understanding of God and in Jesus's understanding

---

27. All of them are given only in a plural form. This is also true of Jesus's understanding of God, which is accessible only through the different versions of the different Gospels. Jesus's life and teaching take up and focus the understanding of God communicated to him along with Israel's prophetic and theological traditions: his understanding of God as the "Father in heaven" is a condensed concentration and a practical focusing of Israel's traditional understanding of God. This understanding of God, which Jesus lived and proclaimed, ran into a decisive crisis at the cross that could have been the end of Jesus's intensification of the theological traditions of Israel. But in fact the reverse took place: what appeared to have come to an end at the cross became the framework for understanding that end. By understanding the cross of Jesus in the light of his understanding of God and through the work of God's Spirit, who opened their eyes to interpret the cross in relation to God's resurrection of the crucified one, the followers of Jesus learned to cope with his crisis at the cross and to allow the crisis itself to determine the Christian image of God.

of God as Father the very precondition for recognizing that in Jesus's life and death a love is at work that creates new life out of death. It is not God who sacrifices Jesus on the cross, nor does Jesus sacrifice himself, but out of love for those to whom he proclaims the advent of God's benevolent rule, he goes all the way to his death on the cross. Precisely this life of unconditional love for others, leading to Jesus's death on the cross, proves to be an irreversible sign for those whose eyes the Spirit has opened through Jesus's resurrection. It is a sign that, at the cross of Jesus, God discloses himself as unselfish, altruistic love, a love that stays near its creatures until death, doing them good and making them new. Even where they themselves cannot realize this any more, others will.

For, on the one hand, God's love experiences and endures the suffering and death of his creatures as his own passion, as is seen on the cross. On the other hand, this divine passion transforms the suffering of others into the determination of God's own life to create new life out of this suffering, as is shown in the resurrection. Evil suffered is not thereby abolished or revoked; it is overcome in such a way that something new and good comes out of it. Sacrifice terminates violence through other violence, and self-sacrifice terminates violence against others through violence against oneself; but this merely replaces one evil by another. The passion of divine love, on the other hand, overcomes evil with good, not with evil, by determining itself through its love for others to create new life out of suffering and death, thus giving the dead a future and the hopeless hope. Neither sacrifice nor self-sacrifice can do that. For the chasm between old and new, between death and life, cannot be bridged through violence, nor through violence against violence or sacrifice against sacrifice, but only through love that inexhaustibly creates new life.

But is it appropriate, using this condensed theology of the cross, to conceive of God completely and unconditionally as love? Does the idea of God's love embrace who and what God truly is? Does it capture at least a part of it? Or does it completely bypass the mystery of God? Does the basic metaphor of God's love provide the Christian faith and Christian theology with an idea of God that in vital ways must be conceived of differently if one wants to think of God as he really is? Or is Christian theology on the track of an insight into God's essence when it says not only "God loves" but also "God is love"? Does it thereby allow God and love to determine each other so closely that the mystery of God can be perceived, not epistemically as the incomprehensibility of the infinite by the finite, but existentially as the inexhaustibility and unfathomability of love, the love as which God can rightly and without reservation or constraint be comprehended?

6

Becoming Human

Compensation for a Deficiency or Excess of Love?

1. The Aporetic Idea of God: Absolute Perfection

"The incarnation," writes Hans Blumenberg in his *Matthäuspassion*, "was not the hyperbole of a divine love but compensation for a divine lack of experience."[1] God had reached his limits. Precisely because he wanted to be fully God and nothing else at all, he came up against a deficiency that is all too familiar to us humans: the deficiency of having to live and act without really knowing what one needs to know in order to be able to live and act properly. According to Blumenberg, God discovers himself to be a deficient being like us, so he tries to compensate for this deficiency in a way that can only be described as paradoxical, by becoming in his incarnation, expressly and in a manner that could never be surpassed or reversed, what he already is: a deficient being.

---

1. H. Blumenberg, *Matthäuspassion* (Frankfurt am Main: Suhrkamp, [3]1991), 126. What follows is a discussion of this argument, not of the question as to whether this is Blumenberg's own position.

What Blumenberg focuses on so allusively in his discussion of the incarnation is an aporia of the traditional European philosophical idea of God. Plato's metacriticism of the natural philosophical and sophistic critique of myth established a ground rule for philosophically adequate thinking about God: "God, surely, and everything that belongs to God is in every way in the best possible state."[2] Hence, Plato's Socrates emphasizes, "For the good we must assume no other cause than God, but the cause of evil we must look for in other things and not in God."[3]

Aristotle regarded even that as too worldly: even a God who is thought to be responsible only for the good in the world is still regarded, in relation to the world, in a manner inappropriate to the reality being considered: "God is too exalted even to conceive of the world. According to Aristotelian tradition he conceives only of himself."[4] One therefore must not even begin to consider the world as having been created by God—at most one may perhaps think in these terms of a cosmos that is coeternal with God and, fascinated by God's absolute self-sufficiency, strives toward that which is perfectly realized therein: complete self-realization, free from any defect.

But what if the world is not eternal and in fact could not exist, given that at one time it did not exist and that soon it will no longer exist, because it is not as it should be? What happens if such an idea of God enters the realm of fundamental Judeo-Christian experience: the idea that the world not only is other than it could and should be, but that it would not exist at all if God had not wrested it from nothingness, so that it only exists because, to the extent that, and as long as, God in fact does that? What happens to the idea of an absolutely self-sufficient God in the light of an insight into the absolute inadequacy of an ontologically contingent world that has to be re-created eschatologically? Does one hold on to such an idea? Does one need complicated workarounds such as this: "Although God does

2. Plato, *Republic* 381b: Ὁ θεός γε καὶ τὰ τοῦ θεοῦ πάντηι ἄριστα ἔχει. (Translation in *Plato in Twelve Volumes*, vols. 5 and 6, trans. Paul Shorey, Loeb Classical Library [Cambridge, MA: Harvard University Press; London: William Heinemann, 1969].)

3. Plato, *Republic* 379c: καὶ τῶν μὲν ἀγαθῶν οὐδένα ἄλλον αἰτιατέον, τῶν δὲ κακῶν ἄλλ' ἄττα δεῖ ζητεῖν τα αἴτια, ἀλλ' οὐ τὸν θεόν. (Translation in *Plato in Twelve Volumes*, Shorey.)

4. Blumenberg, *Matthäuspassion*, 122.

not conceive of the world, he nonetheless *allows it to be conceived of*. That is why he has the angels: it is in them that the world was 'designed'; it is from them that it was 'called forth,' without its having been conceived of by the highest authority, and it is ultimately the human spirit that has shaped it."[5] In the above, Blumenberg is quoting the sixteenth-century Platonist and humanist Charles de Bovelles: "Before God created everything, he designed it in the spirit of the angels; then he called it forth and brought it into being. Finally he shaped it in accordance with the human spirit."[6]

2. Deficiency Compensation by Incarnation

This answer, in its affinity with Neoplatonism, bears the hallmarks of grasping at straws. Might it not be more appropriate, in view of the insufficiency of being of the created world, to conceive of God in a manner distinct from that of antiquity? This was the path taken by the Christian doctrine of the Trinity—with implications that have not yet been thought through, even today. Blumenberg proceeds differently. He seeks to propel the actual idea of an absolutely self-sufficient God into an aporia so as to extract from it the contingency that necessitates God's incarnation. His argument is simple but revealing: if it is this God, seen in this light, who created the world in this manner—if, in other words, he enacted the thoughts of angels because he himself was incapable of thinking those thoughts—then in fact "God did not know what he was doing when he created the world. . . . God did not know what lay ahead because he *could not know it*."[7]

Blumenberg takes the creation of humankind as an illustration: God could not know what lay ahead "when he molded a creature like himself, allowed it to become accustomed to life in paradise, and then drove it out into naked self-preservation." The action was unavoidable for God's self-preservation but nonetheless carried consequences that even God could not have foreseen. "God separated human beings from

5. Ibid.
6. Ibid.: "Deus antequam fierent omnia, ea concepit in angelico intellectu, deinde omnia protulit et fecit. postremo ea in humano intellectu descripsit."
7. Ibid., 124–25.

the fountain of life because there they would inevitably become *his* rivals. By means of death he made them *each other's* life and death rivals. . . . Thus it was that 'sin' came into the world with death, not the other way around . . . : life had become a 'trouble,' and indeed, very quickly, serious trouble: the motive for the first murder."[8] All of this must have remained completely incomprehensible to God. "How could he know the retrospective effect death would have on life since he himself could not be aware of death in any form?"[9] He could not know, just as *"no one* can know what 'pain' is until they have *experienced* it."[10] Thus God had no choice but to experience it himself: "The absolute subject cannot endure its carefree existence; it takes upon itself the cares of the world and saddles human beings, its image and likeness, with the troubles of human existence. However, even one who is omniscient cannot know *in advance* what trouble is, but only when he is condemned to death and marked by pain as a result of the perfidiousness of those by whom he is betrayed."[11] It follows that God could only overcome his lack by means of his own experience, and he could only follow this path by becoming a deficient being: a deficient being just like human beings, who only in this way—albeit in a manner wholly unanticipated—could attain the godlikeness that had been promised them.

According to Blumenberg, therefore, it is God's inevitable lack of experience as a divinity, his "divine . . . ignorance" and "essential . . . divine stupidity,"[12] that prompts him to take on human form.[13] In order to remedy his lack of experience as a divinity, he takes our lack of being into consideration. Now he knows what trouble, pain, and dying are, just as we do. The Creator and his creatures now share a

8. Ibid.
9. Ibid., 125.
10. Ibid.
11. Ibid., 126.
12. Ibid., 125.
13. Blumenberg's argument is one version of an argument already found in Plato's *Parmenides*: Just as we can hardly have real knowledge of the ideas appropriate to the divine, so also the divine can hardly know us or know about us (134e2f), since our knowledge always relates to an individual being (134b1). Knowledge of the universal is one thing, knowledge of the individual is another, and the divine can only have knowledge of the former, not the latter, even if it θαυμαστὸς ὁ λόγος, εἴ τις τὸν θεὸν ἀποστερήσει τοῦ εἰδέναι (134e7f).

common knowledge. But they also share a common being, with the result that their distinctiveness is at risk of becoming blurred. What kind of a God knows as we do, but also dies as we do? And what kind of incarnation leads to the overcoming of God's lack of experience as a divinity, but not to the elimination of our lack of being?

Blumenberg sees the problem, but his proposed solution merely reformulates it. Both God and his creatures "share a common memory of an existence involving pain and death, and what had been reality gives rise to the possibility of an infinite 'free variation,' of the balancing of actual destinies with the subjunctive of possible destinies."[14] Both "God and his creatures" thus become "consorts of the subjunctive":[15] what would have been, and what could have been? Thus they live—if they live—"under the ultimate sovereignty of the subjunctive."[16]

3. Lack of Being instead of Lack of Experience

But do they really? The shared memory of the infinite range of possibilities that remain possibilities is not enough, and in itself it is nothing at all. For how can someone who does not exist in the indicative—not just someone who *has* existed in the indicative—live in the subjunctive, as Blumenberg says? Merely "no longer to *be* what one *had been*" is too little:[17] memory of an existence involving pain and death is available only to those who *are* there, not just those who were there. What kind of God is a God who only exists in our memory? How do the dead benefit from the fact that we remember them? And how do we benefit from the fact that a few people remember us for a short while? To speak of "balancing . . . actual destinies with the subjunctive of possible destinies"[18] would be pure euphemism and a wholly inappropriate belittlement. A life that is merely *remembered* is no real alternative to living. And a God who is *merely* remembered is too little to be a real God, as Anselm proved to the fool. If one

14. Ibid., 128.
15. Ibid., 129.
16. Ibid.
17. Ibid.
18. Ibid.

can remember God, he must have existed. But if God has existed, it is impossible that he no longer exists, if indeed one is speaking of God. Recollection of God presupposes God's reality—whether we understand this memory in terms of a subjective genitive (God's memory) or an objective genitive (memory of God). Only someone who exists can remember. And only someone who has existed can be remembered by others. But if God has existed in the past, then God also exists in the present, whatever Nietzsche's Overman thinks. And if God is not in the present, then he was not in the past, and there is nothing to remember.

For Blumenberg, there is still a problem with the *being* of God if his discussion of the consort of the subjunctive is not to be meaningless. And there is still a problem with the truth and justice of the lives of those who no longer exist. Blumenberg has no solution to either problem. His argument reduces the incarnation to the (thoroughly traditional-sounding) statement that God has become like us and we have become like God. As does the theological tradition, he traces this back entirely to an action by God, although the meaning and basis of this action is reversed: God now knows more but is less. We, on the other hand, neither know more than we did nor are more than we were. For Blumenberg, God's taking of human form has no real consequences for us, but only for God, nor are they the best consequences for him: God is still only like us. Now "both the Creator and his creatures know what trouble death introduced into life."[19] The point of the theological doctrine of the incarnation, namely, that through and as a result of God's having taken human form we are on God's side because God has chosen to be on our side, has eluded Blumenberg. For him, God and his creature encounter each other within the memory of what has happened even though it did not necessarily have to happen and therefore might have been otherwise: "what had been reality becomes" for God "the possibility of an infinite 'free variation,'" whereas for the creature, by contrast,

19. Ibid. For Blumenberg, this is the only knowledge that "has been won for human beings": humans can now know "that, as a result of the passion, they *could* have a different God than they had before, if they wanted: a God who at last comprehends them and who will not let them bear alone the 'consequences' of the divine entanglement in the world, as was the case after the expulsion from paradise" (127–28).

the possibility is finite.[20] Both "have in common the memory of an existence involving pain and death";[21] it is only in the mode of that memory that they are still distinct from each other—if they are in a position to remember.

4. Incarnation as an Inversion of the Resurrection

The aporia of the traditional philosophical idea of God described by Blumenberg thus leads into the aporia of his own description. For how are we to conceive of God's being if not only we but also God himself are to realize the infinitude of the subjunctive? How are we to conceive of our being if we and God are to be consorts of the subjunctive? And what ought one actually to think when one attempts to think of incarnation? One has to go beyond Blumenberg in order to answer these questions, and when the questions are asked from God's perspective, the answers will be different from those to be found when they are asked from our perspective.

We have not yet begun to think through what Christian theology means by "incarnation" if we are talking merely about the involvement of the infinite God in the finite reality of creation and of the human race. What really is at stake here is not the fact that God became a created being and took physical form, nor the fact that God, by becoming human, has replaced the absolute distinction between Creator and creature with the relative distinction between a specific human, in whom and as whom he is present, and the rest of us human beings, even though this does matter. Rather, what is crucial is to understand the idea of the incarnation as the inversion of what the Christian faith expresses when it confesses its belief in the resurrection of the crucified Jesus Christ. It is not a matter of just any incarnation of just any god, but of the incarnation of the God who, according to the Apostles' Creed, raised the crucified Jesus from death into his eternal life. And this is not a question of God's involvement in just any human story, but of his making himself present in the story of Jesus Christ: incarnation is the idea of the *resurrection of the crucified one*, reflected in

20. Ibid., 128.
21. Ibid.

his death on the cross. Both events deal with the same question from
a different point of view. Whatever our thought encompasses when
we use the key term *incarnation* must also be encompassed when
we use the expression "raising of the crucified one," and vice versa.
And whatever cannot be encompassed by the use of the expression
"raising of the crucified one" cannot be encompassed by the idea of
the incarnation either.[22]

These doctrinal metaphors are not concerned with a generalized
transaction or a universal relationship, either between God and creation or between God and humans. Rather, what they refer to is the
very specific eschatological event we call "Jesus Christ"—in such a
way that the objective reality of the event is preserved and its universal
soteriological meaning is heeded. *Incarnation* and *resurrection* are
not universal concepts that could be expressed in various ways or
would be freely definable semantically, depending on the context. They
are basic metaphors or abbreviated metaphorical formulae for that
foundational eschatological event that, through the advent of what is
new—and can never become old—in the life of Jesus Christ renders
what is old in creation (not creation itself!) irrevocably old. These
basic metaphors cannot be properly understood except in narrative
form as a story—and indeed as one and the same story—in which
the eschatological coming of God to his creatures in his creation is
recounted. It is through this coming that the creation is fundamentally
renewed and brought to its goal.

5. Humans' Passive Gain of Being through God's Active
Giving of Being

Both these basic eschatological metaphors of Christian theology thus
give rise to similar problems. If in the resurrection Jesus "became God"
while retaining his humanity, then in the incarnation God "became
human" while retaining his divinity. How are we to conceive of the
being of the crucified Jesus in union with God's eternal life without
either negating Jesus's humanity (thereby blurring the difference from

22. See Ingolf U. Dalferth, *Crucified and Resurrected* (Grand Rapids: Baker
Academic, 2015), chaps. 1 and 3.

God) or understanding it as, among other things, a being that is merely remembered by God (thereby disregarding its relevance for God himself)? And how are we to conceive of the being of God in union with the life of Jesus, ending in his death, without either neutralizing God's own being as God (thereby obscuring the distinction between God and his creatures) or relating it only superficially and not essentially to this life (thereby overlooking God's self-determination of his being as God through his commitment to this life)? If there is any answer at all to these questions, they cannot have different answers, provided that the *resurrection* and the *incarnation* are concerned with the same eschatological event from different points of view. The two questions must receive one and the same answer, even if the form of the answer places particular emphasis on the specific aspect of the fundamental eschatological event that is addressed in the question.

How then can what is eschatologically new in Jesus's "becoming God" be encompassed under the key word *resurrection* in such a way that Jesus's humanity is preserved and the universal relevance of the event is simultaneously made clear? It must be done in such a way that we do not start from a preconceived idea of humanness. Instead, in the resurrection event we recognize the *humanness* of human "being" as that which is destined for eternal being in the presence of the life of God through what God did for the crucified Jesus so that he "became God." The true nature of human "being" is to be destined to live in union with God within the realm of God's eternal life. What human "being" truly is becomes evident in Jesus Christ's "becoming God."

And how can the eschatological newness of God's "becoming human" be contemplated using the key term *incarnation* in such a way that God's "Godness" is preserved and, at the same time, his relevance for everything else is made plain? The answer to this second question is wholly in keeping with the first. We are able to do this when we do not start from a preconceived idea of Godhead. Instead, we recognize God's *Godness* in this event to be that as which God has irrevocably defined himself: to be present to his creatures and to be there for humans. The true nature of the divine being as which God has defined himself is to be found in his living his eternal life in union with our human life: what God truly is became evident when he "became human."

That does not mean that in both instances a completely new understanding of "God" and "humans" has been established. This would
be a semantic impossibility if what we say is not to be ambiguous.
Rather, what we are saying is that the meaning of the word *human* is
to be unfolded theologically in such a way that every understanding of
humanness that is used as a hermeneutical starting point (and there
is always some kind of prior understanding) is refined, modified, and
given emphasis in the light of the resurrection: humans are beings
who, together with their world, are destined for eternal life in the
presence of God. Correspondingly, the meaning of the word *God* is
to be unfolded theologically in such a way that every understanding
of God that is taken as a starting point is refined, modified, and given
emphasis in the light of the incarnation. One must therefore make it
clear that, from an eschatological point of view, only the one who acts
in resurrection and incarnation deserves the name "God" and that his
Godness consists only in what he defines as such in the resurrection
and the incarnation. *God* is the one who is present to his creatures,
not only in life but also in death, just as he was present to Jesus Christ.
He is the one, therefore, whose creative work does not end with his
creatures' passing away, just as it did not start with their coming into
being. And similarly, God's *Godness* is the creative love with which
he remains present to his creatures even in death and brings them to
new life, just as he remained present to Jesus Christ and brought him
to new life. It is the love to which all new being owes its existence and
that indeed is the source of all being.

The basic eschatological metaphor of the incarnation thus points
to God's *specific* presence in *this specific* life: God is present to this
life in such a way that, within the realm of creation, God's presence
is manifest with and for us *sub contrario* (hidden beneath its opposite). Just as the earthly nonpresence of the raised crucified one
proves the effective presence in the world of the one who raises from
the dead, so too the earthly presence of the incarnate one in the life
and death of Jesus proves the apparent nonpresence of God to be
his hidden presence in the world. Considered from the perspective of
the resurrection, therefore, God's presence may be defined as present
nonpresence or *revealed hiddenness*, whereas considered from the
perspective of the incarnation, it may be defined as absent presence

or *hidden presence*. From both perspectives, however, it may be defined as that without which nothing real or potential would or could be, since it owes its existence wholly and entirely to the presence of God's effective love. Only where the objective reality of the incarnation metaphor is heeded can the presence of God, which is the focus of this metaphor, be defined in such a way that the character of its efficacy and the universality of its operation can be conceived of in concrete terms.

6. Blumenberg's Lack of Concreteness

If one takes the concrete specificity of the incarnation metaphor seriously, there are implications that render Blumenberg's variations on the theme problematic from the outset. One cannot begin within a preexisting understanding of God (even one from the Christian metaphysical tradition) and ask how incarnation could or would have been understood within that context. Nor can one begin with a preconceived understanding of humanity and ask how God could or would have become human in that sense. Thus in both cases the primary task must be to derive from the eschatological event, as summarized by the basic metaphor of the *incarnation*, an adequate understanding of God and humankind. In other words, we must arrive at a critical revision and redefinition of the received, existing understanding of God and humankind from the perspective of the incarnation. We are to define our idea of God within the context of his having taken human form, rather than defining the incarnation within the context of our (or any other) idea of God.

This is what Blumenberg does not do. He adheres firmly to the idea of the absolutely self-sufficient God of the metaphysical tradition and attempts to modify the incarnation story from his own perspective so that the *essential insufficiency*, and hence the inevitable *contingency*, of this God emerges who is conceived of as strictly absolute. Blumenberg reduces the issue of incarnation to the question of God's inevitable appropriation of contingent reality, and thus to the inevitable contingency of the absolute. Yet this covers at best a part of what is involved in envisaging God from the perspective of the incarnation. What is required is that we envisage not the unspecific appropriation of contingent reality as such, but God's engagement in precisely *this* life, so as to accomplish his *essential being-for-us* in the transformation of human life from old into new. Not only can God not be God without his appropriation of contingent reality, as Blumenberg seeks to show, but also he is only God for us at all as a result of his having "become human."[23] God is not God simply because he is distinct from the world, but because he is discernible *in* this world *as God* and can be understood *in his Godhead* in his presence with all that is real. No world exists without there being a reality that belongs to it; there is no God who relates only to a world but not to the reality in that world; there is no relationship between God and reality that does not constitute his effective presence with that reality, for it is only through his presence that that reality exists; and God's presence cannot be perceived as real in the world unless God makes a specific reality his own in such a way that in it he is perceived *as God* and understood *in his Godhead* in the world.

Allowing himself to be perceived as God within a reality, however, is different from becoming a reality within what is real. God's presence in and with what is real does not make him one reality within a series of realities that are mutually different from each other. For anyone who seeks God as an other among others, as an *ens* (being) among *entia* (beings), God is nothing. Even if nothing existed without God's presence, we are not able to apprehend this presence even if we apprehend the contingency of our existence. To know that I might not exist and that I do not owe my existence to myself does not mean knowing that I only exist because and to the extent that God is present. For that to be the case, God's presence must be discernible in the context of creaturely reality in a way that makes it distinguishable both from the presence of other creatures and from the nonpresence of something that does not exist. This takes place when God intensifies his presence with created beings to a presence among them that is discernible to them. He has done this by committing himself to and adopting a specific human life in such a way that

23. See Ingolf U. Dalferth, *Becoming Present: An Inquiry into the Christian Sense of the Presence of God* (Leuven: Peeters, 2006), esp. chaps. 3 and 4.

in it and through it he is manifest for us as God, thereby becoming identifiable as God in his Godness.

7. Appropriation of Contingency versus Actual Adoption of a Specific Life

Appropriation of a very specific world reality by God himself is therefore absolutely central to the incarnation. But this reality is the contingent, transitory reality, disfigured by evil and ending in death on the cross, of a very specific life. And the point of God's appropriation of this life is that, whatever else we might have thought, he has thereby proved himself irrevocably, within the sphere of the world, to be in his very essence a God for us. Unless one thinks of God as the God who has defined himself and made himself real as God in this human life, one is not thinking of God. One does not have to think of God; one can think of many things as God, and one can think of many things other than God. But one cannot think of *God* in any other way than the way in which he has made himself real in Jesus Christ. If God has defined and made real his Godness in the life, death, and resurrection of Jesus Christ, then God cannot be truly conceived of as God in any possible world in any other way. As far as understanding God is concerned, there are thus two central aspects to the incarnation metaphor: that God is only God in the appropriation of this specific reality, and that it is only therein that he demonstrates his Godness as a very specific kind of being, namely that of being God for us—as love. We must keep both in mind if we vary this incarnation and this specific story of becoming human.

Blumenberg's rereading of the incarnation disregards this, its objective reality, reducing it to a vague, unspecific appropriation and comprehension ("memory") of contingent reality by God. In reducing the details of the story of Jesus Christ to this generalization, Blumenberg's version of the incarnation retains only a vague and unspecific phenomenological nucleus. For to say that God represents the "possibility of an *infinite* 'free variation'"[24] would be an empty definition

24. Blumenberg, *Matthäuspassion*, 128 (emphasis added).

if nothing "that had been reality" were remembered.[25] Unless God remembers a contingent reality, one cannot speak of the "*possibility* of an infinite 'free variation.'"[26] Only what is real can be transposed into the subjunctive and then varied; only because God has an infinite recollection of contingent reality does he think something that is true, thus becoming conceivable (admittedly not as God for us, but) as a methodological boundary concept of a possible, recollective mode of dealing with the contingent reality of this world that is radically different from our own mode of recollection. This is the first important philosophical and theological consideration that emerges from Blumenberg's retelling of the incarnation event if we pursue it beyond Blumenberg: only a God who incorporates finite reality into his infinite memory, and thus into his own life, is in any way definable, within the horizon of our world and in contrast to us, as the *infinite* "free variation" of the finite.

8. More Than Just a Subjunctive

On its own, this of course is an idea of God that is philosophically and theologically minimalized and has highly problematical implications. This idea of God's infinitely recollective mode of dealing with finite reality is not only an obscure boundary concept that cannot be defined in more detail. A further implication is that in the divine memory our actual human life is apprehended as just one of an infinite series of possible lives. Thus, not only is its contingency recognized, but it also is at risk of becoming downright negligible—of less significance than a drop of water in the ocean. The envisaged "balancing" of our actual destinies by the subjunctive of our potential destinies thus appears to consist in the dissolution and extinction of our actual life in the ocean of possible lives.

Moreover, this underestimates the individuality and significance of human life. According to Blumenberg, however, God's reality and thus the "possibility of an *infinite* 'free variation'"[27] is also thereby

25. Ibid.
26. Ibid. (emphasis added).
27. Ibid. (emphasis added).

called to mind, or at any rate can, and probably also should, be called to mind. But what does this mean—not just for God's recollection of human life, and therefore for God, but for our recollection of God and hence for our human life? This is the other philosophical and theological question that arises from Blumenberg's problematic recasting of the incarnation event. What does it mean for finite human life that it recollects this infinitude? What happens when the horizon of infinite possibility opens up within finite factuality? What does human life turn out to be when God, in his divine presence, becomes manifest and perceptible within it?

We need to go beyond Blumenberg in emphasizing that then there is more to be recollected *eschatologically* than merely an "existence involving pain and death,"[28] namely, the determination of each actual life by the presence of God, a presence that is at work within it, whether discerned or not.[29]

This is not discernible as such, but only through the medium of its resonance in the human life—in other words, either as faith (the discerned presence of God) or as unfaith (the ignored presence of God).[30] This resonance manifests itself in a given life, not as one event among or alongside others, but within its fundamental existential passivity, the reverberation of the basic experience to which that life owes its existence. This passivity is the experiential correlation of the presence of God in the life of faith and (*per negationem ignorantiae* [through the negation of ignorance]) even the life of unfaith. Hence, when one speaks about God in faith, what one says is not to be understood in a theistically objective sense; rather, it is to be understood from the perspective of the experience of passivity. It is the anaphoric/cataphoric reference to the origin and perpetual determinant of life in its passivity, on which it is focused as the goal and fulfillment of its possibilities. And this experience of passivity is not an experience of deficiency but of gifting, distinction, enrichment, and empowerment.

This is what makes plain, in an *anthropological* sense, the degree to which human life is more than its actual enactment (i.e., as a successful

28. Ibid.
29. See Dalferth, *Becoming Present*, chap. 4, §5.
30. Cf. Ingolf U. Dalferth, *Radical Theology: An Essay on Faith and Theology in the Twenty-First Century* (Minneapolis: Fortress, 2016), chap. 11.

or an unsuccessful life, depending on whether it contradicts its destiny to be enacted in accordance with the effective presence of God's love).

And this also makes it clear in a *cosmological* sense that the world in which human beings live is not merely the actual world in which they find themselves, nor even merely the actual world including the possibilities in which they could find themselves. It is the sum total of the actual and the possible *as creation*—in other words, as the place whose existence is due to God himself and in which humans live out (or fail to live out) their destinies in the effective presence of the love of God.

9. Excess of Love

However, it is not the success or failure of a life that decides whether God is present in it or not. God's love is not a reaction but an action (or better, an activity): it precedes human conduct, rather than following it. It is only because God's love is at work in their lives before they ever concern themselves with it that humans are able to live a life that—measured in those terms—is successful or unsuccessful. The mode of their conduct (living their lives in faith or in unfaith) is a consequence of the presence of God's love in their lives, not a condition or prerequisite.

The fact that God is like that has no other ground than his love itself. His love does not seek to remedy a deficiency, either in humans or in God. It is what it is (love), which is why its effect is what it is (love). As love, it is the free surrender of the self to another, opening itself up to that other in order to foster his or her well-being (love of the other) and its own well-being (self-love). Its aim is to achieve a response, although it does not require one. As excessive affection for the beloved, it precedes the latter's conduct in a very specific way, while determining it in such a way that, whatever form it takes (whether rejection, acceptance, or disregard), it becomes a reaction to the proffered love. One who is loved can behave however he or she wishes: the lover will understand that behavior as a reaction to the proffered love. And one who loves creates a situation for himself or herself and the beloved in which nothing is neutral, excluded, or unrelated to this love. Where there is love, a life is determined by that love, not just partly but wholly and entirely.

If God is love, then, because he is God, he is free self-giving and self-opening for others. As God, he thus is always open to what he loves, whether or not this love is either returned or heeded. As love, God's self-mediation in the human life is not tied to any precondition on the part of his creatures. It comes about purely of its own accord and of its own free will, not as a reaction to a deficiency in created beings nor because of a deficiency on God's part. As such, love is surplus, prodigality, excess, the abundance of the more for the other. It contains its grounds in itself and needs no other extrinsic grounds. As love, God wants to be near those whom he loves. And as divine love, he comes so close to them that the excessiveness of his love is always more than they can grasp. That is all, and that is enough. It makes God's love unfathomable, but only because it is unambiguously love. God is not infinitely incomprehensible; rather, he is love in excess, love beyond which nothing greater can be contemplated, for it proves to be unfathomable, immeasurable, inexhaustible. Here everything depends on positioning the negative correctly. *God's love is unfathomable, but the fact that God is love is not.* To be able to say this positively is indeed the only good reason to speak of God at all. It is not lack but abundance that impels us to do so.

It is no accident that love has become the basic metaphor Christians use when they are speaking to or about God. This is not suggested by each and every life experience, as we all know; it took a lengthy period of historical development before Christianity arrived at an unqualified statement of this basic metaphor. Christianity does not describe God as love because it is a blatantly obvious truth that stares us in the face at every turn, but rather because the eye of faith recognizes him as excessive love for his creatures. And faith itself, as the mode of living rightly before God, only becomes conceivable when God is its source and origin. In order to understand what faith is, faith must be understood from God's perspective. Human life as such provides no convincing answers. Faith does not come naturally to it; indeed, it does not even allow faith as possible, let alone probable or plausible. Insofar as life is lived in unfaith—and this is how it is lived by us all—faith is not an issue, neither an actual nor a potential one.

One lives as one lives, and there is no reason to give any thought to the manner of one's life before God, or even to render account for it.

Of course we can find ourselves pondering it even so, since we are very likely to have questions concerning God, or the meaning of life, or the nature of what is good, true, and beautiful. But our questions are scarcely more than groping in the dark, since we do not know what we are looking for. We seek for "God," but we have no idea how we would know whether we have found what we are seeking. At one moment, the answer appears to be too small and slight in view of the vastness and weightiness of the question with which we are struggling. At another, we ask ourselves whether the answers are unsatisfactory because our own questions are too shortsighted. Neither the questions one has nor the answers one comes up with are beyond all criticism.

10. Radical Interruption

This is why faith, when we finally arrive there, is not a continuation of our question-and-answer search. Rather, it constitutes a radical interruption, dislocation, and discontinuity, even if in practice it happens not dramatically but very gradually and even if various different elements from before and after the faith event are still discernible. No deficiency can pave the way for the new event of faith to such an extent that our deficiency is removed and the questions we already had are answered. Faith is always more: surplus living out of surplus. If it were merely the removal of deficiency, then the deficiency would define what faith needs to accomplish in order to be existentially and intellectually convincing. However, this is a functionalization of faith, which squanders its incomparable newness and underestimates the way it appears from nowhere. Even when faith provides answers to the questions we had, we do not find answers alone: the questions change, and new questions are triggered. There are many questions in every life, and we do not find answers to them all. With faith it is no different: many questions remain open in faith too, and what is more, it generates new questions that one did not have before. For faith is not itself a phenomenon of life but a whole new field of vision by which to orient oneself among the complex and confusing phenomena of the human life.

As such a radically new orientation, faith would remain incomprehensible even to itself if it tried to understand itself from the perspective of what we had sought and found in our lives so far. Both biographical and autobiographical endeavors reach their limits here, for they neither lead to faith nor derive from it. Psychological, historical, sociological, or economic explanations give us a better view of some things. But they can only make the transition to faith comprehensible superficially, because they seek to understand it within the continuity of a story that does not recognize or allow for any complete breaks, but maps any discontinuity in terms of a sustained or wider continuity. But this is precisely not what faith is, even if one can describe it historically and biographically as something that does not continue a progression of this kind, but initiates a new progression. Thus it finds its purpose not in what has preceded it historically or autobiographically but in the interruption of these continuous processes that do not take it into consideration. It is rooted not in the antecedent life story but in the event that brings to light the truth that has hitherto lain concealed.[31]

So, in order to understand the conversion event from which it emerges, faith must begin with itself. It does this by postulating its own roots anaphorically, so that it relates itself to and comprehends itself from the perspective of that to which it owes its existence. This is precisely what it is expressing when it acknowledges the love of God. It gives the name "God" to its "whence" and the name "love" to that to which it owes its existence. "God" is the one who, in his love, enters the life of the other unreservedly so that he is in truth the infinite excess of love. And "love" is this unconditional self-giving by God without which it would be impossible to live one's life in faith. Both of these are strictly event-related definitions, and without their relationship with faith, which seeks to comprehend itself within that relationship, they lose their Christian meaning. Nothing merits the

31. This structure has been aptly worked out in detail under the category of a "truth event"—independent of all theological considerations—by A. Badiou, *L'être et l'événement* (Paris: Seuil, 1988). Cf. E. Pluth, *Badiou: A Philosophy of the New* (Cambridge: Cambridge University Press, 2010), chaps. 2 and 3.

name "God" unless it can function as the basis of the conversion from unfaith to faith and thus as the "whence" of faith. And nothing can function as that unless it can be called "love." This does not even begin to scratch the surface of the meanings of "love" and "God." But at least it identifies the event context that sheds light on their meanings. The event is the occurrence of God's love in a human life in such a way as to bring about its radical dislocation and disorientation in relation to what has occurred up to that moment and to open it up and give it new orientation in relation to what is to come. This occurrence of divine love is the indicative to which every subjunctive variation must be continuously related in order to be considered as a possible version of this event. If this relationship is withdrawn or ignored, then the subjunctives become meaningless, however delightful they sound.

11. The Inversion of Indicative and Subjunctive

To live in faith—to live at all, in fact—would be impossible without the prior gift of God's self-giving. But life itself does not provide proof of this—neither through its finiteness, nor through its contingency, nor through the heights and depths experienced in its good and bad times. All life's phenomena, both positive and negative, can always be understood differently, so they do not make it necessary for anyone to speak of God or even of God's love. On the contrary, they tend to encourage the opposite, even when there are equally few valid rational or experiential grounds to support either impulse. Only from a position of faith, whence it becomes plain that one's own prehistory was one of unfaith, does the fact emerge that life is more than what one experiences. Anyone who wants to talk about this has two stories to tell: how one used to experience one's life (as one's former life) and how one regards it now (as a life lived in unfaith). Both refer to the same life, but it can never be possible to draw them both into the unity of a single story. One did not experience one's former life as a life lived in unfaith, and faith does not originate from within what one then experienced, but from something wholly other: the prior gift of God's self-giving. As a prior gift, the latter never functions as compensation for a deficiency—whether of the created being or of the Creator. Rather, it is nothing other than an excess of love, and its origin is in nothing but itself, with which God becomes present in his creatures' present in such a way that their present no longer is merely the transition between the future and the past, but becomes the place where eternity becomes present in time.

In this way the present receives an added value in terms of meaning and possibility that we could never have extracted from it as it is. This means that it too must be assigned an irreducibly double meaning. If we understand this present as one of the three temporal modes of past, present, and future, in which human life relates to or orients itself in time, then the new possibility of living that begins here must be referred to in the subjunctive mood rather than the indicative. It is an unexpected possibility that could not have been garnered from the horizon of possibilities available in our human life; it only becomes a possibility for human life by defining this horizon in a new and different way. It is not a possibility intrinsic to this life: it transplants this life, with all its possibilities, into another horizon of possibilities, namely, that of the love of God.

On the other hand, if we understand this present as the place where eternity is present in time, then indicative and subjunctive are inverted, since we now must speak of the event of the love of God in the indicative, whereas we must speak of human life, within which this love eventuates, in the subjunctive: it could have been, and ought to have been, different. What would it have been like if that had been the case? What could it have been? And what might it have become?

This inversion of indicative and subjunctive at the location of the present is the expression of the fundamental reorientation that takes place when unfaith is exchanged for faith. What hitherto had been referred to using, at best, the subjunctive of the possible and for the most part only the *irrealis* (hypothetical) of the impossible now becomes the indicative of the actual and truly real. And what had up to now been expressed in the indicative of the past, present, or future now becomes the subjunctive and *irrealis* of something that, through the event of the presence of the love of God, is proved to be at best possible and at worst impossible. While it had been possible to live one's life in ignorance of having turned one's back on God, this state of affairs now proves to be an impossible possibility—a possibility that, within the horizon of the indicative of the love of God, cannot be conceived of as possible, but only as the negation of a possibility.

12. Analogy, Dialectic, Unity, Difference

Given the inversion of indicative and subjunctive in the light of the fact that the presence of God's love has intervened, the boundary line between possibility and impossibility must be redrawn. Therefore we now must differentiate between the indicative discourse and the subjunctive discourse, not just in one but in several ways. In that case, however, the possibilities to be contemplated from a philosophical point of view are not the same as those to be explored from a theological point of view. Even where both are endeavoring to elucidate the possibilities, the theological and philosophical thought processes do not coincide.

A philosophy focused on the possible alone admittedly would seem to run the risk of failing to see the indicative forest for the subjunctive trees. And yet it is essential to avail oneself of the indicative in order to recast something in the subjunctive: not everything can be recast in the subjunctive, because we can recast anything at all only in the indicative but not in the subjunctive. The subjunctive discourse remains grounded in the contingency of an indicative from which it cannot argue without availing itself of it as an indicative. This in itself leaves open, in principle, the possibility of imagining another indicative discourse that cannot be reduced to the philosophical one, but whose indicative can be recast as a subjunctive by calling on a different indicative, not the philosophical one. This is precisely what theology does.

Theology is confronted by three possibilities. First, it can draw everything as subjunctive into the indicative of the event, thereby resolving the indicatives of the human life into subjunctives of the divine event. But this would underestimate the relative independence of the contingent indicative of human life, and the distinction between *possible creation* and *contingent creation* would be withdrawn. But what is only possible does not coincide with what is in fact, even though in fact it might not have been. Only the contingent can be recast in the subjunctive, because it bears a relationship to an indicative. What is possible, on the other hand, can only be itemized, and a mere list of possibilities is not a recasting of them but a sequence of different items.

Alternatively, theology can take the contingency of the indicative of the discourses of everyday life, the sciences, and philosophy seriously but relate this indicative to the indicative of the divine event in such a way that this event turns out to be the full realization of that at which they can only hint in a vague and precursory way. The details of this model were worked out in the classical doctrine of analogy, which brought not only the possibilities but also contingent created reality and noncontingent creative reality together in a well-ordered relationship. Admittedly, it constantly had to identify the possibilities of this reality context and incorporate them into a common frame of reference, so as to require only one system of the possible and one hierarchically tiered system of reality. That could be convincing on the premise of an Aristotelian concept of possibility (the possible is all that was, is, or will be actual, and only that), but it became untenable, or at any rate highly questionable, on the premise of a Scotist concept of possibility (for every actual reality there is an infinite number of possibilities, most of which never were nor ever will be actual). For how, on these premises, is a plurality of worlds to be excluded in principle so that one can avoid pluralizing not only the concept of possibility but also the concept of actuality, thereby calling into question the unity of the one created reality? It was not, as is sometimes asserted, the univocity of the concept of being as applied to God and creation, but rather the concept of possibility that was the explosive charge that irreversibly shattered the medieval synthesis between the philosophy of the ancient world and Christian theology.[32]

This fragmentation then gave rise to the third possibility, which was realized in Luther's theology and determined not just modernity but

---

32. See Ingolf U. Dalferth, "*Possibile absolutum:* The Theological Discovery of the Ontological Priority of the Possible," in A. K. Min, ed., *Rethinking the Medieval Legacy for Contemporary Theology* (Notre Dame, IN: University of Notre Dame Press, 2014), 91–129.

also late modernity. The contingent indicative of the created and the
noncontingent indicative of the creative cannot be analogously related
so that they are integrated into the unity of a mixo-philosophico-
theological reality discourse; rather, theology has to shift into (at
least) two indicative discourses, with their respective forms of the
subjunctive and the *irrealis*, which are not reducible to each other
even though neither allows the other to be bypassed or avoided. From
its respective standpoint, namely, on the one hand *sapientia humana*
(philosophy—in the broad sense of all nontheological sciences)[33] and
on the other hand *plenitudo sapientiae* (theology),[34] each of these discourses represents a comprehensive universal discourse within which
everything can be encompassed. The philosophical discourse takes
as its starting point the perspective of this life (*huius vitae*),[35] from
which it can speak of God, his love, and a future form of human life
at best in the subjunctive or *irrealis* mood. The theological discourse
in contrast takes as its starting point life in both this and its future
form (*futurae formae suae vita*).[36] In order to do this not purely in
the subjunctive or the *irrealis*, theology has to relate to both from
a third standpoint, one that is not absorbed into either discourse.

It finds this standpoint at the point where God is not presented
as a "something," a topic for consideration (God as "object"), but
as a "someone" who presents himself for our consideration (God as
"subject"). This takes place when theology starts from the point where
we find not humans talking about God but God speaking to humans
(utterances in the first person: "I am the Lord, your God"), and where
humans speak not about but to God (utterances in the second person:
"You are my God"). The formula adopted by Reformation theology
to express this was "Word of God," and it unfolded this by moving
from the *verbum Dei aeternum* (the Second Person of the Trinity)
to the *verbum Dei personale* (Jesus Christ), thence to the *verbum
efficax* of word and sacrament, and finally to the *verbum externum*
(proclamation of the gospel) and *verbum internum* (Spirit-effected
assurance of the truth), treating this as the fundamental effective

33. WA 39/I:175.3–4.
34. WA 39/I:176.5–6.
35. WA 39/I:175.
36. Ibid.

context to which theological discourse concerning God must relate if it wants to speak about God from God's perspective and not ours. To speak about everything from the perspective of the Word of God, however, means that we must state everything twice over: from the perspective of this life and from the perspective of the life to come. This means, first, that theological discourse expresses everything, not from a single perspective but rather in the light of uncircumventable distinctions. Thus it talks, for example, not about *human beings* but about *sinful beings* and *righteous beings* or *justified sinners*; it refers not to *God* but to *Father, Son,* and *Spirit* or to *Creator, Redeemer,* and *Reconciler*; it speaks not of the *church* but of the *visible and invisible church, the church of experience and the church of faith,* and so on. Second, this means it sets up a reciprocal relationship between itself and philosophical discourse in such a way that the latter's indicative-subjunctive-*irrealis* framework is not resolved in the former's indicative-subjunctive-*irrealis* framework, but both are held together in the form of double descriptions. It thus is impossible to engage in theological discourse concerning God, humanity, reason, or love without distinguishing between philosophical and theological discourse concerning God, humanity, reason, and love and relating each to the other while remaining mindful of their differences.

The central theological task is not the preservation of the unity of a unified-discourse context along analogical lines, but accurate distinction between and disciplined handling of the differences inherent in an irreducible diversity of discourse along dialectical lines, translating the other discourse into one's own discourse, but in such a way that the differences are not eliminated but in fact multiplied.[37] The mark of this theological tradition is sensitivity toward distinctions, not the implementation of a unified perspective on everything. It does not shun the controversial diversity of life by retreating into a unified metaphysic that ultimately recognizes only one true and correct way of viewing everything. Rather, it seeks to draw attention in the individual life to the fact that—and the ways in which—life is open to more than what it can become of itself within its allocated

---

37. For a systematic and historical development of this idea, see Ingolf U. Dalferth, *Theology and Philosophy* (1988; repr., Eugene, OR: Wipf & Stock, 2002).

span. Only that which is more than it can become in its allocated span becomes more than it ever is within its allocated span. Only a life that is not classified categorically within the whole of reality is a living life. And only a living life, whose identity is not found in what it will and can become in and of itself, but in what God's love apportions to it, makes possible for it, and preserves it from, is the kind of life that has grounds for hope and whose future lies not in death but in the end of death.

7 ————————————

Creative Passivity

The Self-Belittlement of Human Beings

1. Who Are We?

Theology proclaims nothing new about heaven. It concerns itself entirely with the lives, beliefs, and hopes of human beings here on earth. It does not tell us anything fresh, but reminds us of what we have long known, or at any rate what was once well known to us all.

This means that many today are suspicious of it. In a situation of continuous change and innovation, the memory of the familiar can easily come to be seen as superfluous. But that is a fundamental misapprehension, and not just as regards theology. Sometimes even astronomers need to correct this misconception. In August 1845 King Friedrich Wilhelm IV of Prussia visited the newly erected observatory at the University of Bonn. His jovial greeting to the director, the astronomer Friedrich Wilhelm August Argelander, "Well, Argelander, what's new in the heavens?" received the reply, "Is Your Majesty well acquainted with what's old?"

The astronomer's answer is just as relevant today, and not just where royal personages are concerned. What is old is easily undervalued because one is no longer familiar with it. This is evidence not merely of a deficit of information but also of a loss of orientation. Many new things appear less fascinating when one compares them with the old, whereas others can be properly appreciated only when so compared.

Without the capacity for comparison, there is no ability to make a judgment, and to do this, one must be familiar with the new *and* the old.

2. Strange Questions

This applies to the question about ourselves as well. "Who are we?" We rarely pose this question. "Where are we?" is a much more frequent inquiry, especially in an unfamiliar city. Even "Who are you?" is a question with which we are familiar, even if we normally encounter it in the form "And your name is?" from friendly receptionists. It would be rather odd, to put it mildly, to respond with a ruminative query "Who am I?" And to respond by asking the question in the plural would be even more remarkable: we would be placing the other person in a position of uncertainty entirely inappropriate to the situation. To ask the question "Who are we?" randomly, without further explanation, is to invite misunderstanding.

When it is asked, however, it indicates that we have become uncertain about something that has been self-evident up to now. Generally speaking, we have no problem knowing who we are. If we are asked, we introduce ourselves, pull out our ID, or describe our role or position. But it would be a little strange when we are asked, "Who are you?" to reply, "a human being," and many, indeed, would find it inappropriate to answer, "God's creatures."

Anyone who asks us who we are assumes that we are human beings. It is precisely this out-of-the-ordinary question "Who are we?" that constitutes the uncontentious premise for ordinary questions we are asked. For if we reply, "human beings," that does not put the question to bed. It opens up further questions: What are human beings? Why are we asking? To whom is this of interest, and why?

The answer "God's creatures" is another matter entirely. Whereas the answer "human beings" has recourse to an uncontentious premise, the answer "God's creatures" does not. We take it for granted that we are humans when we ask questions of others or answer their questions to us, even if we have different notions of what exactly is to be understood thereby. That we are God's creatures, however, cannot be similarly taken for granted, for not only are there differing notions as to what is to be understood by "creatures," but also, and above all, as to whether one can, should, and wishes to understand oneself as such. If someone denies being a human, we regard that as a sign of confusion or assume that the person has not understood what "human" means. If, on the other hand, someone argues not to be God's creature, we regard that as the expression of a legitimate conviction, protected by the right to freedom of religious persuasion. It is not essential that we share this conviction, but we cannot impute it or its opposite to others. To dispute one's own humanity appears to us confused, whereas to dispute that we are created beings does not.

3. Our "History of Dis-illusion"

That was by no means always the case. There were times when it seemed just as self-contradictory to say "I am this or that—but not a creature" as it was to say "I am him or her—but not a human." The fact that we make a categorical distinction between the two instances has to do with the way in which we differentiate between the situations and the orientation systems in which we answer questions about ourselves. Police officers usually want to know different things about us than our children do; biologists are looking for different information than tax inspectors, shrimpers, doctors, or clergy. Anyone who answers such a question with "human" takes his or her place as a particular species of living being among other living beings. One who says "creature" places oneself, together with everything else, in a relationship to God, the Creator, and defines oneself as a special creature among creatures. In one scenario the question "Who are we?" is answered by reference to differences between living beings, that is to say, those differences one considers to be relevant. In the other scenario it is answered by reference to precisely two distinctions by which one orients oneself: those between *Creator* and *created being*

as well as those between *ourselves* and *other creatures*. In the one
case we are adopting a biological frame of reference; in the other, a
theological one.

They are two different horizons of orientation that we use to answer questions about ourselves, and they are not the only such horizons with which we are familiar. But that is not an end to the matter,
as is evident from our various approaches to challenging our own
humanity or creatureliness. Peter Sloterdijk calls the evolution that
led to differentiation between these two horizons of orientation "the
human history of dis-illusion."[1] Once—according to the well-known
myth of the expulsion from paradise—everything was "clear and
straightforward: the earth was the center of the universe and humankind was the crown of creation. Then, along came Copernicus and
displaced the earth from its central position. Charles Darwin followed,
declaring humankind to be one stage in the evolution of life."[2] And
today evolutionary biology and neurobiology are making increasing
efforts to level off this step and to rank human beings not simply as a
family on their own (Hominidae) alongside the anthropoid primates
(Pongidae) under the dry-nosed primates (Haplorhini), but instead
directly as anthropoid primates: the human being (*Homo sapiens*)
is the only surviving species of the genus (*Homo*) belonging to the
anthropoid primate family (Hominidae).

This would seem to provide as clear an answer to the question "Who
are we?" as one could possibly wish for: we are a particular species
(*sapiens*) of the human genus (*Homo*) of the anthropoid primate
family (Hominidae).

What is exciting about that? In what way is it dis(-)illusioning or
liberating, grounds for scandalization or, conversely, for celebrat-
ing the critical and enlightening achievement of modern science?
If the question "Who are we?" is concerned purely with a scientific
problem, all of this would be wholly incomprehensible. But there
are clearly other issues at stake here. Disillusioning, scandalizing, or
even liberating, we can only find a biological answer if we have posed
a question that in fact is not biological, if our question as to who

---

1. Peter Sloterdijk used this term in a lecture titled, "Weltglashaus und leeres
Firmament" (Hamburg Planetarium, July 10, 2006).
2. Hans-Arthur Marsiske, "Wer sind wir?," *Hamburger Abendblatt*, May 9, 2006, 12.

humans are deals not with a scientific problem but with something rather different. But what?

4. We Experience How We Live Our Lives

The reflexive format of the question "Who are *we*?" gives us a clue. We are not concerned with just anything, but with *ourselves*. Our inquiry is about ourselves, and even in our most lucid moments our interest in ourselves is never purely academic. In our changing circumstances we want to be perceived not simply as *the very same*; rather, we want to be taken seriously *as ourselves*. We are not just a special example of a biological species, but a unique self. We remain an example of the *same* biological species (*sameness*) throughout our lives, no matter what we become. A *self*, on the other hand (*selfhood*), is something that we become during our lives, not because we are different from crocodiles in the way we are but because we experience how we live our lives: we enjoy them, take pleasure in them, find them irritating or boring, want to hold on to them, or cannot wait to move on. In good times as in bad, life does not leave us cold: our attitude to it is not neutral; rather, we experience how we live our lives.

This has far-reaching consequences. Because we experience how we live our lives, we do not just live out our lives—we respond to them.

As Charles Taylor phrased it, we are "self-interpreting animals,"[3] whose relationship to ourselves is always one of self-understanding, so that we live our lives in the light of our own view of our lives.

The neuronal mechanisms of these processes currently are being intensively researched, with the result that the following, at least, can be said: the emotional, cognitive, and empathetic states of our body and its interactive processes are represented in the neuronal mechanisms within the modular structure of our brain. We experience how we live our lives (a difference between *living* and *experiencing*). As a result of this differentiation, there is an increasingly clear distinction between self and situation, in that, in a spiral movement of differentiation and patterning, our autobiographical self evolves as a mental

3. Charles Taylor, "Self-Interpreting Animals," in *Philosophical Papers*, vol. 1, *Human Agency and Language* (Cambridge: Cambridge University Press, 1985), 45–76.

function controlling the neuronal representations of our emotions, cognitions, and empathetic relationships (a differentiation between *self* and *situation*). Its first-person perspective (singular or plural) cannot be traced back to any second- or third-person perspective (a differentiation between *first person* and *third person*). As ourselves, we create our own view of ourselves and our world, so that we can and must respond to ourselves and our changing circumstances: interpretatively, by forming images of ourselves and our life situations; and creatively, by responding to the fact that we live thus and not otherwise, within specific parameters, even though we need not live in this way but in fact could live otherwise.

5. Choosing, Wishing, and Wanting

Our manner of life, then, is not self-evident: on the contrary, it results from decisions that allow some possibilities to become realities, while others do not. We can never become all that is possible, only what is possible in reality. We all have our dreams, but we know that much of what we dream will always remain impossible. Many languages rightly distinguish between *potentialis* and *irrealis*, the potential and the hypothetical; what can be, even if it is not; and what could be, even though it never can be. But the really possible is always more than what nonetheless can be realized consistently. Given the abundance of possibilities, we are compelled to choose, whether by actually living this way and not the other, or by deciding, deliberately and judiciously, in favor of one and against another.

What we can choose is also subject to time-related restrictions. It is dependent on what comes our way. What we and others have previously chosen and decided is a contributory factor, as is what we have become during our life so far. For any discussion to be meaningful, it is only against the background of this double conditionality that we can be said to be *free* to shape our lives: we are only ever recipients of the possibilities that come our way from time to time, and we are always tied to the reality of what we have become as a result of our own and others' decisions that have led us to live our lives in this way and not otherwise. The paths of our lives evolve as a series of contingent decisions within a realm of contingent decisions in which only one thing is constant: not only can we choose; we must choose. And while in most cases we could have chosen differently, we could never not have chosen.

6. Self-Image and Other-Image

But even this frequently invoked contingency of our life is not what is most important. Sometimes in fact we *cannot* live otherwise than we do, and not just because certain possibilities are not accessible to us here and now. In other words, the real world is not the way we would like it to be, but what is more, we have not wanted or been able to take hold of certain possibilities that were readily available to us, because they were incompatible with our self-image and our idea of what it means to be human. It is not the world or logic that prevents us from living thus, but we ourselves. Extortion and trafficking in drugs and human beings are lucrative areas. For human beings, it is perfectly possible to live this way, as we know. But *for us*, it is not possible, since we neither want to nor can, and the reason we neither want to nor can is that it is incompatible with our idea of what it means to be human. For us, it is not an actual impossibility, but an existential one. What this includes can and does change over time. But as selves, we are never without a self-image that sets us goals and boundaries.

However, how *we* experience ourselves and our lives is one thing; how *others* see it is quite another. Even the most precise scientific description of our life from the perspective of others is not a seamless rendering of how we, from our own perspective, experience what such a description documents scientifically. And no real-time monitoring of our experience with the aid of noninvasive imaging procedures to represent our brain activity, such as positron emission tomography (PET) or functional magnetic resonance imaging (fMRI) technologies, gives us anything more than neuronal corollaries of our experience. Our experience can be observed. But what is observed (our other-image) and how we experience it (our self-image) are not exactly the same.

7. Biography and Autobiography

One can see this from the difference between the *biography* and the *autobiography* of a life. Biographies can give an account of things that cannot be told autobiographically based on one's own experience: of the beginning and end of one's life, for instance, or of one's genetic, family, or educational background—matters of which one may never have become aware oneself. On the other hand, autobiographies can provide information about experiences, opinions, and value judgments that are inaccessible to a biographer unless the actual subject of the biography has imparted them.

Neither of these two ways of viewing a life is superior to the other in principle. Even if every last detail of a human life were plain for all to see (which never happens), the way in which the person experienced it would be far from being common knowledge. And indeed, what we ourselves believe we know about our own lives is never the whole truth. Contrary to what the Romantics thought, we do not have privileged access to our lives, but neither, as some empiricists have asserted, do others. Both we and others know some of what there is to know, but even together, we do not know it all. Each approach has its blind spots, which cannot easily be remedied by adding in or combining various approaches.

Briefly stated, our life is always more than we know or can know. What we know of ourselves is always less than others can know of us. But from another point of view, we also always know more than they are able to know of us. This is not self-contradictory but gives expression to the fact that human life is concealed, not just from biographers and scientists of all stripes, but also from itself, and from both in different ways.

8. Questions of Orientation

There is therefore more than one fundamental question concerning human beings and more than one answer to each question. The question "Who are we?" can be asked from either a biographical or an autobiographical perspective. It can raise a *scientific* problem to be solved scientifically by the appropriate research. But it can also raise a *practical* issue, an issue of life orientation, to which the sciences as well as philosophy and theology have a genuine contribution to make.

Such contributions are not rival answers to the same question. Theological anthropology is not a transcendental, nor even a "transcendent," biology of human beings, and neuroscientific insights into the way the human brain functions are no substitute for an epistemological philosophy of mind. Each of these disciplines asks and addresses the human question from a different key point of view: the sciences aim to explain reality, philosophy thinks through possibilities, and Christian theology seeks to provide direction. The former are carrying out experiments, the latter thought experiments: theology thinks through faith-life experiments that deal not merely with some issue or another but with the total orientation of a life. This makes them high risk, but the alternative is not risk-free security but a different life experiment, just as high risk. In critical comparison with other life orientations, both historical and current, Christian theology gives the following orientation to Christian life orientation: it is a second-order orientation discipline.

In fact, orientation is not only given in relation to orientation; it is in itself already a complex process, more complex than describing something, explaining it, or thinking it through in thought experiments. Orientation includes the reliable ordering of the world in which we live so that we find our place intelligibly within this order and are able to identify the standpoint, perspective, and horizon of the world in which we live, act, and perceive ourselves and what is other than ourselves.[4] Without a map of Hamburg, I would have had some difficulty finding the route from the airport to the planetarium. But the map on its own would have been little use if I had not known where I was (at the airport) and where to find the airport on the map. Both a shared order and our own positioning in the world are important for orienting ourselves.

If we ask the question "Who are we?" in this sense as a question of orientation, then it becomes a question about the ordering, orientation points, waymarks, and guidelines that give us direction in

4. For a more detailed analysis of the concept of orientation, see Ingolf U. Dalferth, *Die Wirklichkeit des Möglichen* (Mohr Siebeck: Tübingen, 2010), part 1.

an unpredictable world as together we seek, in our life experiments, to transform the improbability that our life will succeed into consciously chosen life risks.

It is the job of science to expand the knowledge that is important for just such an orienting of our lives. But science itself does not achieve this orientation. What is important is not just what the world is like and what we are like, but also what it and we could be, should be, and want to be. Even though we can never know enough to answer these questions from a scientific point of view, scientific knowledge on its own is never enough to answer them. Science, philosophy, and theology do not give different answers to the same question; they are dealing with different questions. Hence they can never be played off against each other. If we forget that, we will always be disappointed with their answers.

9. Lessing's Hesitation

This is precisely what characterizes the "history of dis-illusion" alluded to near the beginning of this chapter: it is a history of misunderstandings, and it has taken us a long time to detect this.

There are methodological reasons for this. In order to orient ourselves, we have to place ourselves in relationship with what is other than ourselves and compare ourselves with it. But comparisons are always drawn between things that are different in a certain respect and under certain conditions. If we compare ourselves with what is other, or from another viewpoint with what is the same, we will understand ourselves differently; and if the conditions change, familiar comparisons will lead to other results.

This is clearly expressed in a brief couplet from Lessing's *Religion* (1753).

> *Der Mensch, wo ist er her?*
> *Zu schlecht für einen Gott; zu gut fürs Ungefähr.*[5]

5. G. E. Lessing, "Die Religion. Fragment," in *Werke und Briefe in zwölf Bänden*, ed. Wilfried Barner et al. (Frankfurt am Main: Deutscher Klassiker Verlag, 1985–2003), 1:265: "Man, whence is he? Too bad to be the work of a god; too good for the work of chance."

There are two things here that are noteworthy. First, Lessing's question with regard to human beings is *whence they come*. He is looking backward, not forward. In his search for orientation, he is looking for an answer regarding the origin, not the future of human beings.

Second, Lessing's question about human beings uses *comparison*. In order to say who and what we are, we need orientation points we can use for direction in our search for an answer. We find these by comparing ourselves with others or with what is other. Two or more variables are compared with a third: *a* and *b* with regard to *c*; God and humans with regard to their mortality/immortality; humans and anthropoid primates with regard to use of tools, ability to learn, faculty of speech, and so on.[6] Without this kind of comparison, from specific perspectives generally deemed relevant, we cannot establish anything as regards our humanity, nor can we therefore assert our humanness at all.

Traditionally, there are three ways of carrying out this comparison. One compares the human being

1. with the *superhuman*, the divine, the gods, or God;
2. with the *nonhuman*, with animals, or specific animals (anthropoid primates); or
3. with what is *human*, with oneself, or with other humans.

All three approaches have been used from time immemorial;[7] each has its own difficulties, but they all share the problem that, in order to make the comparison, we need to know from the outset what we mean by "human." Just defining the reference parameters (superhuman,

6. F. de Waal, *Der Affe in uns: Warum wir sind, wie wir sind* (Munich: Carl Hanser, 2006).

7. Human beings, as is emphasised in Psalm 8, are neither God nor animal, but only "a little lower than the angels." In his *Pensées sur la religion et sur quelques autres sujets*, Pascal takes this up in his own way, commenting: "L'homme n'est ni ange ni bête, et le malheur veut que qui veut faire l'ange fait la bête" (Blaise Pascal, *Pensées*, ed. Michel Le Guern [Paris: Gallimard, 1977], fragment 572, p. 370). ("Man is neither angel nor brute, and the unfortunate thing is that he who would act the angel acts the brute.") Precisely because of our balancing act between two orientation points, humans are constantly in danger of plummeting headlong into superhuman hubris and inhuman bestiality.

nonhuman, human) demonstrates the basic methodological problem that they are framed from a human point of view and are therefore couched in anthropomorphic terms.

But with what should we compare ourselves in order to come up with acceptable answers? There was a lack of clarity about this even during the Enlightenment period, as Lessing's couplet shows. The old answers—God's creature, God's image—no longer carry weight; new and convincing answers are not yet in prospect. Lessing therefore left everything up in the air undecided and restricted himself to commenting on where humans do *not* come from: they are neither created by God (how could such a perfect being create so imperfect a creature?), nor have they simply dropped down from heaven.[8] Somewhere between accident and necessity is where humans are to be located. Lessing was unable or unwilling to say more.

10. Darwin's Provocation

To oversimplify a little, we may say that Lessing's comment sits on the borderline between the classic *ontological* and the modern *evolutionary* paradigms, between the type of thought that used categories of *being* and the type that used categories of *becoming*. In the ontological paradigm the world is perceived as *cosmos*, in which humans take their ontological place as living beings endowed with reason (*animal rationale*) or, in Christian terms, as the image of God (*imago Dei*). In the evolutionary paradigm, by contrast, the world is viewed as a cosmic process and the human being as an emergence phenomenon within the process of biological evolution. The implication of this for both the traditional philosophical understanding (*animal rationale*) and the theological understanding (*imago Dei*) of human beings remains an open question. Can these traditional definitions from the ontological paradigm still be considered valid in today's world, or does their evolutionary and neurobiological provenance mean that

8. See E. Jüngel, "Der Gott entsprechende Mensch: Bemerkungen zur Gottebenbildlichkeit des Menschen als Grundfigur theologischer Anthropologie," in *Neue Anthropologie*, vol. 6, *Philosophische Anthropologie*, ed. Hans-Georg Gadamer and Paul Vogler (Stuttgart: Georg Thieme, 1975), part 1, 342–72 (the quotation here appears on 346–47).

they have passed their plausibility expiration date once and for all and must be consigned to the refuse heap of history?

Even if the answer to this is no, the Christian understanding of humanity ought not to be equated with the formula found in the ontological paradigm. Otherwise, nothing remains from a theological point of view but the unhappy choice between adaptation or opposition. Moreover, in the face of the cultural paradigm shift toward evolutionary thinking, neither orthodox rejection nor modernistic *aggiornamento* is of any help. The crucial question is not, "How can the old understanding be sustained under the new conditions?" Rather, it is, "From a Christian point of view, what can we say in theological terms *under present conditions*, regarding the human race?"

To answer this question, we need to change our direction of sight so that our understanding of human beings is no longer defined from the perspective of their origin, but from that of their future: what defines who we are is not where we come from but what we are becoming.

This change in the direction of the question is the result of the paradigm shift in the understanding of the human race that Darwin initiated, although he himself did not begin to work through it fully in a systematic way. He too still took the question of origin as his basis, but he altered the point of reference for the orientating comparison: the human question is to be answered from the animal, not the human point of view. Ever since Plato it had been held that the human being possessed an immortal soul since our universally accepted basic ideas could not be convincingly derived from experience but require a preexisting soul as a presupposition.[9] Darwin, however, countered this laconically with the words "read monkeys for pre-existence."[10] The scientific affront to the traditional conviction

9. Plato, *Timaeus* 90a2–7: "We are a plant whose roots are not in earth but in the heavens."

10. "Plato says in Phaedo that our '*necessary ideas*' arise from the pre-existence of the soul, are not derivable from experience.—read monkeys for pre-existence"; see Charles Darwin, "Notebook M," in *Notebooks 1836–1844: Geology, Transmutation of Species, Metaphysical Enquiries*, ed. P. Barrett et al. (Cambridge: Cambridge University Press, 1987), 520–60 (the quotation here appears on 551, dated September 4, 1838).

of the special status of the human being could hardly have been more succinctly put. The outcry was proportionately loud, and the discussion between his advocates and opponents has been fiercely contested ever since.[11]

11. Nietzsche's Appeal

Moreover, there was not simply either assent or contradiction, but even contradiction within the assent. Nietzsche was a prime example of this. "We have changed our minds. We have become more modest in every way. We have stopped deriving humanity from 'spirit,' from 'divinity'; we have stuck human beings back among the animals."[12]

Nietzsche was far from wanting to revise this. But he does not entirely hold to it either. "Has the self-belittlement of man, his *will* to self-belittlement, not progressed irresistibly since Copernicus? Alas, the faith in the dignity and uniqueness of man, in his irreplaceability in the great chain of being, is a thing of the past—he has become an *animal*, literally and without reservation or qualification, he who was, according to his old faith, almost God ('child of God,' 'God-man'). . . . Since Copernicus, man seems to have gotten himself on an inclined plane—now he is slipping faster and faster away from the center."[13] Where once we saw a "child of God," we now see an animal, without the quotation marks.

The new aspect of the evolutionary-biology answer is not comparison with animals, nor even with apes, but rather the point that, in order to eliminate the distinction between animals and humans—as Nietzsche does—human uniqueness must be understood wholly from the perspective of human animality (rational *animals*), and no longer from that of a human rationality (*rational* animals) that is or

---

11. See E. Haeckel, *Die Welträthsel: Gemeinverständliche Studien über monistische Philosophie* (Bonn: Emil Strauß, 1901).

12. Friedrich Nietzsche, *Der Antichrist: Versuch einer Kritik des Christentums*, §14, KSA 6:180. English translation: *The Anti-Christ, Ecce Homo, Twilight of the Idols, and Other Writings*, ed. Aaron Ridley and Judith Norman, trans. Judith Norman (2005; repr., Cambridge: Cambridge University Press, 2006), 12.

13. Friedrich Nietzsche, *Zur Genealogie der Moral*, Dritte Abhandlung, §25, KSA 5:404. English translation: *On the Genealogy of Morals*, trans. Walter Kaufman and R. J. Hollingdale (New York: Random House, 1967), 155.

can be differentiated from it. As Heraclitus put it, "In comparison with God, the wisest human seems like an ape in terms of wisdom, beauty and all else."[14] But he immediately added, "The most beautiful ape is ugly when compared to a human."[15] Just as the dissimilarity between God and humans exceeds their similarity, so it is between humans and animals. No animal is like a human, even as a human is not God. Humans are indeed animals, but—and this was the evidentiary basis for every idealistic model—they are *rational* animals, animals with reason.

Darwin made it clear that even the rational animal is first and foremost an *animal*. Nor does Nietzsche dispute this, although he reminds us that it is true that humans are animals, yet no animal is like a human. But what marks out the human animal from among the animals?

The traditional answer—relationship with God, evident in reason and rationality—was not an option for Nietzsche. "God is a conjecture, but I want that your conjecturing not reach further than your creating will. Could you *create* a god? Then be silent about any gods!"[16] We should limit conjectures to things we can make ourselves. God is not among them. Human beings are distinguished from the rest of the animals by what they can make, and what they can make of themselves.

This is the precise nub of Nietzsche's diagnosis of "the self-belittlement of humankind": only human beings can belittle themselves, and only human beings can understand themselves as mere products of the evolutionary history of life. Precisely the human "will to self-belittlement" proves to be a paradoxical indication of the uniqueness of human beings. As animals they can desire to be *mere animals*. But as mere animals they can also desire to be *more than animals*. They can reach out beyond what they indisputably are: animals.

Nietzsche's Zarathustra puts it like this: "All creatures so far created something beyond themselves; and you want to be the ebb of

14. Heraclitus, *Die Fragmente der Vorsokratiker*, ed. H. Diels and W. Kranz (Zürich: Weidmann, 1951), 1:6, 169 (B83).

15. Ibid., 1:169 (B82).

16. Friedrich Nietzsche, *Also sprach Zarathustra II. Auf den glückseligen Inseln*, KSA 4:109. English translation: *Thus Spoke Zarathustra: A Book for All and None*, ed. Adrian del Caro and Robert B. Pippin (Cambridge: Cambridge University Press, 2006), 65.

this great flood and would even rather go back to animals than overcome humans? What is the ape to a human? A laughing stock or a painful embarrassment. And that is precisely what the human shall be to the overman: a laughing stock or a painful embarrassment. You have made your way from worm to human, and much in you is still worm. Once you were apes, and even now a human is still more an ape than any ape."[17] We face the decision as to whether we want to be mere animals or more than humans. We are compelled to choose both options because we are not simply what we are but make ourselves into what we want to be: animal—or more than animal, human—or overman.

It is here that we first encounter the crux of Nietzsche's objection to Darwin: human beings are wholly animal, but they are what they are only because and to the extent that they *want to be* it. However, if they want to be animals, they in fact could be more than that—more than animal and more than human. And if they could, then they should: human beings are who they *want* to be and what they *make of themselves*. We cannot make God. "But you could well create the overman. Not you yourselves perhaps, my brothers! But you could recreate yourselves into fathers and forefathers of the overman: and this shall be your best creating!"[18]

Nietzsche's appeal is unambiguous: we can and should be *more* than we are. This more is not to be sought in what we share with animals (our capacity for pathos and passion, for suffering and distress), but in what differentiates us from them. And what differentiates us from them above all is the ability and possibility we possess to use thought and action, reason (*logos*) and will (*ethos*) to make more of ourselves than we are. We can belittle ourselves, but this very capacity for self-belittlement demonstrates our capacity for self-aggrandizement. We can surpass ourselves: humans are not transcendent beings, but *self-transcending beings*, animals who can and should raise themselves, not just above their animal nature but even above their human nature.

It is impossible to say in advance where that will lead. We are stepping into a new and open realm, governed by just one principle:

17. Ibid., 14 (*Thus Spoke Zarathustra*, 6).
18. Ibid., 109 (*Thus Spoke Zarathustra*, 65).

we are who we become, and we will become what we make ourselves. We are the products of our will and our action, of our will to power.

12. The Will to Power

That is—as Nietzsche constantly insisted—rejection of the herd mentality and the herd morality, rejection of the misconception that "the *meaning of all culture* is to breed a tame and civilized animal, a *domestic animal*, out of the beast of prey 'man.'"[19] This merely has the result "that things will continue to go down, down, to become thinner, more good-natured, more prudent, more comfortable, more mediocre, more indifferent, more Chinese, and more Christian."[20] Yet what everyone wants, what is held by all to be good and right for all,[21] is not what is good, right, and proper for me just because it makes me into me. Rather, I become who I can be only by wholly and exclusively following and making space for my own will, so that instead of striving for equality and conformity with others, I cultivate the "pathos of distance."[22] Otherwise there is an inexorable slide into mediocrity, into the "degeneration and diminution of man into the perfect herd animal," the "animalization of man into the dwarf animal of equal rights and claims."[23]

Nietzsche recognized that this was possible. But it does not have to be like this. For if human beings can turn themselves into dwarf animals, they also can do the opposite. It is our "*will* to self-belittlement"[24] that is decisive, not our will to *self-belittlement*. We are *will*, the will to power, and "man would rather will *nothingness*, than *not* will."[25]

19. Nietzsche, *Zur Genealogie der Moral*, Erste Abhandlung, §11, 5:276. English translation: *On the Genealogy of Morals*, trans. W. Kaufmann and R. J. Hollingdale (New York: Vintage Books, 1989), 42.

20. Ibid., §12, 5:278 (*Genealogy*, 44).

21. Ibid., §14, 5:282 (*Genealogy*, 47–48).

22. Ibid., §2, 5:259 (*Genealogy*, 26).

23. Friedrich Nietzsche, *Jenseits von Gut und Böse*, §203, KSA 5:126–28. English translation: *Beyond Good and Evil: Prelude to a Philosophy of the Future*, trans. Walter Kaufmann (New York: Vintage Books, 1989), 117–18.

24. Nietzsche, *Zur Genealogie der Moral*, Erste Abhandlung, §25, 5:404 (*Genealogy*, 155).

25. Ibid., §28 (cf. §1), 5:412 (cf. 339) (*Genealogy*, 163 [cf. 97]).

This is where one must begin, and then one can see that there are grounds to hope that humans can turn themselves into something entirely different from what is suggested by present-day herd humans, with *resentment* as their guide. Then it becomes plain that, so far, the human being has been a self-misunderstanding, a being who wanted to be something different from what he or she is, not an animal but a rational being, one who therefore has made himself or herself into something wholly false, into a morally mythical being.

The crux of Nietzsche's argument is clear: human beings are to be understood decisively as animals that can make something of themselves and whose primary life instinct is the will to power. No one can breed this will out of them, however much it may have been distorted and belittled by the cultural control mechanisms of a reason controlled by resentment, which is why human beings are able to redesign themselves taking this will as a starting point. Of course they can only do it *themselves* and do not need anyone to stipulate what they are to make themselves into (self-becoming as *self-creation*). That presupposes that, as the "poets of [their] lives,"[26] they first of all design and develop themselves, whatever implications this may have for others (self-creation as the *will to power of the strong*, who care nothing for the ideology of equality of the weak, arising as it does out of resentment). To achieve this, they must act entirely on their own behalf, without heed to their fellow humans (self-creation as *a heroic existence without one's fellow humans*). This drives them into a fundamental solitude, as Nietzsche powerfully portrays in the figure of Zarathustra: only as a solitary can we follow the path to ourselves.[27] Those who make themselves independent of the opinions of others and who go in search of themselves find their home in solitude.[28] Instead of the agreement of others, their opposition, hostility,

26. See Friedrich Nietzsche, *Die fröhliche Wissenschaft*, Viertes Buch, "Sanctus Januarius," §299, KSA 3:538; Nietzsche, *The Gay Science*, ed. Bernhard Williams (Cambridge: Cambridge University Press, 2008), 170.

27. See Nietzsche, *Also sprach Zarathustra*, vol. 1, "Vom Wege des Schaffenden," 4:80 (*Thus Spoke Zarathustra*, 47: "Lonely one, you go the way to yourself!").

28. Ibid., vol. 3, "Die Heimkehr," 4:231 (*Thus Spoke Zarathustra*, 146: "Oh solitude! Oh you my *home* solitude! I lived wild too long in wild foreign lands to not return to you with tears!").

and exclusion indicate that one is on the right path: "You lonely of today, you withdrawing ones, one day you shall be a people: from you who have chosen yourselves a chosen people shall grow—and from them the overman."[29] Alone, he follows his own will to power, like a lion that pays no heed to others, but is what he is by being what he wills himself to be: "Hungry, violent, lonely, godless; thus the lion-will wants itself."[30]

13. Barth's Critique

Karl Barth saw clearly, as few others have, that this is where the real problem with Nietzsche's concentrated philosophical endeavor lies: Nietzsche promulgates a "humanity without the fellow-man."[31] His systematic direction of the vision toward the individual's will to power isolates and abstracts such an individual from a social context with a sense of shared humanity: the only human being in whom Nietzsche is interested—"We are weary of *man*"[32]—is not the herd human but the lion, who, proud and solitary, goes out hunting. This human without fellow humans is strikingly portrayed in Nietzsche's Zarathustra. For Nietzsche, Zarathustra is the "most affirmative of all spirits,"[33] who in no sense understands himself as opposed to others and is therefore free from all resentment. "At every moment here, humanity has been overcome, the idea of 'overman' has become the highest reality—everything that was considered great about people

---

29. Ibid., vol. 1, "Von der schenkenden Tugend," 4:100–101 (*Thus Spoke Zarathustra*, 58).

30. Ibid., vol. 2, "Von den berühmten Weisen," 4:133 (*Thus Spoke Zarathustra*, 80).

31. Karl Barth, *Die kirchliche Dogmatik*, III/2, 273 (*Church Dogmatics,* III/2, 233). I learned what follows from a seminar paper by M. Böger ("Humanität. Ein Vergleich zwischen Karl Barth und Friedrich Nietzsche," University of Zürich, fall semester 2010.

32. Nietzsche, *Zur Genealogie der Moral*, Erste Abhandlung, §12, 5:278 (*Genealogy*, 44). Cf. Nietzsche, *Ecce homo: Warum ich ein Schicksal bin*, §6, KSA 6:371 ("*Ecce Homo:* Why I Am a Destiny," chap. 6 in Friedrich Nietzsche, *The Anti-Christ, Ecce Homo, Twilight of the Idols, and Other Writings*, ed. Aaron Ridley and Judith Norman, trans. Judith Norman [2005; repr., Cambridge: Cambridge University Press, 2006], 148: "My danger is *disgust* with people.").

33. Nietzsche, *Ecce homo: Also sprach Zarathustra*, §6, 6:343 (*Ecce Homo: Thus Spoke Zarathustra*, §6, 129).

lies infinitely far *beneath* him."[34] Such a human being recognizes none other but himself. In Zarathustra, according to Barth, Nietzsche allows the overman character to appear on the scene "without condition or restraint, in all its nakedness."[35] There are no others, where he is concerned, which is why it is not accidental but essential that he is alone. "If there were others, he would not be Zarathustra."[36]

Nietzsche viewed Zarathustra as his greatest gift to humanity: "With it, I have given humanity the greatest gift it has ever received."[37] This gift consists precisely in the fact that it preaches neither moral code nor faith, for "these are not the words of some fanatic, nothing is being 'preached' here, nobody is demanding that you *believe*."[38] This gift raises up no ideal figure to set us on a predefined path, since each of us can only find out for ourselves who we are by listening to our own will and living it out. "I will go by myself, my disciples! You go as well, and alone! This is what I want. . . . You admire me: but what if your admiration *subsides* someday? Be careful not to be killed by a statue!"[39] Where there is such an emphasis on solitude and aloneness, the reference to "gift" becomes a problem, in Barth's view: "To whom is he, the overman, the absolute 'I am,' to give himself?"[40] Here there can be no reference to self-surrender, self-giving, love, let alone excess of love. Zarathustra can only will "lion-will," and one cannot give this to others as a gift. One can only bring them to the point of making themselves into lions—into animals that, without regard to others but simply to themselves, make of themselves whatever they can. This cannot be called a gift-giving or "bestowing virtue"—it neither gives anything, nor is it a virtue.[41] It gives no gift; it is not even an aid to self-help; it is a challenge to pay heed to oneself without regard to one's fellow humans and, abandoning the mediocrity of the herd, turn oneself into a free beast of prey, a hyperborean overman.

34. Ibid., §6, 6:344 (*Ecce Homo: Thus Spoke Zarathustra*, §6, 130).
35. Barth, *Kirchliche Dogmatik*, III/2, 279 (*Church Dogmatics*, III/2, 233).
36. Ibid.
37. Nietzsche, *Ecce homo*; Vorwort, §4, 6:259 (*Ecce Homo:* Preface §4, 72).
38. Ibid., 260 (*Ecce Homo:* Preface §4, 73).
39. Ibid.
40. Barth, *Kirchliche Dogmatik*, III/2, 279 (*Church Dogmatics*, 234).
41. See Nietzsche, *Also sprach Zarathustra*, vol. 1, "Von der schenkenden Tugend," 4:97 (*Thus Spake Zarathustra*, 55).

14. Open Horizon

What in Nietzsche's day might have sounded untimely has long since entered current thinking. Whereas he still believed that humanity has rolled away from the midpoint of things since Copernicus, today we no longer have any idea what and where such a midpoint might be. Hence we can no longer describe ourselves as beings who have rolled to the edge: midpoint and edge are not the metaphors that mark out the location of human existence in the world, but accidental position and open horizon. If, in addition, we take into account the breathtaking speed of the development of global consciousness on the internet, accessible as it is from everywhere, it would appear that metaphors of location have served their purpose, as regards the definition of what it is to be human. We can no longer answer the question as to who we are by pointing to where we are. Our location does not define us; rather, we define our location—socially, cosmologically, and biologically.

This results in a significant shift. The monistic image of a unified world with a center and a periphery is replaced by the pluralistic image of a plethora of world perspectives, framed from varying positions: humans are not located somewhere or other in the world, at the center or on the periphery; rather, they frame their world themselves from their respective standpoints. World is whatever is related to humans, in the multiplicity of their situations, as their primeval world, their environmental world, their social world, and the world of their posterity, together with whatever the neural network of their brains represents to them as world.

Whereas at one time humans could be defined by the categories of their existence and location, today the categories of time, process, and construction must be included. "I am. But I do not possess myself. That is why we are still only becoming," wrote Ernst Bloch forty-five years ago, with a cogent change of tense and number.[42] Today, in our biotechnical age, we need to give this extra focus: "I am. But I do not possess myself. That is why *we are still making ourselves*." From being an ontological topos with a stable horizon of possibilities, the

---

42. E. Bloch, *Tübinger Einleitung in die Philosophie* (Frankfurt am Main: Suhrkamp, 1963), 11. The focus of his thesis on self-possession clearly shows the limits of his turn toward shared becoming.

human being becomes an open utopia shaped by himself. It is not what we are that determines our humanness, but what we are yet to become, not our reality, in which the story of our biological, social, and cultural origins is summed up, but the opportunities we have grasped, that open up to us a future in which we become what we make of ourselves. No longer are we defined by our position in the world; rather, we define our position, which is why our existence is literally utopian. We become what we make of ourselves, and it is impossible to tell where we will end up as a result.

This leads to a radical intensification of something that began in the Renaissance: the discovery of the creative power of the human being, experienced as liberation. In the Renaissance era it took the form of a return to an idealized antiquity; today it is instead an anticipation of a utopian future. But then as now, human beings are represented as makers—then as those who make something new, today as those who make something new of themselves.

15. The Rational Animal as the Image of God

The ancients understood the world as a well-ordered cosmos and humans as determined by the details of their ontological position within the cosmos. They are *animal rationale*, and as such they are classed in their entirety as living beings (not inanimate objects) who differ from all other living beings because of their *ratio* (their reason, rationality, and language). They share with the animals the pathetic (the capacity for suffering and distress) but are distinguished from them by *logos* and *ethos* (a reason that has a capacity for truth and a will that is guided by reason).

Ancient thought saw this specific difference as derived, from a source other than the animality of the human. "The gods plant reason in mankind / Of all good gifts the highest," writes Sophocles in *Antigone*.[43] The idea takes many and various forms,[44] but the statement of

43. Sophocles, *Antigone*, lines 683–84.
44. See Pythagoras: "We humans come from another life and nature into this life," cited by Cicero in his *Tusculan Disputations* (Zurich: Artemis & Winkler, 1992), 323 (line 9).

the essentially human in terms of the divine, rather than the animal, remains the predominant answer to the human question until late in the eighteenth century.

That applies even when—as with Lessing—the origin of the specifically human is left open or—as with Herder—is described as a particular way of reorganizing the animal traits of the human being: "While still an animal, man already has language," writes Herder in his *Treatise on the Origin of Language*,[45] although at the same time he maintains that it is nonsense to seek to derive human language from the cry of animals.[46] But Herder also holds the traditional thesis that reason and language have been implanted in humans from elsewhere to be philosophical nonsense,[47] on the grounds that this makes the human being into an inconsistent amalgam of finite and infinite, temporal and eternal, conditional and unconditional. Herder therefore seeks to develop them "from the general animal economy"[48] but is unable to do so because he lacks the necessary categories. Even when one tries to categorize human beings as wholly animal, they are still *animal rationale*, a type of being that, until Darwin, was extraordinary and whose individuality distinguished them from other living beings, not merely in degree but by category.

After its own fashion, Christianity accepted this traditional view of humans and reconstructed it in the light of biblical creational thinking. Thus the cosmos is defined theologically as the creation, and the *animal rationale* as the image of God and hence as the goal and crown of creation: human beings are those for whose sake everything is created and who are created to praise and revere the Creator.

45. J. G. Herder, "Abhandlung über den Ursprung der Sprache," in *Werke*, ed. U. Gaier (Frankfurt am Main: Deutscher Klassiker Verlag, 1985), 1:695–810 (the quotation here appears on 697–98).

46. "I cannot conceal my amazement that philosophers—people, that is, who look for clear concepts—ever conceived of the idea that the origin of human language might be explained from these outcries of the emotions: for is not this obviously something quite different?" (ibid., 708).

47. "The attempt has been made to think of man's reason as a new and totally detached power that was put into his soul and given to him before all animals as a special additional gift and that, like the fourth step of a ladder, with three steps below, must be considered by itself. And that to be sure—no matter how great the philosophers were who said so—is philosophical nonsense" (ibid., 717–18).

48. Ibid., 716.

This means that humans are not so much the focal point of creation as its apex. They are distinguished from all other creatures as the "image *of God*," whereas they are distinguished from God as his created "*image*." If we interpret the idea of image according to the logic of archetype and copy, then the human being becomes the mirror in which we recognize (albeit brokenly) the essential features of the divine and the creaturely. As reason and will they are finite and imperfect copies of the perfect reason and infinite will of God. At the same time, it becomes apparent in them what is true of the whole world as experienced by the senses: it is the temporal copy of the eternal creation in which God's perfect ideas are the timeless archetypes of all temporal realization processes—with the result that nothing can become real in our world unless it has been intended in advance as a possibility in the archetypes of the divine spirit and its final realization has been planned for.

The consequence of this way of seeing things is that there can be nothing new under heaven—or at any rate nothing new that is not a temporal, imperfect copy of an eternal and perfect archetype. This is true not only for all phenomena in the world, the condition of whose possibility and source of whose reality are the eternal ideas of God, but also for humans themselves, who in their state (as fallen sinners remote from God) are historical copies of the Adamic archetype (the old self), and in their redeemed and delivered state (as believers) are a historical copy of the archetype Jesus Christ (the new self).

16. The Secularization of the Idea of Human Godlikeness

Toward the end of the Middle Ages, however, it was this image that led to the abandonment of a view of humanity and the world erected on correspondences between the eternal and the temporal. The more we see the similarity between Creator and creature not just in the *logos* and *ethos* of humanity but also in human creative activity, so that human creativity shifts to become the central focus of interest, the clearer it becomes that, under the logic of the idea of human likeness to God, human beings are indeed *created* beings, but, as the *image* of the Creator, are themselves "minicreators," *homo faber* (man as

maker), *homo pictor* (man as artist), *homo creator* (man as creator)—
those who make, create, and depict themselves and their world. The
human is not merely one who copies divine archetypes; the human
brings forth genuine innovations, both scientific and technological,
that previously did not exist and, furthermore, are not based on any
paradigm of the Spirit of God.

In his dialogues with a layman, reflecting the scholarship of his period, Nicholas of Cusa places words in the mouth of a simple craftsman
who takes a spoon as his example: The spoon has no divine archetype
beyond the spirit of the spoon carver. It is a free human creation.[49] The
example is as trivial as it is far-reaching. Human godlikeness is not
rooted in human beings' createdness but in their role as creators, in
human creativity, since through generating knowledge and the products
of their activities they create themselves and their world.

Thus human beings *confront* the world in a manner previously
unimaginable. They become *subjects* who use and consume what
the world provides as *objects* from which they shape themselves and
their environment. Human beings have no locus in the world; they
create their world and today to an increasing degree themselves—*their
world* by permanently remodeling nature in culture, and *themselves*
by the cultural and biological reshaping of their own nature. *Causa
sui*, self-creator, once exclusively the divine predicate, is increasingly
a predicate applicable to humans, who create themselves and their
world. We are what we make ourselves into; we are the designers of
our world and of our humanity.

17. The Debasement of the Human Being's Special Status

In the intervening time this view of humankind has become fully
emancipated from its theological background. Hence the question as
to who we are is now answered from the perspective of the biological
evolution of life. Such an evolution gives rise to endless new forms of
life that presuppose earlier life forms from which, however, they are
not causally derived. How animals could have become human and

49. N. von Kues, "Idiota de Mente," in *Philosophisch-theologische Schriften*, ed.
L. Gabriel (Vienna: Herder, 1967), 3:479–609 (the quotation here appears on 492).

how the human spirit could have developed out of animal life was an
insoluble mystery for the entire classical tradition right on into the
nineteenth century. The concept of emergence, however, renders it
conceivable without recourse to the idea of a divine origin of spirit
or a Creator of humankind. If reason, spirit, and free will are emergence phenomena and hence products of evolution, then they are no
longer signs of the divine in humankind. Once these are viewed as the
reasons for the human being's special status among the animals, the
anthropological basis for a knowledge of God and creation crumbles
as well, and epicyclic rescue attempts such as the anthropic principle,
the fine-tuned-universe argument, or the intelligent design model do
not change anything.[50]

The debate being conducted so fiercely at present concerning the
neuroscientific challenge to the concept of free will is, from a theological point of view, a sideshow. In the debate over the neurophysiological questioning of free will, we find remarkable coalitions between
representatives of the contemporary image of the human being as
characterized by autonomic subjectivity ("We are autonomic subjects")
and defenders of the classic Christian view of humankind ("We are
finite copies of the infinite freedom of the Creator"). Both defend
human freedom against the neuroscientific claim that human beings
are human by virtue of their capacity for free self-determination. The
essence of this is that, where one's will and actions are concerned,
one is not at the mercy of one's own desires and greed but is able to
decide *against* what one wishes and desires because it is inconsistent
with one's own self-image. To be free means that one does not have
to want what one wishes for: one can want what one ought to. This
capacity for freedom is the rock to be defended against every neuroscientific attempt at debasement.

That people can also decide *against* what they wish and desire because
it is inconsistent with their self-image is sufficient evidence that one
does not have to want what one wishes for but also can want what one
ought to. To that extent the central issue of human autonomy remains
unaffected by the neurophysiological critique. However, as regards the

50. V. J. Stenger, *The Fallacy of Fine-Tuning: Why the Universe Is Not Designed
for Us* (New York: Prometheus Books, 2011).

defense of freedom alone, nothing has yet been gained from a theological point of view: the capacity for freedom too becomes emergent in the evolutionary paradigm and is then understood without reference to God.

Today the central challenge is not the denial of reality but the *use* of freedom, as is borne out by the profound remodeling of the human being by human beings. With the replacement of more and more body parts by implants, the insertion in the body of chips that can take over more and more body control functions, the targeted manipulation of the brain by neural implants and hormones, and indeed the development of intelligent materials that act and react like a second human skin, the borderline between humans and their environment is being increasingly blurred and dissolved. Where do I end and where does my environment begin? What elements of my physical and mental circumstances are essential and indispensable to my identity? How much technology and electronics can we install in our body before we become a type of machine or a mere node of the global information network? It is not merely the *self-destruction* of human beings as a result of atomic or biological catastrophes and ecological disasters that is an impending scenario today, but also the *self-abolition* of humans in the sense known hitherto, that is, their *remodeling* as beings who—as Nietzsche would have said—are as far removed from present-day humans as they are from animals.

From a theological point of view it is insufficient, in the face of these contemporary trends toward the self-aggrandizement, self-belittlement, and self-dissolution of the human, to invoke the classic Christian view of the human. For one thing, the discovery of human creativity is inherent in the Christian view. When we adopt the biblical prehistory, the human is understood as a being of possibility, a being that misses its own mark because it wants to be other than it is and therefore is less than it could be, even though this misuse of its possibilities does not nullify their right use but rather requires and *ex negativo* confirms it. Modernity, with all its consequences, is thus a wholly legitimate child of Christianity, albeit not one wished for or beloved by all. For another, from a theological point of view this classic image of the human is far from being a timeless and binding one. Rather, it is the result of a questionable interpretation of the idea of human godlikeness, one in serious need of correction.

18. The Fallacy of the Traditional Understanding of Human Godlikeness

The traditional Christian image of the human being is the result of a one-sided theological interpretation of a one-sided philosophical understanding of human nature. In defining human distinctiveness, mainstream ancient thought one-sidedly emphasized the characteristics *logos* and *ethos*, while *pathos* was inappositely left out of account. This is not because they had overlooked the pathic, or emotive, side of the human, but because it was so very present that, in the face of individual and collective eruptions of fervor, suffering, pathos, and passion, they saw the essence of the human being in the capacity to keep these forces, experienced as destructive, under control, to rein them in by reason, will, *logos*, and *ethos*. Thus the spirit was contrasted with the body; reason, which was held to be directed toward the common good, was contrasted with one's own wishes; and the will, led by reason, was contrasted with sensory desire.

Christian theology built on this by locating the evil of sin in the pathic, sensory, and corporeal. It located the relationship with God in the *logos*, on the other hand, and with it the orientation to the good, the true, and the beautiful; and the goodwill and true life associated with it were located in the *ethos*. But Christian theology could only arrive at this reinforcing position on the basis of a highly problematic interpretation of the *imago Dei* idea. Its interpretation of Genesis 1:27 ("So God created mankind in his own image, in the image of God he created them; male and female he created them," NIV) highlights the human imaging of God as that which distinguishes human beings from all other creatures: as male and female, they alone are intended to reflect God.[51] At the same time, their godlikeness is seen in what distinguishes them from other living beings: their reason, their erect gait, their duty of care toward the rest of creation, and their mandate of dominion over it.

51. Pope Benedict XVI said in his Regensburg lecture "Faith, Reason and the University: Memories and Reflections," not in relation to woman and man, but in a more abstract sense in relation to human "reason," that is our "sense of the true and good," of a "mirror of God" (http://www.vatican.va/holy_father/benedict_xvi /speeches/2006/september/documents/hf_ben-xvi_spe_20060912_university-regens burg_ ge.html).

But to link these two ideas is neither necessary nor illuminating. That humans, as the image of God, are distinguished from all other creatures does not mean that it is their godlikeness that distinguishes them from the other creatures. The distinguishing marks of their species, which set them apart biologically from other living beings, offer no basis for reconstructing the uniqueness of their (destiny to) godlikeness. "There is no fundamental difference between man and the higher animals in their mental faculties,"[52] as Darwin emphasized, and this applies to every other point of biological comparison between humans and animals. But this should not surprise us. As the image of God, human beings are of course distinct *from God* and simultaneously *from all other creatures*. But what constitutes their godlikeness can only be defined *in comparison with God*, not in comparison with other creatures.

For a long time theology has allowed its adoption of the traditions of antiquity to inveigle it into ignoring this and to see in phenomena such as reason, spirit, conscience, the faculty of speech, and such, which appear to distinguish humans categorically from other living beings, the manifestation of human closeness to God. It was thought that taking this as a starting point and drawing conclusions by analogy could offer true insights into the nature of God on which to base the unique dignity of human beings in comparison with all other creatures.

For those who hold this viewpoint, evolutionary and neurobiological insights into the only slight difference in degree between humans and other primates are nothing but a provocation: not only do they call in question the concept of human godlikeness, but they also remove the anthropological basis for knowledge of God.

Yet the whole debate renders itself superfluous if we drop the ill-considered identification of what differentiates humans from other living beings with what they have in common with God. It has long been clear we are barking up the wrong tree with this view: if God is supposed to be the perfect exemplar of what humans, as rational beings, are imperfect exemplars, then the biblical marking

52. Charles Darwin, *The Descent of Man, and Selection in Relation to Sex* (1871; repr., Princeton: Princeton University Press, 1981), I:35.

out of humans by God becomes a dogma of God's occupation by humans. The whole thought form thus leads us to define God from the perspective of humans, not humans from the perspective of God: what humans are as distinct from other beings, God is in the highest degree. Praise of God's greatness thus becomes—as Feuerbach rightly saw—human beings' backhanded praise of themselves.

Darwin pulled the rug out from under this kind of thinking: "Man in his arrogance thinks himself a great work. Worthy [of] the interposition of a deity, more humble & I believe true to consider him created from animals."[53] This was perceived as a fundamental affront, but this is to misunderstand what Darwin was saying. If humans are distinguished from all other creatures by being God's image, and if reason, rationality, self-awareness, use of symbols, and such mark out humans and anthropoid primates at best by degree, not categorically, this does not call in question human godlikeness. Rather, from a theological point of view just the opposite is true: human godlikeness does not consist in these mental capabilities. Reason, self-awareness, and free will are not evidence of human beings' godlikeness, but of the fact that their dissimilarity to other hominids is only relative. The findings of evolutionary biology and neuroscience do not represent a challenge and can be discussed calmly as what they are: empirical hypotheses.

19. Orientation to God

Theologically, human godlikeness is revealed not by comparison with other creatures but solely in relation to God. God, not the rest of creation, is the normative orientation point for a theological definition of what it is to be human.

This does not make the matter any simpler. Methodologically, this means that one cannot arrive at a theological definition of the human being without knowing God. But knowledge of God is notoriously controversial territory, to which different religions take a different

53. Charles Darwin, "Notebook C," in *Notebooks 1836–1844: Geology, Transmutation of Species, Metaphysical Enquiries*, ed. P. Barrett et al. (1838; repr., Cambridge: Cambridge University Press, 1987), 237–328 (the quotation here appears on 300).

approach. Admittedly, there are images of God in abundance, but Feuerbach comes closest to the truth with his conjecture that most of these represent human beings' projection of their own desired ideal into heaven.

Thus, for all revealed religions there is reliable knowledge of God only at the point where, according to their insight, God allows himself to be known in such a way that human projections of God can chafe against this knowledge and be corrected by it. According to Christian conviction Jesus Christ is the paramount example of this. It is no accident that in the New Testament the "image of God" predicate is first and foremost ascribed to him.[54] But this is not about what distinguishes humans from other creatures, but purely about the fact that in this crucified one God reveals himself in such a way that he becomes accessible and comprehensible to others in his trustworthy generosity to them.

We only have to recall this key New Testament point to see the questionableness of the classic Christian view of human beings. There is much that distinguishes humans from other living beings, and much that they have in common with them, but they are distinguished from them only by being *made in the image of God*, and this mark of distinction consists purely in what they *become* through God's generosity, what *befalls* them, what *benefits they receive* from God: that God reveals himself to them and through them to others as the one who allows them to become what is best for them.

So one cannot be said to *be* God's image: one *becomes* it, and humans become God's image by becoming the place of his presence to such an extent that their lives become the place of God's presence *for others*.

20. Creation as the Place of God's Presence

What humans are becoming by God's generosity cannot be seen if we ignore the new perspective on things by which their lives are oriented.

---

54. See Ingolf U. Dalferth and E. Jüngel, "Person und Gottebenbildlichkeit," in *Christlicher Glaube in Moderner Gesellschaft: Enzyklopädische Bibliothek in 30 Teilbänden*, ed. Franz Böckle et al. (Freiburg: Herder, 1981), 24:57–99, esp. 70–86.

It is in this perspective, not in the things themselves, that it becomes apparent what has changed: they now have come to see themselves and the world differently, which is why they now live their lives differently. They experience the world as creation, and they live in the world as created beings.

It follows that the meaning of creation is to be apprehended differently. One cannot tell by looking at the world that it is God's creation. Whichever phenomena are cited—the laws of the universe, the miracle of life, the improbability of there being life and consciousness in the world—alternative explanations can always be put forward: the obvious disorder, wickedness and evil, the avoidable and unavoidable destruction of life in the process of the preservation of life, senseless natural disasters, and the irrelevance of human efforts in the face of the inexorable approaching end of the universe.

Yet just to search for such objective evidence for creation is mistaken. Just as in the world there is neither left nor right, neither front nor behind, because our spatial juxtaposition that triggers our need for orientation is what leads to these distinctions, so, equally, the world cannot prove to be creation without reference to us. Those who label the world "creation" are not describing it but orienting themselves within it in a particular way: they are not highlighting observable differences in the world but locating the world with all its differences in relationship with God. It exists in and through God's presence.

That the world is creation is thus not a possible topic for scientific research. From a scientific point of view one can only research which changes trigger observable differences that give rise to a need for explanation. But nothing in the world, either real or possible, differentiates itself from anything else by being created. It is not that some things are created and others are not: either everything is created or nothing is.[55]

The only difference that the creation predicate delineates is that between Creator and created being: the world is viewed as creation that owes its existence to God, and God is seen as the one to whom the world owes its existence. This does not mean that he might have

---

55. We could not orientate ourselves in relationship to God in the world if anything were omitted as being irrelevant to orientation.

engendered it causally, but that without God's creative presence the world neither would nor could exist. God makes creatures make themselves (thus A. Farrer), but whereas the making of the created being is a realization process in time, the making of the Creator is apparent in the opening up of the possibilities without which there could be no realization processes in time. Time is the structure within which we come into being and pass away; creation is the endlessly new opening up of possibilities whose interaction gives rise to the creative new and without which there would be no coming into being or passing away in time.

However, this is not a description of the world but a statement of orientation. To be able to speak of creation in this way, we must understand ourselves as created beings and hence as the place of the creative presence of God. Without this as one's self-image, the world does not reveal itself as creation. In the light of this self-understanding, however, everything that comes to us is given a fresh luster: not just the exceptional and the unique, but also everyday things such as "clothes and shoes, food and drink, house and homestead, wife and child" (thus Luther), along with everything else that is part of life. None of this is self-evident. Nothing must, but everything can be understood as a gift of creation. When we view ourselves as created beings, we adopt a different attitude to both the good and the bad aspects of life: they are experienced as God's good gifts for which we give thanks, as a dark burden about which we complain, or as a reason to turn to God in thanksgiving, petition, and intercession. If we view ourselves as created beings, we see God everywhere; if not, then we see God nowhere.

Hence it is not *that* we are created beings that makes a practical difference, but *how* we live as created beings. If human beings are created beings because they become the place of God's creative presence, then they are distinct from other creatures in that they cannot help but behave as such: actually, by orienting or not orienting their lives to God's presence, or intentionally, by wanting to live in one way or another. *Those who apprehend themselves as created beings live with a different attitude to the world.* And because every human apprehends or does not apprehend himself or herself in this way, all live either in faith or in unfaith, as Christians put it: *in faith*, in the

sense that, in the changing circumstances of their lives, they turn
to God in thanksgiving and petition, complaint, and accusation; *in
unfaith*, on the other hand, in the sense that they do not do this but
ignore, fail to notice, or actively dispute God's presence.

We are not created beings because we live like created beings;
rather, because we are created beings we are able to live as such—or
indeed not. Nor do we cease to be created beings, even if we do not
apprehend ourselves as such or live as such. Being a creature is not
something for or against which one can decide: it is what gives one
the ability to decide for or against anything at all. One is a created
being only because one *becomes* one, and what one is becoming is
apparent not from one's origin but from what one will become in
the future.

Seen in this light, the essence of the Christian understanding of
humanness can be treated as theologically valid, even within the evolutionary paradigm, without fallacious modification or apologetics
on behalf of earlier modes of expression.

21. Active Creativity

Who then are we—theologically? The answer is familiar and remains:
we are created beings, for whom God's presence makes the world into
God's good creation. But what does that mean?

In the old paradigm it was clear that we are rational beings and, as
such in *logos* and *ethos*, finite copies of the infinite Creator: created
creators. This persists in its secularized form, in that while humans
are no longer viewed as God's creatures, they nonetheless are still
viewed as creators: they themselves are creators, and today they are
becoming self-creators—an open-ended process.

This demonstrates the altered perspective of the current paradigm.
It is not where we come from but what we are becoming that defines
who we are as humans. Who we are is not determined by our origin;
it will become evident in our future.

What this means receives a different emphasis in the secular and
the Christian perspectives. In the one case it is our active creativity
that is highlighted, so that our *becoming* is understood as *making*,

while the other focuses fundamentally on the creative passivity that defines us, so that our *becoming* is thought of as *gifting* and *empowering*.

From a secular perspective we are viewed essentially as actors or protagonists: we are who we become, and we become what we and others make us. But this has its limits. For one thing, we cannot make everything we want to. The range of our possibilities is restricted and remains so, even if they are constantly changing. There is a constant line of distinction to be drawn between the actually possible and makeable on the one hand, and the possible but now (as far as we can see) never to be makeable on the other. For another, we do not have to make everything that we can make. We have available to us a range of decisions that we neither can nor must exhaust. We are required to exercise the kind of responsibility that weighs up consequences, and what we consider responsible is never independent of the image that we have of ourselves and others. Third, we can only ever become what we are not, but we cannot become all that we are not, nor can we even become everything that we could become. When the time comes in which one could, often the time has passed in which one can, as Marie von Ebner-Eschenbach once put it. The reality of the world, the structure of time, and the normativity of our image of ourselves and of the world basically condition what we make and can make.

Hence it is inadequate to examine human life merely from the point of view of logical action as the execution of decisions made in time. It is true that the decision process can be described as taking up and carrying forward decisions, but this does not mean that life consists only in decision making and nothing else. It is only because possibilities come our way that we can decide, but our decisions constantly render some things impossible, while others become possible, so that in the course of time the scope of our lives, that which opens up to us the allocation of possibilities, changes. We make use of things that are not due to us, and we bring about things that we can no longer undo.

Nevertheless, it is not the scarcity but the abundance of the possibilities that come our way that is the fundamental problem. This makes it necessary for us to choose and decide. If it were any different, we would not have to choose, and if we did not have to choose, life would not be an existential challenge for us. Not only can we choose, we must, and we do it every time we live one way and not another.

22. Creative Passivity

Christianity does not dispute any of this. However, it does not accentuate the activity chain: can, choose, wish, want, and should. Rather, it stresses what precedes and accompanies this chain: the opening up of possibilities, without which there could be no can, choose, wish, want, and should. *Who we are* will certainly only become apparent in the future. But from a theological point of view, this orientation toward becoming shifts the focus away from human activity to human passivity. It is neither our making nor that of others that decides who we are becoming; rather, this comes from the concrete possibilities that come our way and on whose creative potential our making remains constantly reliant.

When Christianity speaks of creation, it is referring to this uncontrollable bursting in and unanticipated supervention of life opportunities. Creation is gift, one that provokes a thankful and inquisitive attitude to life. The decisive premise for the Christian life orientation, life perspective, and way of life is not that humans are protagonists but *that God, the reality of the possible, is present in the opening up of creative life opportunities*, thus provoking us to responsible use of our freedom.

Anthropologically, too, it is not human beings' activity and creativity that are the central focus of theological attention, but their passivity, radically understood, their life arising out of God's creativity, to which they owe not just the fact that they exist rather than not existing, but also who they can be and will be. The whole activity chain of can, choose, wish, want, and should depends on which concrete possibilities have been opened up to each of us. We have practically no influence on this, and indeed this very opening up of possibilities—so essential to our lives—that does not compel us but enables us by opening a window of life options, is conceived of theologically as God's presence and God's gift.

If creation is gift and gifting, then what corresponds to it where the created being is concerned is passivity, but not as it has been traditionally understood.

First, this passivity is not merely the capacity for suffering and change found in animal nature, which humans share with animals and is overcome by their rationality; this passivity is that without which there would be nothing to which *pathos*, *logos*, or *ethos* could be attributed. Not that humans are passive; rather, it is through passivity that humans become those whom they become in their activity and (relative) passivity: the passivity that is consistent with creation is creative.

Second, from a theological point of view, this human passivity is not conceived of as deficiency, but rather as *gifting*: it is creative because it alone enables humans to become those who, via the can, choose, wish, want, and should activity chain, can make themselves into those they become. To define it in terms of an anthropology of lack as absolute dependence, or existential deficiency, or creaturely imperfection obscures its essence.[56] As long as passivity is understood in this way, it is possible to propagate the denial of createdness as the liberation of humans from heteronomy to autonomy, as Nietzsche—and others—have taught. However, this is a misapprehension. Human creative passivity is not a sign of ontological deficiency; quite the reverse, it is a sign of special gifting. To be created means to be gifted and endowed by God, and humans are the image of God, not primarily as free and creative protagonists but first and foremost in their *creative passivity*. They are the ones to whom God makes himself present as God by opening up to them possibilities through which they become those they can become within the scope of the possibilities that come their way.

No one can make himself or herself the place of God's presence (that is to say, a created being). We can only become this place. And we cannot decide of ourselves to become this place; it is the result of the divine opening up of life opportunities and chances through

56. It was against this type of misunderstanding of Schleiermacher's discussion of "consciousness of absolute dependence" that A. Schweizer protested in his *Die Christliche Glaubenslehre nach protestantischen Grundsätzen dargestellt*, 2 vols. (Leipzig: S. Hirzel, 1863/1869, ²1877).

which humans become humans, in the sense that they become able to live as humans. Not until we have become this place are we able to choose, decide, and act for ourselves, but we do not reach this place through our own choice, decision, or activity. Just as no one can make herself an heir, but can only behave as an heir when she becomes one by accepting or rejecting her inheritance, so too no one can make herself the place of God's presence, but can only behave as such by her assent or rejection.

To *become* a created being thus precedes any kind of behavioral response on the part of the created being to its createdness. To become a created being, however, means to be gifted and endowed by God in the sense that life opportunities come our way over which we never have control but they allow and enable us to become human and to live as humans with an open future, but without being able to extrapolate, on the basis of our own origin, as to what we are to become as a result. *Who we are* is not to be decided by us by what we *become for others*—for other people, for other creatures, and for God.

23. Beings of Possibility

My thesis has been that in the Christian view humans are *beings of possibility* who are what they become, but who always become more than they can make of themselves, in either positive or negative terms. They can fail to fulfill themselves if they want to be other than they are becoming, and will consequently be less than they could be. But conversely, they can surpass themselves by becoming other than they make themselves and more than they wanted to become. One way or another, they are headed for a future that has not been determined by their origin. They are open to the new, the new into which they make themselves, and the new that they simply become but into which they can never make themselves.

This is why nothing that they are, neither reason, nor will, nor feeling, nor whatever else they hold in common with other living beings, albeit in different degrees, manifests human *godlikeness*. This does not consist in their capacity for freedom, for recognition of the truth, or for the inventive creation of something new, and it therefore is not cast into doubt by evolutionary and neurobiological challenges to the uniqueness of these capabilities.

Rather, it consists in what makes humans passively into something that, with all their activities, they can never make themselves, but that they cannot in any way prevent: namely, that God makes them into the place of his creative presence in such a way that they are able not only to respond but also, through the reality of their lives, to behave in such a way that they obscure or illuminate this presence *for others*. They *become* God's image, either as their lives obstruct, obscure, and distort God's presence for others, or as they become for them a place where this presence is revealed, clarified, and made accessible. We do not have to want this in order to become it; we can want one or the other but still not become it; but we become it even if we do not want it—simply by living as we live and thus becoming for others what we are not of ourselves and could never make ourselves: the image of God.

Author Index

*

205

Scripture Index

*

Subject Index

*